THE DISCOVERY OF BRITAIN

THE DISCOVERY
OF BRITAIN

The English Tourists

1540
to
1840

ESTHER MOIR

ROUTLEDGE & KEGAN PAUL
London

First published 1964
by Routledge & Kegan Paul Limited
Broadway House, 68–74 Carter Lane
London, E.C.4

Printed in Great Britain
by The Anchor Press Ltd.
Tiptree, Essex

TO MY FATHER
PREBENDARY A. L. MOIR

CONTENTS

ILLUSTRATIONS

ACKNOWLEDGEMENTS

I AM grateful to the librarians and staff of the British Museum, the Cambridge University Library, the Bodleian Library, the Cardiff Public Library, the York Public Library and the Wigan Public Library for much kindly help in connection with their MS. collections.

I should like to thank Miss F. F. Andrews for permission to quote from *The Torrington Diaries*; Mr. E. M. Forster for a short passage from *Marianne Thornton*; Mr. Christopher Morris for the extensive use of his *Journeys of Celia Fiennes* in chapter 4; Mr. Gerald Yorke for allowing me to make use of the Yorke papers at Forthampton Court; and Dr. A. N. L. Munby, Librarian of King's College, Cambridge, for much help and criticism.

My thanks are due to the following for permission to reproduce prints or drawings in their possession: Tunbridge Wells Public Library for the Johannes Kip etching of Tunbridge Wells in 1718; the Department of Prints and Drawings of the British Museum for Thomas Rowlandson's *Comforts of Bath*; *Country Life* for the frontispiece of the guide-book to Houghton Hall, and the water-colours of Wilton House and Hawkstone Park; the National Museum of Wales for the water-colours of industrial scenery by Paul Sandby and J. C. Ibbetson; Miss F. F. Andrews for John Byng's sketches; Major J. R. Abbey for Paul Sandby's *Pont y Pair* and J. Farington's *Waterfall at Rydal* from his *Scenery of Great Britain*.

Parts of chapters 2, 6, 7 and 8 have appeared in the pages of *Country Life* and *History Today*, and I am grateful to their respective editors for permission to quote from them here.

ESTHER MOIR

INTRODUCTION

THE old English noun 'travel' used in the sense of a journey was originally the same thing as 'travail', and it implied trouble and discomfort. The hardships endured by the tourists of Britain in the three centuries from 1540 to 1840 will become all too apparent in the following pages. Yet, despite the many trials, the purpose of the travels here described was pleasure. This was travel for its own sake; journeys undertaken for themselves rather than as some necessary evil to be endured for some other end. The merchants, pilgrims and scholars of the Middle Ages travelled for material wealth or spiritual gain. But when Thomas Platter, a Swiss Protestant visiting this country in 1599, described the purpose of his journey as 'mere curiosity to see' he supplied an admirably succinct definition of the newly emerging tourist, pinpointing wherein he differed from earlier travellers.

This study, however, is not concerned with the foreign tourists who from the sixteenth century began to flock to this country, nor with the equally large numbers of English youths who made the Grand Tour of Europe, for these are sufficiently familiar. Both were essentially conventional, following a set pattern of visits to the more important cultural and political sights, so that while the sons of the English nobility and gentry, accompanied by their tutors, followed the well-worn paths to Italy and back, European visitors in return were making their round of London, the courts and the universities. The intention of this book is to consider that hitherto neglected subject, the Tour of Britain.

It is remarkable that the *Gentleman's Magazine*, which always recorded with scrupulous care in its obituary notices the time spent in youth on making the Grand Tour of Europe, rarely or never thought it worth while to mention the time spent on the Tour of Britain. Yet such travels so commonly undertaken by members of the English upper and middle classes must have contributed much to their general education, promoting a knowledge of contemporary social and economic developments, and encouraging the growth of aesthetic awareness, whether of antiquities, industrial sites or mountain scenery. The habit of touring their native land began in the sixteenth century; it is a Tudor phenomenon. Better roads and improved cartography were making travel easier and safer, but the motive force was pride in the greatness of Tudor England, and a curiosity both in the historic roots of that greatness and its contemporary manifestations. Bound by no tradition or convention, lacking the established routes and rituals of the Grand Tour, it became a popular pastime amongst gentlemen of leisure to travel for weeks, even months, in the discovery of their own country.

To follow these journeys through three centuries is not only to watch the changing English landscape through the eyes of contemporaries, it is also to see the change in the vision itself as the interests and concerns of the tourists grow and develop from one generation to another. The earliest tourists showed an uncritical and all-embracing enthusiasm which ranged from prehistoric antiquities to the most recent industrial undertakings. Their concern was to present a *Speculum Britanniae*, a looking-glass of Britain, which should mirror faithfully the country in all its aspects. Increasing knowledge and widening possibilities of travel encouraged rather more sophistication in the later tourists, and by the mid-eighteenth century a man would be more likely to pride himself on being first and foremost an antiquarian, an authority on the Picturesque, or an expert on gardens. Approval of Gothic but dislike of Norman; appreciation of a Palladian house but dismissal of a Baroque one; acclaim for Van Dyck but scorn for Rubens; pleasure in the work of Capability Brown but horror in the sight of a formal garden—from the tourists' accounts a picture emerges of what a gentleman of taste in the eighteenth century liked and admired in natural scenery and in the arts. Perhaps the most fascinating change to follow is in the attitude towards mountains. Originally hideous obstacles to be skirted or avoided wherever possible, these ultimately become objects of beauty to be sought out and enjoyed almost to the point of worship. So the mountain scenery of North Wales and the Lakes (as also of Scotland, which for reasons of space has not been included here) was discovered and explored, and a new arena added in which the tourists might employ their notebooks and sketching-pads.

The Tour of Britain remains, during this period, the prerogative of the governing classes, and the tourists who feature here are, with very few exceptions, members of the nobility and gentry. This is particularly true of the visitors to the great country houses, for their owners were willing to open their doors to who-ever presented themselves on the tacit understanding that the low and common sort of people did not take such a liberty. Similarly the Welsh mountains or the attractions of the Wye drew only those whose sensibilities had been correctly nurtured on the reading of Payne-Knight, Burke, Gilpin and those other prophets of the Romantic and the Picturesque. A great many remain anonymous, and of even more we know only the names. To give shortened biographies of those whose works are quoted in these pages, even if it were possible, would only be tedious. These tourists must be taken to represent a fair cross-section of the upper and middle ranks of English society between the mid-sixteenth and the mid-nineteenth centuries.

Well-informed curiosity, a real love of the English countryside and a willingness to undergo considerable discomfort—if these are the criteria of the true tourist they were undermined by the coming of the railways. The most obvious change was that as travel became easier it became available to a much wider mass of people, and with this popularization lost much of its character as a venture of personal discovery. A readiness to suffer discomfort in the pursuit of pleasure can hardly be deemed a feature of the typical Victorian middle-class tourist. For now he has become essentially passive, a sightseer who expects everything to be arranged for him. Well-planned excursions appealing to the middle classes are a far cry from the solitary travels of the early pioneers in the art of touring. The change comes in the 1840's. It is said that the very first railway excursion was made in 1838 to take the people of Wadebridge to the neighbouring town of Bodmin to witness the execution of two murderers, where, since the gallows stood in full view of the station, the passengers were able to watch the scene from their uncovered carriages without even leaving their seats. The greatest organizer of railway travel was, of course, Thomas Cook, whose special-rate excursions soon gained immense popularity. On July 5th, 1841, he took 570 people from Leicester to Loughborough for a temperance convention at a reduced round-trip fare of a shilling per head. Before long he was sending hundreds to Ireland and Scotland, and in 1851 he brought literally thousands to London for the Crystal Palace Exhibition. A round of well-selected 'beauty spots' under the care of a well-briefed conductor left little room for individual initiative, and the whole idea of travel as exploration and discovery disappears. 'Going by railway I do not consider as travel at all', commented Ruskin; 'it is merely being "sent" to a place, and very little different from becoming a parcel.'[1]

But the clock could not be turned back, and as Cook said in defence of these developments, it was not only foolish to wish that places of interest should be excluded from the gaze of the common people and kept for the select of society, it was also now impossible. As the coaches and the charabancs take over from the railways the early tourists seem increasingly remote. Lest they be entirely forgotten they are here presented, with their account of the country they set out to discover.

[1] Quoted Daniel J. Boorstin, *The Image*, London, 1962, 96.

ARS PEREGRINANDI

The Art of Travel

T seems natural to travellers to write of their travels. They mostly wish, as John Caprove put it, to add their own 'smal pyping of swech straunge sites as I have seyn'.[1] The tourists of Britain are no exception. Long winter evenings were spent in transcribing the notes taken in the previous summer's tour, and they produced their accounts, sometimes for publication, often for circulation in manuscript form amongst friends and neighbours. The simplicity and spontaneity of their writings stand in refreshing contrast to much other tourist literature, and when other travellers' tales grow tedious it is good to turn again to these eye-witness accounts of the English countryside which they knew and loved.

'Ars peregrinandi' might almost be called a European cult of the sixteenth century. 'All nations espying this realm to be so commodious and pleasant have a confluence to it more than to any other region',[2] wrote Andrew Boorde, and indeed England was always popular with the foreign visitor. But whether he came as a member of an embassy or as a private individual, his sight-seeing was centred mainly on London, Oxford and Cambridge, and the inevitable tour of royal palaces: Greenwich, Richmond, Hampton

---

[1] *Ye Solace of Pilgrims*, (ed.) C. A. Mills, London, 1911, 67.
[2] *Thomas Platter's Travels in England 1599; rendered into English from the German and with introductory matter by C. Williams*, London, 1937, 77.

Court, Windsor. This almost mechanical round produced stereotyped writings, and the interest of such accounts lies less in their
topographical descriptions than in their comments on those
English racial characteristics and idiosyncrasies which have
always intrigued and bewildered the foreigner, a fascination
which was none the less great for being coupled with the general
idea, which persisted practically down to the time of Victoria,
that they were really beyond the pale of civilization. It was therefore with scarcely concealed satisfaction that visitor after visitor
discovered that the English loved sport and were oblivious to art;
that they lived in cold, damp houses; that they were heavy
smokers; had 'little mode for gallantry' and disliked foreigners—
generalizations which appear with such monotonous regularity
that they seem like the plagiaristic borrowings of successively
baffled tourists turning to see what foreign visitors before them
had made of the English race.[1]

In return the English travelled in Europe. The Grand Tour
held an important place in English life, and was backed by a
formidable literature which demonstrated that travel alone could
bring that experience necessary to crown a liberal education.
Innumerable essays appeared on the subject in the sixteenth and
seventeenth centuries, some justifying travel with moral and
rational arguments, others giving practical advice and guidance,
all determined to mould both the route and the impressions of
the young tourist. They tended to follow much the same pattern.
The goal was Italy, the aim a veneer of culture. Typical of the
Elizabethan traveller making the Grand Tour is Sir Philip Sidney,
who spent two years abroad, passing through France and Germany to Italy, accompanied by three servants, and attaching
himself to some official or diplomatic mission whenever possible.
During the next three centuries this changed little. The raw
English youth spent two or three years moving about Europe in
the company of an experienced tutor who was expected to shield
him from its moral and religious hazards. He followed the well-
worn paths through Paris, Florence and Venice to Rome, read the
stereotyped guides, and returned with his collection of artistic
trophies and conventional views to impress his contemporaries
who had been doing exactly the same thing.

[1] See Francesca Wilson, *Strange Land, Britain through Foreign Eyes, 1395–
1940*, London, 1955, *passim*.

2

'The tour of Europe is a paltry thing, a tame, uniform, unvaried prospect which affords nothing but the same polished manners and artificial policies.'[1] There had, however, been considerable debate upon its merits, acrimonious attacks and optimistic defences, before Bishop Hurd summed up the views of those in opposition so defiantly in his supposed dialogue between John Locke and Lord Shaftesbury. Even those who advocated it most strongly had been aware of the dangerous lengths to which a young man might be tempted, and had counselled moderation. Thomas Nashe had been one of the first to pour his scathing wit on the idea that 'hee is no bodie that hath not traveld' and he painted only too mercilessly his picture of the assiduous tourist: 'Hee that is a traveller must have the backe of an asse to beare all, a tung like the taile of a dog to flatter all, the mouth of a hogge to eate what is set before him, the eare of a merchant to heare all and say nothing; and if this be not the highest step of thraldome, there is no libertie or freedome.'[2] The question was discussed with increasing heat throughout the eighteenth century. But by then the fashion was at its height and unlikely to be influenced either by the commendations of Josiah Tucker, whose *Instructions for Travellers* set out the system of travel he considered most profitable, or by such satires as Cowper's *Progress of Error*. *Inglese Italianate, diavolo incarnato* was a favourite tag, and Adam Smith's picture of the tourist returning more conceited, more unprincipled, more dissipated and more incapable of any serious application represented a widely held view.

The Tour of Britain, however, aroused no such passions, called forth no fierce controversy and created no particular philosophy to justify itself. Its devotees were content to travel, to describe what they saw and encourage others to follow them. And while the foreign visitor wrote of the peculiarities of the English people as he found them, while the voyager to the East returned with his gloriously embellished romantic tales, and while the young nobleman brought back his careful impressions of the riches of Europe's cultural heritage, the British traveller does not fit into any easy category. He was essentially an individualist: he was not a member

[1] *Dialogues on the uses of foreign travel; considered as part of an English gentleman's education: between Lord Shaftesbury and Mr. Locke*, Dublin, 1764, 98.
[2] *The Unfortunate Traveller*, 1594; illustrated by Michael Ayrton, with an introduction, London, 1948, 94.

of a caravan trekking east, nor did he move perpetually surrounded by a miniature court of English secretaries, chaplains and servants, as though he, 'like the king's ambassador was leading a tiny mission to the continent'.[1] Travelling alone, or at most accompanied by a servant, he was unlikely, at least before the end of the eighteenth century and the cult of the Picturesque, to have had his outlook and taste fashioned by treatises which set out the ideals of touring. Nor did he leave a common society of Whitehall or the university and return to report the fruit of his journeyings to contemporaries of the same background and ideas as himself. A royal librarian, a Cheshire landowner, a spirited young woman, an army lieutenant, a hack journalist, a philanthropic cleric—it was an extraordinarily mixed company which set out to discover their native land, with motives and interests as varied as themselves.

Celia Fiennes, standing equidistant in time from the Tudor topographers and the mid-Victorian travellers, well symbolizes the English tourist, and is untypical only in being a woman. Her curiosity was unbounded, her writing vivid and spontaneous, her interests ranged over all that she came upon in her travels, and she would describe with equal enthusiasm natural wonders or the most recent developments in mining. And probably no one ever held firmer views upon the value of making the Tour of Britain.

> If all persons, both Ladies, much more Gentlemen, would spend some of their tyme in Journeys to visit their native Land, and be curious to inform themselves and make observations of each place, with the variety of sports and recreations they are adapt to, would be a souveraign remedy to cure or preserve from these epidemick diseases of vapours, should I add Laziness? It would also form such an Idea of England, add much to its Glory and Esteem in our minds and cure the itch of over-valueing foreign parts.[2]

The wise tourist did not set out upon his travels without careful preparation beforehand to ensure at least a minimum of physical comfort in the face of hazardous roads and squalid inns. The Rev. James Plumptre had reduced this to such a fine art that by 1794 he was actually designing a special form of dress for himself and his companion, which was intended to be at once handsome,

---

[1] J. W. Stoye, *English Travellers Abroad, 1604–67, their Influence in English Society and Politics*, London, 1952, 27.

[2] *The Journeys of Celia Fiennes*, (ed.) C. Morris, London, 1947, 1.

neat and light. They wore nankeen breeches with garters, short blue coats with large lapels which could be buttoned over in case of rain or cold, and Scotch plaids, and they carried knapsacks covered with goatskin. These latter had to be of very considerable size, for not only did Plumptre equip himself with such necessities as seven shirts and three pairs of well-seasoned shoes but he would never venture forth without what he was pleased to call his knick-knacks: a small telescope; a pocket compass; a pocket knife and fork; drawing and memorandum books; a silver pen and pencil; a drinking horn; a pocket pistol; magnifiers for botany; a sixteen-inch tape-measure and, finally, Cowper's poems, 'a book which breathes the finest poetry with the truest religion and morality—a book I shall never think I have read sufficiently till I can retain it all in my Memory'.[1]

Almost every tourist had hints and suggestions to offer to his fellows, based all too often on hardly won experience. But Dr. William Kitchinir said all that there really was to be said in his *Traveller's Oracle: or Maxims for Locomotion, containing Precepts for Promoting the Pleasures and Hints for Preserving the Health of Travellers*, published in 1825. He covered every possible aspect of his subject, from advice on personal defence to hints for care of the feet, and he enlivened his pages with his own musical compositions, *An English Grace*, *A Father's Advice to his Son*, and a patriotic hymn, no doubt intended to cheer on the flagging traveller, *All Hail, Britannia, Queen of Isles*. His concern was to send the traveller forth equipped for any emergency, yet not festooned with cumbrous baggage, and to achieve this end he had designed, with very considerable ingenuity, a thermometer which was housed in a toothpick case; a barometer for measuring heights in a walking stick; a sword inside an umbrella; a knife, fork and spoon folded into one large pocket-knife; and a night-lamp placed in a little lantern which could carry on its top a tin cup that would hold half a pint of water. For personal comfort he advised the wearing of gaiters, or, better still, a pair of fisherman's worsted hose drawn over the shoes, and he advocated a Welsh wig as a cheap and comfortable travelling cap. To ensure against the worst evils of the inns he produced his *pièce de résistance*: a portable canteen which contained leather sheets as a precaution against

[1] 'Narrative of a Pedestrian Journey . . . in the Summer of 1799', Camb. Univ. Lib. Add. MSS. 5814, f. 35.

damp beds, a kettle, knives and forks, and 'Soldier's Comforters, consisting of two Saucepans, Lamp and Stand, Spice Box, all contained in one Saucepan'. He did not allow his tourist that dilettante plaything the Claude-glass, but instead recommended that he should take an 'Invisible Opera Glass or Traveller's Vade Mecum' of his own invention, so that on arrival at any place he might at once climb to the top of the highest building and gain a general idea of it.

Thus equipped, and carrying those stout notebooks which they were determined to fill, the optimistic tourists set out along roads whose appalling state called forth some of their most violent diatribes—though none was to jeer quite so heartlessly as the foreign traveller who said of the English that they had roads 'as the lazy Italians had fruits, namely what God left them after the Flood'. On the borders of the country, in Devon and Cornwall, Wales and the Peak, such conditions might be expected, and it was hardly surprising to find that in the far west roads became mere narrow lanes through which a single horse might pass only with difficulty, and in the north they were little more than steep and stony tracks following the hillsides. Some of the very worst roads, however, were to be found near London. The liquid mud of Sussex, churned by the constant traffic, was the most famous of all, and it was said that respectable Sussex women went to church in ox-drawn coaches, and Sussex men and animals had grown long-legged through pulling their feet through the clay. 'If you love good roads . . . be so kind as never to go into Sussex', wrote Horace Walpole to George Montague. 'The whole country has a Saxon air, and the inhabitants are savage. . . . Coaches grow there no more than balm and spices. . . . Sussex is a great damper of curiosities.' In open or unenclosed country, roads were often not clearly defined, and any traveller felt himself at liberty to choose whatever way seemed best, even at the risk of traversing good agricultural land. In country where stone was scarce the local surveyor of the highways felt no compunction in regarding any prehistoric remain or ancient monument as a public quarry, and the traveller who congratulated himself that the way leading to some well-known antiquitity was in good repair generally failed to realize that this had been achieved only by the destruction of the goal of his journey. Each season brought its own particular dangers, and few travelled for pleasure except in the summer when they had nothing worse to face than clouds of dust, for in the spring and autumn they might expect ruts filled with water, and in the winter snow, which if followed quickly by a thaw made any journey extremely disagreeable and frequently dangerous.

All roads deteriorated seriously during the sixteenth and seventeenth centuries, owing largely to the great increase in wheeled vehicles. Medieval traffic had consisted mainly of riding horse, packhorse or litter, with agricultural carts or ploughs with some box attachment for short-distance travel, and the waggons used by royal and noble households. The mid-sixteenth century saw the introduction of the four-wheeled English wain; private coaches were becoming increasingly popular, and the stage coach first began to appear sometime between 1600 and 1650. Already by 1622 John Taylor was complaining 'the world runs on wheels —this is a rattling, rowling, rumbling age', a fact which encouraged him to make several journeys by water, notably those from London to York and Salisbury, which he described in *A Merry Wherry-Ferry-Voyage* and *A Discovery by Sea*. But he concluded that travel by river and sea was even more beset by travail and danger, and clearly there could be no serious alternative to road travel, with, as its corollary, a constant increase in the amount of wheeled traffic. A succession of Acts passed at regular intervals throughout the seventeenth and eighteenth centuries made ineffectual attempts to regulate wheels, horses, loads and so on. Even the Rev. Richard Burn, author of that indispensable guide for the country Justice of the Peace, had to confess himself bewildered by the number of repeals and revivals, so that often it had become impossible to conclude with certainty how the law stood in many instances. Underlying this confused mass of legislation was the tacit assumption that the wheeled carriage was an intruder, and as such must be suppressed or at least restricted, a wildly unrealistic attitude which inevitably proved ineffective. A more constructive approach to the question lay in the large number of Highway Acts passed under Mary and Elizabeth, the most important being that of 1555 which laid upon the parish the responsibility of the upkeep of the roads within the parochial boundaries, ordering the annual election of two surveyors and the setting aside of certain days around the Feast of St. John at midsummer for the remaking of the roads by the local inhabitants. Even as set out in the statute book the drawbacks to the Act were obvious. Labourers naturally begrudged six days' work without wages, particularly in June at the busiest time of the agricultural year, and if a local Justice were to be negligent in making his ruling a stretch of road might well be left untouched for several years. William Harrison nicknamed the labourers 'the King's Loiterers', and Burn described the surveyors as 'spiritless, ignorant, lazy, sauntering people'. But theirs was an invidious task, and it is scarcely surprising that the roads should receive the minimum of attention at their hands.

The earliest manual of road repair was not published until 1675, but it was soon followed by a stream of similar pamphlets giving practical advice. The general spread of turnpike trusts throughout the eighteenth century brought the first really considerable improvement. The earliest Turnpike Act was passed in 1663 and allowed the Justices of the Peace responsible for Hertfordshire, Cambridgeshire and Huntingdonshire to raise funds for the maintenance of their roads by the erection of toll-bars or turnpikes. Eventually there were over a thousand such trusts administering 23,000 miles of road, on which toll-bars occurred with a frequency that caused considerable delay and expense to the traveller. The main work of the trusts lay in widening and straightening, though occasionally they also constructed new roads. But they found themselves hampered by lack of professional surveyors with a competent knowledge of technical problems, and there was no real advance here until the two great engineers Thomas Telford and John MacAdam turned their attention to scientific roadmaking. De Quincey's eulogy of the latter may be an exaggeration, but it is a pardonable one: 'All the roads in England within a few years were remodelled, and upon the principles of Roman science. From mere beds of torrents and systems of ruts, they were raised universally to the condition and appearance of gravel walks in private parks.'[1]

Milestones and signposts were rare throughout the greater part of this period, and even where they existed travellers complained of their inaccuracy. This was perhaps hardly surprising since, although the statute mile had been defined in 1593, it was not put on the map until Ogilby used it in 1675, and even then in many parts of the country the old British mile of 2428 yards was still usual. Celia Fiennes frequently noted that the roads she

[1] Quoted Thomas Burke, *Travel in England*, London, 1942, 93.

followed were measured in long miles. Lancashire was exceptional in being well signposted, and she noted with pleasure that at all crossways there were posts with hands pointing to each road with the names of the towns that it led to. The majority of roads, however, remained quite inadequately marked until the mid-eighteenth century, and the general erection of milestones came only with the establishment of the turnpike trusts. At first they were put up voluntarily on a few roads, but from 1744 most Acts contained a clause requiring the trustees to measure their roads and to set up stones or posts giving distances. Post-houses generally had professional guides available for those travelling post, but others were forced to depend upon local men, particularly carters and carriers who might be expected to have some first-hand knowledge of the danger points on the route. At harvest-time or in bad weather it was frequently impossible to find anyone willing to help, or only on payment of some exorbitant fee in addition to their food and lodging. William Cobbett had a particularly vivid story of the uselessness of such guides which is only too typical of the experiences of many other travellers. In November 1822 he gave a man three shillings to take him from Headley to Hindhead, and set off following his guide's white smock through the drizzling rain. After a hazardous progress of seven miles, three of them down a hill so steep that they could move only at a foot's pace, the man confessed himself lost, and it fell upon Cobbett himself to extricate the pair of them.[1]

The first real road-book appeared in 1577: chapter XVI, of Holinshed's Chronicle, *Of our Innes and Thorowfares*. It gave an account of hostelries and inns with warnings and observations, and set out a table of roads with distances in miles for each stage. After this the only man who attempted to deal methodically with such matters before the time of John Ogilby was John Norden, whose *England, An Intended Guyde for English Travailers* was published in 1625 and gave forty plates of triangular distance tables. All the road-users of the seventeenth and eighteenth centuries owed their greatest debt to Ogilby, who not only established the statute mile of 1760 yards instead of the old British mile, but produced a road-book which was to remain the pattern for all future itineraries, 100 folio plates showing the principal roads of England and Wales, engraved on strips or bands, and

[1] *Rural Rides*, London, 1830, 95–6.

giving short particulars of the road itself and of the surrounding countryside. A shortened version went through successive editions and became the foundation of all eighteenth-century road-books, being displaced only in 1798 with the appearance of Cary's *New Itinerary*. Ultimately all itineraries and road-books were to be superseded by the accurate and technical mapping of the Ordnance survey which began to produce their fine series of maps in the early years of the nineteenth century.

Yet in spite of such advances the terrible condition of the roads remained a constant theme in the writings of all travellers. Their appalling state was described time after time with a wealth of vivid detail and an outpouring of vituperation, in which none could excel Arthur Young in the bitterness of his tirades, and he shall be allowed to speak for the others. He denounced those he found in Yorkshire as 'detestable, full of ruts whose gaping jaws threaten to swallow up any carriage less than a waggon'; in Wiltshire they were 'little better than ponds of liquid dirt with a scattering of loose flints just sufficient to lame every horse that travelled them'; while in Bedfordshire he would scarcely allow the name of road to 'the cursed string of hills and holes' he traversed between Newport Pagnell and Bedford.[1] In Wales he was driven to interrupt his narrative to interpolate an impassioned plea to his readers:

> But, my dear Sir, what am I to say of the roads in this country! The turnpikes! as they have the assurance to call them; and the hardiness to make one pay for. From *Chepstow* to the half way house between *Newport* and *Cardiff* they continue mere rocky lanes, full of hugeous stones as big as one's horse, and abominable holes. The first six miles from *Newport* they were so detestable, and without either direction-posts or mile-stones, that I could not well persuade myself I was on the turnpike, but had mistook the road; and therefore asked every one I met, who answered me, to my astonishment, Ya–as.[2]

Time and time again he sums up the general verdict.

> Of all the roads that ever disgraced this kingdom in the very ages of barbarism, none ever equalled that from Billericay to the King's Head at Tilbury. It is for near twelve miles so narrow that a

---

[1] *Northern Tour*, London, 1770, I, *389*; *Six Weeks Tour*, London, 1768, *318–20*; *Northern Tour*, I, *41*.

[2] *Six Weeks Tour*, London, *161–2*.

mouse cannot be passed by any carriage; I saw a fellow creep under
his waggon to assist me to lift, if possible, my chaise over a hedge.
The rutts are of an incredible depth—and a pavement of diamonds
might as well be sought for as a quarter. The trees everywhere
over-grow the road, so that it is totally impervious to the sun,
except at a few places.[1]

'Intolerably disagreeable', 'inexcrably bad', Arthur Young's
epithets and denunciations continue, and it would be only too
easy to parallel them from the accounts of his fellow travellers.

Yet the English tourists were not to be deterred by such
hazards, and with a curiosity that was only matched by their
courage they set out upon the discovery of their native land.

[1] ibid., 87–8.

A LOOKING-GLASS
OF BRITAIN

The Tudor Topographers

Y a curious piece of irony John Leland has become known
to posterity as the first and only bearer of that proud
title *King's Antiquary*. In fact he never held any such
office and the title itself is to be traced no further than a
seventeenth-century biography of Camden.[1] But the result has
been that he is generally acclaimed as the earliest antiquary and
the first of that long line of writers who stretch through Camden,
Dugdale and Plot to those countless authors of eighteenth-
century county histories. Yet Leland's place may be said to lie
more justly with the topographers, those who travelled the
countryside and described its face, modern as well as ancient, and
their descent may be traced less from him than from William
of Worcester in the later fifteenth century.

William of Worcester, or William Botoner as he liked to call
himself, was born in Bristol, went to Oxford in 1431 and five years
later became retainer to Sir John Fastolf of Caister Castle in
Norfolk. His travels were based on his two homes, Bristol and

---

[1] Arnaldo Momigliano, 'Ancient History and the Antiquarian', *Journal
of the Warburg and Courtauld Institutes*, XIV, 1950, Appendix I, *313–14.*

Norfolk, his most important journey being made in 1478 from Norwich to St. Michael's Mount in Cornwall. The manuscript he left is a day-to-day account of his expedition:[1] his interests ranged widely and he would recite with equal pleasure the foundation charter of a town or a list of the newly built ships of William Canynge lying in Bristol harbour. Numbers and figures, measurements of any kind, seem to have held a fascination for him and he would note the distance between towns, the courses of rivers, the numbers of fords or bridges. It seems that he was collecting material for a 'Description of Britain', and, although his notes were left to lie neglected until an eighteenth-century edition by Nasmyth, all the Tudor topographers were in fact pursuing the same purpose, concerned less to produce a strictly historical survey than to write a *Speculum Britanniae*, a looking-glass in which the country should be mirrored in all its aspects.

The earliest topographical writers took all England as their province, then later turned to their own counties: lest, as William Burton of Leicestershire put it in 1622, 'my native countrie should any longer lye obscured with darkness I have adventured (in some sorte) to restore her to her worth and dignitie'.[2] Men utterly unalike, the discursive William Harrison, the cold, clear-headed Camden, the poet Michael Drayton, the scientific John Norden, all shared one thing in common: an almost fanatical love for Tudor England. They wanted to write descriptions of their native land, the fruits of their own travel and observation, glorying in her past because of pride in her present greatness. Their approach was generally uncritical; their writing contained more or less whatever they pleased. As Sampson Erdeswicke, who wrote his *History of Staffordshire* between 1591 and 1603, explained: 'I have set down what I can find, or what I can yet learn—and have thought it a very commodious way to follow the Rivers.' Both William Lambard's *Perambulation of Kent* and Richard Carew's *Survey of Cornwall* were in fact leisurely tours of their respective counties in which the reader was taken gently by the hand and led through the countryside by an author anxious to omit nothing of interest and always ready to turn aside to tell a good story or reminisce about some curious happening. Such writing becomes increasingly rare after the appearance in 1656

---

[1] Corpus Christi College Library, Cambridge, MS. 210.
[2] *The description of Leicester Shire*, 1622.

of William Dugdale's *Antiquities of Warwickshire*, for this marks a turning point in English antiquarian scholarship. After this authors become more strictly historical, their chief concern being to trace the descent of the manor in relentless detail, so that inevitably their writing loses much of that freshness and vigour and, above all, the impression of being an eye-witness account, which is the most attractive characteristic of their predecessors.

The squires, lawyers and parsons who vied with one another to praise their country were spurred to their task not only by their own intense patriotism but by the knowledge that this was a subject of burning interest to their contemporaries. When Lambard published his *Perambulation of Kent* in 1576 he dedicated it to his fellow countrymen: 'I know not (in respect of the place) unto whom I may more fitly send it than unto you, that are either bred or well brought up here, or by the goodness of God and your owne good provision are well settled here; and here lawfully possess, and are neere unto sundry of those things that this book specially speaketh of.' For it was with a highly informed and critical public in mind, and frequently with their active support, that these works were written. An interest in antiquity, in genealogy and heraldry, was the common pastime of the age, and numberless country gentlemen were engaged in the study of their locality. Heraldry had become a subject for serious almost solemn pursuit, and many, like William Cecil, must have spent laborious hours constructing and reconstructing the family pedigree, producing, as changing taste demanded, a British or a Roman ancestry. The investigation of origins fascinated men more and more, and an informed interest in anything with an antiquarian flavour encouraged the advances made in all branches of antiquarian scholarship. Genealogical studies received new impetus from the re-establishment of the College of Arms in 1555, and the appearance of John Guillim's *Display of Heraldry* in 1610. The Welshman Humphrey Lhuyd brought his knowledge of his native tongue to bear on the elucidation of English place-names, and Robert Taylor, who identified the Antonine Itinerary routes, provided skeleton material for a map of Roman Britain. The advances in cartography are impressive when seen against the difficulties which faced the early map-makers, who, as Lawrence Nowell said in a letter to Cecil in 1563, 'lacking any certain rule and all craft to aid their judgement, either placing their reliance upon the reports of certain others or trusting to the wavering conjecture of their own eyes, have huddled into their charts places set down and spaced by guess'. By the end of the century the demands of the new landed gentry for estate maps had encouraged the growth of trained surveyors, and it was from these that the earliest makers of county maps, Christopher Saxton, John Norden and Philip Symonson, emerged. Some time about 1572 Thomas Seckford, a wealthy Suffolk lawyer and courtier, commissioned Saxton to survey and map all the counties of England and Wales, and undertook to have them engraved and published at his own expense. Saxton's first two maps appeared two years later, and the others followed in rapid succession, so that the atlas, containing a general map of the country and thirty-four county maps, was completed by 1579. Saxton probably did more than any other man to establish cartography in England, not only because his maps, with their decorative colours and cartouches, were artistically masterpieces, but because they showed that engraved maps could be produced in large numbers. John Norden, although he failed through lack of patronage to accomplish that grandiose project the *Speculum Britanniae*, did yet produce plans of London and Westminster and five county maps between 1593 and 1598, and in them introduced certain radical improvements into English mapping: the marking of roads, omitted by Saxton; a marginal scale and index; inset plans of county towns; the symbol of crossed swords to mark a battlefield; and so on.[1] Meanwhile, a small group of scholars gathered round Archbishop Parker devoted themselves to Saxon studies, and Lawrence Nowell, the most prominent of these, attempted to make a glossary of Old English words.[2] All these were no dry, academic studies unrelated to contemporary life. The membership of the Society of Antiquaries founded in 1572 provides the best commentary on the state of antiquarian studies in Elizabethan England. Here peers and country gentlemen sat side by side with courtiers, heralds, judges and Members of Parliament, meeting frequently (until they were dissolved by James I who suspected them of subversive purposes) to read and discuss papers on every aspect of British antiquities.[3]

[1] Edward Lynam, *The Mapmaker's Art*, London, 1953, 55–74; *British Maps and Mapmakers*, London, 1944, 17–22.
[2] Robin Flower, 'Lawrence Nowell and the Discovery of England', *Proc. Brit. Acad.* 1935.
[3] J. Evans, *A History of the Society of Antiquaries*, Oxford, 1936.

A further incentive to the discovery of their native land, if one were needed, had been the presence of the Italian scholar Polydore Vergil at the court of Henry VII. He came to England in 1502 as the collector of Peter's Pence, and published his *Anglica Historia* in 1534. He dismissed with scant sympathy the *British History*, that mythical extravagance concerning the origins of the country which had been, up to this time, one of the most popular themes in historical writing. Supposedly discovered by Geoffrey of Monmouth in the twelfth century, but in fact largely his own invention, this told of the Trojan Brutus arriving in these islands, conquering the giants whom he found in possession, rebuilding London, which he named New Troy, and founding a great pre-Roman dynasty which reached the heights of its power under King Arthur, ruler of a northern empire stretching from Iceland to Gaul. The storm of indignation which arose when Polydore Vergil ruthlessly revealed all its weaknesses—'He pincheth somewhat smartly upon the antiquity of Britain', remarked William Burton ruefully—led men either to fight in its defence or to investigate the whole subject for themselves. Leland stands out as the greatest of these.

John Leland was born in London in 1503, and as an orphan was adopted by a certain Thomas Myles who sent him to St. Paul's School and then to Christ's College, Cambridge, where he took his B.A. in 1522. For a short time he was a member of the household of the Duke of Norfolk, but on the Duke's death in 1524 he went to Oxford, and from there to Paris, where he studied under Francis Sylvius and many famous scholars. On his return to England in 1529 he took holy orders, and became a royal chaplain, though here his main concern seems to have been with the three libraries established by Henry VIII in the palaces at Greenwich, Westminster and Hampton Court. In 1533 he was granted permission to search all the monastic and collegiate libraries of the country, and so began those journeyings that were to occupy him for the rest of his life. His reading of the historians and chroniclers of England's greatness had already filled him with a determination to see his country for himself, and, addressing his New Year's gift to Henry VIII in 1543, he told the king of his pleasure at this commission:

> I was totally enflammid with a love to see thoroughly al those partes of this your opulente and ample reaulme, that I had redde

of yn the aforesaid writers: yn so muche that al my other occupations
intermittid I have so travelid yn yowr dominions booth by the
se costes and the midle partes, sparing nother labor nor costes,
by the space of these vi. yeres paste, that there is almoste nother
cape, nor bay, haven, creke or peere, river or confluence of rivers,
breches, waschis, lakes, meres, fenny waters, montaynes, valleis,
mores, hethes, forestes, wooddes, cities, burges, castelles, principale
manor placis, monasteries, and colleges, but I have seene them;
and notid yn so doing a hole worlde of thinges very memorable.

He went on to speak of six books and concluded optimistically: 'I
truste that this yowr reaulme shaul so welle be knowen, ons
payntid with his native coloures, that the renoume ther shaul
gyve place to the glory of no other region.' But these high hopes
were not to be realized, for, as his friend John Bale put it, by 'a
most pitifull occasion he fell besides his wits', dying in 1552
with his great *Britannia* still unwritten. But the notes taken on
his travels, still in their manuscript form, soon became widely
known and highly prized, and copies, taken in whole or in part,
were passed from hand to hand, circulating widely amongst all
subsequent antiquaries.[1] For although he left no more than the
skeleton of his projected work, bare impersonal notes lacking the
warmth of detail and the picturesque touches which make much
later writing such delightful reading, in fact it is all there—the
towns and castles, the churches and their monuments, the open
and the enclosed country, the quarries, mines and industries.
He wrote neither as an archaeologist nor as a historian; he felt
no particular pride or pleasure in anything simply because it was
old. The fair new church at Fairford or the nave of Thornbury
built within the memory of man pleased him as much as Glaston-
bury Abbey or Hereford Cathedral; his fondness for standing
stones did not blind him to the existence of salt-workings or lead-
mines. The land over which King Arthur had ruled was equally
a land of new enclosure and flourishing industries. He covered the
country from Land's End to the Roman Wall in a succession of
journeys made over a period of ten years. It is impossible to
discover any continuous itinerary, for he seems to have started from
different places and made several separate tours, basing his excursions
on towns where he might have a chance of examining a library or

[1] The *Itineraries* were ultimately published by Thomas Hearne in nine
volumes, 1710-12. They were edited in five volumes in 1907 (London) by
Lucy Toulmin Smith, the edition used here.

else of enjoying the hospitality and local antiquarian knowledge of some landowner like Mr. Brudenell of Dene in Northamptonshire, whom he mentions several times as showing him rolls.

Perhaps he can be seen at his best and most typical in writing of military fortifications, earthworks and town walls, symbols of England's greatness in the past and still in his day one of the most dramatic features of the countryside. A 'campe of men of warre' would at once catch his attention, and he made constant reference to the dykes, ditches and towers he found in his journeys. It was, indeed, when he came to write of castles and walled towns that he most often managed to break away from his usual dry and unadorned recording. He would speculate whether a mound might be a Pictish fort, would draw attention to the skilful use of mortar or comment on structural details. Although most of the castles he saw were beginning to fall into ruin they must still have presented a magnificent appearance. At Tadcaster he found 'a mighty great hille, dikes, and garth of this castelle on Warfe be yet seene a litle above the bridge; it semith by the plot that it was a right stately thing'; Pontefract stood forth with its eight great towers; Fotheringay was fair and strong with double ditches and an ancient keep. Brancepeth was 'strongly set and buildid, and hath 2. courtes of high building'. He took obvious delight in the building technique he found at Richborough: 'The walles the wich remayn ther yet be in cumpase almost as much as the Tower of London. They have bene very hye, thykke, stronge and wel embattled. The mater of them is flynt, mervelus and long brykes both white and redde after the Britons fascion. The sement was made of se sand and smaul pible.' His imagination was stirred by the sight of the ruins of Tintagel: 'This castelle hath bene a mervelus strong and notable forteres, and almost *situ loci* inexpugnable, especially for the dungeon that is on a great and high terrible cragge environid with the se, but having a draw bridge from the residew of the castelle onto it.'

The first impression which he gave of any town would be a description of its fortifications and gates, its towers and bastions, for most were still enclosed by their medieval walls, and even if some were beginning to fall into ruins many more were still well maintained. At Exeter, although the towers had been allowed to decay, the walls had actually been recently remade; the walls and gates at Hereford were carefully kept in repair by the burgesses;

at Bath the walls were still complete, and Gloucester was still strongly defended by its walls. Many must have added a touch of warmth and colour to the scene, as the brick walls at Hull or those at Coventry of 'a darkesche depe redde, as it were ferragineos colour'. The finest of all he found at Newcastle, built by its medieval merchants, 'the strengh and magnificens of the waulling of this towne far passith al the waulles of the cities of England and of most of the townes of Europe'. Often, however, he found neglect and decay. At Richmond the walls were in ruins with only parts of four out of the five gates remaining; at Barnstaple the wall which used to be half a mile long was almost completely fallen down, while at Totnes nothing was left but the traces of the foundations.

Many of the more prosperous towns were paved by this time, and a few had even progressed towards some form of elementary sanitation, though such developments were still by no means common. Leland's description of Droitwich would probably be true of the average small town. 'The beauty of the towne in a maner standithe in one strete.... The towne of itselfe is somewhat foule and dirty when any reyne faullythe, with moche cariage throghe the stretes, [being] over ill pavyd or not pavyd.' Boscastle he found a very filthy town and ill kept, and he dismissed Padstow summarily as 'onclenly kept'. Yet Nottingham, in spite of timber-and-plaster building, had wide streets and clean paving, while at Manchester he for once forgot his principles and took it as a sign of grace that stones had been taken from the castle to build the bridge. At Durham he saw five conduits for fresh water for the town, and at Lichfield a conduit brought water from a hillside in lead pipes to the town.

The great majority were flourishing but unpretentious market towns, of which Wakefield or Evesham may be taken as typical. 'The toune of Wakefield streachith out all in lengtht by est and west, and hath a faire area for a market place. The building of the toune is meately faire, most of tymbre but sum of stone. Al the hole profite of the toun stondith by course drapery.' 'The towne of Eovsham is metely large and well buildyd with tymbar. The Market-Stede is faire and large. There be divers praty streats in the towne. The market kept at Eovsham is very celebrate.' The general pattern was of one long, well-built street, a market serving the immediate neighbourhood, and probably an annual fair. Such towns were the capitals of their small local kingdoms, vital links in the diversified economy of the sixteenth century. Thus Leland would describe Kingston as the best market for Surrey, and praise Swaffham as one of 'the quikkest markettes of al Northfolk ... it stondith much by handy crafte [men] and byers of grayne'.

Between such 'praty market tounes' the country still lay open, champion land whose fields were tilled in strips as they had been throughout the Middle Ages. The picture which Leland gave of enclosure, however, is by no means as clear as that of the Tudor moralists and pamphleteers, who saw it in only a sinister light as involving enclosure for sheep and the conversion of tillage to pasture, a movement calculated to enrich the landowners and merchants and to cause unemployment and poverty among the rural population. In fact only a small proportion of the country was enclosed at this time and much of that was to improve corn growing rather than for conversion into sheep-walks. The heart of the Midlands was still open country, and as he rode from Nottingham to Beverley Leland noted that it was all champion ground in sight, and between Wellingborough and Northampton marvellously rich corn land, while he saw near Bicester and Brackley 'very fruitfull grownd havynge good corne, grace and some wood, many conies, but litle enclosynge grownd'. But elsewhere the face of the countryside was beginning to change, and these endless vistas of rolling open fields were being broken up into the familiar chequer-board of modern England. As he travelled through the south-west, along the Welsh borders and through Somerset, Leland found hilly ground, rich in corn and grass, with most of the land enclosed by hedgerows, and he noted as he approached Ilchester that all the way along the fields and pastures were enclosed by hedges of elms. In parts of Devon, Cornwall and Wales where timber was scarce stone walls took the place of hedges. 'In tyme of mynde menne usid not in Termone [i.e. Anglesey] to seperate theyr grounde, but now stille more and more they digge stony hillokkes yn theyre groundes, and with the stones of them rudely congestid they devide theyre groundes after Devonshire fascion.' Yet the pattern was often more complex and Leland would frequently record travelling through two miles of enclosed followed by three miles of open country, or through a countryside divided almost equally between the two, as when he rode from Banbury to Warwick through twelve miles of 'champayne ground frutefull of corn and gresse, baren of woodde, and

2. miles by some enclosyd and wooddy ground'. It was unusual for him to say more than this: for an account of farming methods or for information about crops, techniques and the agricultural improvement we must wait for Defoe, or, later still, for Arthur Young and William Cobbett. He found a rich and peaceful country and did not concern himself with searching for reasons for its prosperity. The agrarian England that he described is well summed up in a phrase he used of Yorkshire: 'fruteful of wood, pasture and corne, a very pleasaunt countrey to se to'.

Time and again Leland would say of some small town 'a praty clothinge towne' or 'it stondith muche by clothinge', though he had little to add about the manufacture of cloth. The only detailed account he gave of any industry was that of salt-making at Droitwich, which he described at some length and added in conclusion, 'the people that be about the fornicas be very ille colourid'. He did, however, mention many mining enterprises: Cornish tin, the Forest of Dean iron-mines, lead ore from Swalesdale, coal from Derbyshire or the alabaster from the Isle of Axholme. Sea-coal was found at a number of places along the coasts, notably Pembrokeshire and Northumberland where 'the isle of Coquet standith apon a very good vayne of se coles, and at the ebbe men digge in the shore by the clives, and finde very good'. Inland coal, such as that mined in Yorkshire near Richmond, was of superior quality. 'The vayne of coales sometyme lyethe as a yarde depe of the substaunce of the coale. Sometyme the vayne it selfe is an ele in depthe, sometyme the hole heithe of a man, and that is a principall vayne. The crafte is to cum to it with leste paine in depe digginge. Some vaynes of coales ly under rokks and heades of stones: as some suppose that coales ly undar the very rokks that the minstar close of Duresme standithe on.' Mining often led to the growth of other associated trades nearby. At Rotherham, a mile from the mines, were very good smiths for all cutting tools; at Walsall, with its pits of sea-coals, iron ore and lime, there were many smiths and bit-makers in the town; while Birmingham had already gained a reputation for its smiths and cutters.

And yet the countryside was largely untamed; it was still far from 'the planted garden' of Defoe's day. Vast stretches of land were given up to woodland and forest; much remained waste and uncultivated. There were still great areas where the forest stretched for mile upon mile, stocked with deer and preserved for hunting.

Much of this was royal property, though Leland occasionally mentioned forests in private hands, as Lord Audley's at Stowey filled with red and fallow deer, or that recently created by the Duke of Buckingham at Thornbury and the cause of much unpopularity, 'the inhabytaunts cursyd the duke for thes lands so inclosyd'. Travelling was by no means free of natural hazards and the safe crossing of rivers could not be taken for granted. The bridge at Brecon had recently been carried away by flood-water, 'it was not by rain but by snow meltid that cam out of the montanes. The water ranne a yarde above the toppe of the hy bridge.' The stone bridge which Leland saw in course of being built at Gloucester would be most important, since there was no other below, and none above for eleven or twelve miles. At Stratford, before Hugh Clopton, Lord Mayor of London, had built the great bridge, there had been only a poor timber bridge with no causeway to it, 'whereby many poore folkys [and] othar refusyd to cum to Stratford, when Avon was up, or cominge thithar stoode in jeoperdy of lyfe'. Similarly, at Abingdon, which until a recent gift towards making a bridge had depended upon its ferry, were 'dyvers mischauncis sene at this passage and dyvers persones drowned'.

But there are many hints here of the England which will become familiar in the pages of later tourists. Already Leland's England was one in which monastic houses were giving place to the country houses of a prospering gentry. Milwood Park, a Carthusian monastery in Lincolnshire, had become a good manor; Cateley Priory, near Sleaford, now belonged to one Car, 'a proper gentilman, whos father was a riche marchaunt of the staple'; at Titchfield in Hampshire Mr. Wriothesley had built a stately house in the place of the Premonstratensian monastery there. Whether or not it was under the stimulus of newly acquired monastic property, certainly many of the gentry were rebuilding and enlarging their houses. Mr. Strangeways at Melbury had been improving his house by the addition of a high tower requiring 3000 loads of freestone from a quarry nine miles away; Mr. Gostwick of Willington, having acquired property from the suppressed abbey of Wardon and bought five or six more lordships, had built a fine new brick-and-timber house with water brought in a conduit of lead pipes; Lord Russell had so changed the house at Chenies that little or nothing of the original remained. Begun in 1511,

Thornbury was still unfinished, with the foundations of the court, certain towers and gates, standing as witnesses to the ambitious intentions of its noble owner. Leland scarcely ever mentioned the interiors of any of these houses, though he did describe Ewelme Manor: 'the haul of it is fair and hath great barres of iron overthuart it instede of crosse beames. The parler by is exceding fair and lightsum: and so be all the lodginges there.' He was clearly much impressed, as one would expect him to be, by the library at Wressel. 'One thing I likid excedingly yn one of the towers, that was a study caullid Paradise, wher was a closet in the midle of 8. squares latisid aboute: and at the toppe of every square was a desk legid to set bookes on cofers withyn them, and these semid as yoinid hard to the toppe of the closet: and yet by pulling one or al wold cum downe, and serve for deskes to lay bokes on.' He never felt the slightest hesitation in discussing the wealth of any family, or the sources from which they derived their income. Some were 'ancient gentilmen', many more 'originally marchauntes and after men of land'. The Mr. Palmer of Warwickshire who rose by a successful marriage was worth a passing note. 'He began first with a very smaul portion of lande: and being a galant felow, and clothid yn mightie colowrs, got a riche widow in Lemington to wife, a 80. yers or more hens; and sins there hath plantid themselfes, and buildid a faire house, and bought faire landes to it.' Such were the country squires, the 'gentilmen that have praty landes', an essential part of the England Leland knew, and the ancestors of those tourists who in the next centuries were to follow him in the discovery of England.

'I truste so to open this wyndow that the lighte shall be seene so longe, that is to say, by the space of a hole thousand yere, stoppid up, and the olde glory of your renownid Britaine to reflorisch thorough the worlde.' Leland was right in that he had in fact opened a window that was not to close again. His contribution to English topographical writing was profoundly important. He had determined to go and see his country for himself instead of merely reading about it, and moreover to see it in its entirety, not with the specialist approach of the archaeologist or the antiquarian. Spurred by curiosity, and enflamed by patriotism, he looked at everything, past and present together, since for him they were two inseparably interwoven halves of the Tudor England with which he was in love.

ECCLESIOLOGY AND SCIENCE

The Seventeenth-century Tourists

OHN LELAND had blazed the way and a large band of later Tudor topographical writers followed his lead. Perhaps the greatest of them was William Camden, though he can scarcely qualify as a tourist. For, setting out upon the herculean task of covering the entire country, including the outlying islands, from the Scillies to the Shetlands, he was forced to turn to a band of correspondents for information about those parts which he could not visit himself, and he thereby broke the first canon of the true tourist in failing to see what he described. Later authors were to go even further, depending not merely upon their friends for help but lifting accounts wholesale from earlier works, and compiling treatises which were little more than guide-books listing any noteworthy sites but failing to bring the country itself to life. By the seventeenth century writing of this kind was in full spate. The widespread and growing antiquarian interests promised a good market, and with a sufficiency of material upon which to draw the manufacture of such books could become a pleasant task for winter evenings or old age. Edward Chamberlain sought to win the confidence of his readers by reassuring them that he had made frequent use of such authorities as Glanvill, Bracton, Camden and Selden. His *Anglia Notitia; or, the Present State of England: together with Divers Reflections upon the Antient State thereof* was a careful work for the conscientious traveller, written, as he explained in his introduction, 'so that the whole state of *England* might be seen at once, as in a Map; so every one might without trouble alwayes carry it about with him as a *Companion* to consult upon all occasions'. Edward Blome in his *Britannia* of 1673 made his position even clearer by renouncing any claim to be called *author*. Rather he saw himself as 'the *Undertaker* of this *Work*, it receiving Birth from divers *Manuscripts*, from all *Books* yet extant that have writ of the same *subject*, as well in general, as in particular: and from some *hundreds* of experienced *persons* in the several *parts* of the *Kingdom* of *England*, who have freely contributed their assisting *hands* in the promoting the same, and rectifying or enlarging the *descriptions* of such *places* etc as are known unto them'.[1] Almost equally remote from first-hand experience, though in a very different genre, was Michael Drayton with his *Polyolbion*, a lengthy description of the country in verse which ranged from a mere catalogue of the general characteristics of a county to flights of wildest fantasy and high-flown praise. Offa's dyke, for example, proved the signal for a show of patriotic exultation:

> Offa (when he saw his Countries goe to wrack)
> From bick'ring with his folke, to keepe us *Britons* back,
> Cast up that Mound of eighty miles in length,
> Athwart from *Sea* to *Sea*, which of the *Mercians* strength
> A witness though it stand and *Offa*'s name doe beare,
> Our courage was the cause why he first cut it there.[2]

Eulogies were poured out upon the Fens:

> Of all the *Marshland* Iles, I *Ely* am the Queene
> For Winter each where sad, in me likes fresh and greene.
> The Horse, or other beast, o'rway'd with his owne masse,
> Lies wallowing in my Fennes, hid over head in grasse:
> And in the place where growes rank Fodder for my Neat;
> The Turffe which beares the Hay, is wondrous heedfull Peat:
> My full and batning earth, needs not the Plowmans paines:
> The Rils which runne in me, are like the branches vaines
> In humane Bodies seene.[3]

[1] *Britannia; or a Geographical Description of the Kingdoms of England, Scotland, and Ireland*, London, 1673, *preface, 1–2*.
[2] *A Chorographical Description of all the tracts, rivers, mountains, forests, and other parts of this Renowned Isle*, London, 1622, *158*.
[3] ibid., *24*.

But by no means all were content with second-hand accounts, arid descriptions and turgid verses. There were still many honest tourists who really set out to see the countryside and to write books about what they had actually seen. Most enterprising of them all was John Taylor, the self-styled Water Poet, who was determined not only to see England for himself but to make his writing pay for it. His method was to solicit subscriptions, sending out bills to his friends and promising them in return an account of his journey. The picture he presented of himself to his readers in his introduction was as jaunty and disarming as his verses:

> Like to the stone of Sisiphus, I roule
> From place to place, through weather faire and foule,
> And yet I every day must wander still
> To vent my Bookes, and gather friends good will;
> I must confess this worke is frivalowse,
> And he that (for it) daignes to give a lowse,
> Doth give as much for it as 'tis worth, I know.[1]

The prospects he held out of his subject-matter were equally light-hearted:

> This Pamphlet is not stuft with Triviall Bables,
> Or vaine prodigious undigested fables:
> This is no *Mercury* (with scoffs and jeeres)
> To raise debate and set us by the eares,
> ... My lines are all from feare and horror free,
> And here and there as true as true may be.[2]

Yet he was not entirely the gay and irresponsible bard, for beneath the mask of the clown there was often a hint of tragedy:

> This is a mad world, (my masters) and in sadnes
> I travail'd madly in these dayes of madnes:
> Eight yeares a *frenzy* did this Land molest ...[3]

For though political comment lay outside the scope of most tourists, few in the middle years of the seventeenth century could fail to take notice of the effects of the Civil War and the scars it had left upon the face of the country. In his *Wanderings to See the Wonders of the West* in 1649 John Taylor came across many examples of a country just beginning to recover from its devastations. At

[1] *Wanderings to see the Wonders of the West, 1649*, London, 1670, 21.
[2] *Taylors Travels, from London to the Isle of Wight, 1648, introduction*, Spenser Society, Manchester, 1876.
[3] *Wanderings ... 1649, 1-2*.

Faringdon he saw particularly clearly what it had meant, for here the Royalists had burnt one part of the town and the Parliamentarians had fired the rest, so that between them a handsome market town had been turned into ashes and rubbish. It was now being rebuilt again, with here and there a pretty house, the promise that it would rise phoenix-like from its cinders. The sight of Wells was especially sad: 'I stayd but little and found as little matter of observation, but that these holy, prophane days, and blessed execrable times of troublesome tranquility, have spoyled and defaced one of the goodliest and most magnificent Cathedrall Churches in the Christian world: But for such pious workes as polution and abusing of Churches, wee neede not goe amongst Turkes for proofes.'[1]

The religious conflicts of the early seventeenth century were no doubt responsible for an interest in churches, more marked among John Taylor and his contemporaries than either the tourists who preceded or who followed them. It was an informed and intelligent interest, one which reflected the common concern of an age which forced men to consider their loyalties towards a godly Puritanism or to the Laudian ideals of the beauty of holiness. A few, like Ralph Thoresby or the brothers Edward and Thomas Browne, still followed the more limited antiquarian approach of cataloguing and transcribing inscriptions, measuring the length of altars, counting the numbers of statues and recording details of knights in armour and recumbent figures. But a man like Lieutenant Hammond who made his tours in 1634 and 1635, when the Laudian movement was at its height, looked at churches with particular regard to the worship and liturgical practices carried on within them. His great delight was wherever he went to find that 'the Citizens haue spared no cost, nor forwardnesse to beautify and adorne (a pious, and religious example for all our Kingdome) for they dayly striue in euery Parish, who shall exceed other in their generous, and religious bounty, most to decke, and inrich, those sanctify'd Places, and Heauenly Mansions, heere on Earth, to Gods glory, and good example of others'.[2] He took a special pleasure in listing plate and vestments,

[1] ibid., 3, 4.
[2] *A Relation of a Short Survey of 26 Counties Observed in a Seven Weeks Journey begun on August 11 1634*, By a Captain, a Lieutenant and an Ancient, (ed.) L. G. Wickham Legg, London, 1904, 92.

and noting any particularly splendid examples of copes, crosses or altar cloths. 'The Sumptuous Ornaments, and vestments belonging to this Cathedrall [he was referring to York] are carefully kept in the vestry aforesaid, vizt, the gorgeous Canopie, the rich Communion Table-cloths, the Coapes of embroder'd velvet, Cloth of Gold, Silver, and Tissue, of great worth, and value. There Mr. Verger shew'd us St. Peter's Chair (which we made bold to rest in), wherein all the Archbishops are install'd: Two double gilt Coronets, the tops with Globes, and Crosses to set on either side of his Grace, upon his sayd Instalment, when he takes his Oath, these are call'd his Dignities.'[1] He listed the rich profusion of vestments he saw at Winchester with obvious pride: 'One of Velvet wrought with Gold for the High Altar, which was given by Bishop Fox, others of Cloth of Tissue and faire Cushions, which were given by Sr. John Paulet. Another of Cloth of Gold, fill'd with Pearle Wire. A rich, and faire Canopie of Cloth of Gold to carry ouer the king. 12. faire Cushions of red and blew Velvet with Lions and flower de Luces in them wrought in Gold.'[2] He always noticed the organ for he was interested in church music, and whenever possible joined in the services. At Exeter he enjoyed the 'delicate, rich and lofty Organ, which has more additions then any other, as fayre Pipes of an extraordinary length, and of the bignesse of a man's thigh, which with their vialls, and other sweet Instruments, the tunable Voyces, and the rare Organist, togeather, makes a melodious, and heauenly Harmony, able to rauish the Hearers Eares'.[3] He looked upon the statues of the west front of a cathedral such as Wells or Exeter less as fine examples of medieval carving than as reminders of his Christian heritage, and was glad to spend his time at Canterbury reading the legends of the stained-glass windows, or at Winchester deciphering the wood-carving, tracing the scenes portrayed there from the Creation to the Passion. He was clearly at his happiest gazing at the 'Patriarkes, Prophets, Apostles, Fathers, and other blessed Saints of the Church, from the Creation, in their admir'd Postures, artificially cut in Freestone', or listening to 'voyces and Organs at Prayer'.

[1] ibid., *18*.

[2] *A Relation of a Short Survey of the Western Counties made by a Lieutenant of the Military Company in Norwich in 1635*, (ed.) L. G. Wickham Legg, London, 1936, *49*.

[3] ibid., *44*.

This impression given by the Lieutenant of the richness of ecclesiastical furnishing is echoed in the accounts of many of his fellow tourists who comment on the recent adornment of churches and cathedrals. Even the Brownes were distracted from their single-minded pursuit of antiquities at Boston when they saw a font newly built of black and white marble with 'a cover in the fashione of a crowne, which might bee lifted up higher or lower as you please by a cord, which was fastned to it and the top of the church'.[1] Roger Gale found St. Mary Redcliffe, that magnificent Gothic church in Bristol, had recently been repaired, the pillars being painted like marble and the capitals filled with gold 'so that it seemed new-built when I saw it'.[2] His picture of Salisbury was equally full of colour:

> The church within is adorned with a great number of small marble columns, of a greyish mixture, such as adorn many of our sacred edifices, and seem to be of Sussex marble. . . . The choir is spacious, regular, and beautiful, and lately new-built. Over the great door there is a great organ, the pipes covered with gold, and the case of wainscot, finely carved. The stalls are decently painted and gilt. The frontispiece of the altar is hung with crimson velvet, fringed with gold, and the antepedium is of the same.[3]

It was mainly for the splendour of its chapels that Gale enjoyed Oxford, the pride of place going to New College:

> It is a curious structure, and so decently adorned, that a view of it leaves a religious impression upon the mind; it is paved with black and white marble. The windows are large, and represent the sacred histories in painted glass. The wood-work of the choir is painted, and the carving gilt; the backs of the stalls are adorned in lively colours with the effigies of the patriarchs, prophets, and apostles in full proportion. The frontispiece of the altar is beautified with painting, and a good picture of the Salutation; above which, upon the wall, there is a cupola well designed in good perspective. The roof is also painted and gilt. This chapel brings to my thoughts Mr. Milton's desire, which he thus expresses in the poem by him styled *Il Penseroso*:

---

[1] *Journal of Edward and Thomas Browne's Tour into Derbyshire in 1662, Sir Thomas Browne's Works*, (ed.) Simon Wilkin, London, 1836, I, *24*.
[2] *A Tour through Several Parts of Britain*, 1705, J. Nichols, *Bibliotheca Topographica Britannia*. London, 1790, III, *16*.
[3] ibid., *28–9*.

> But let my due feet never fail
> To walk the studious cloisters pale
> And love the high embower'd roof
> With antique pillars massy proof,
> And storied windows, richly dight,
> Casting a dim, religious light.[1]

In cathedral after cathedral that he visited in his travels in 1635 Sir William Brereton found frequent evidence of moves under Laudian influence to increase a sense of the reverence and dignity of divine worship, and he had cause to comment a number of times on the refurbishing of the Lady Chapel for the daily saying of Morning Prayer. At Hereford, for example, where Matthew Wren was then bishop, the altar had been railed off and might be approached only at times of communion; at Gloucester two small oratories on either side of the Lady Chapel had been made ready for private devotions. At Durham Brereton attended a celebration of the Holy Communion with full vestments and ceremonial.

> A stately altar-stone all of fine marble, standing upon a frame of marble pillars of the same marble of the font. When the Communion is here administered, which is by the bishop himself, here is laid upon this altar, or rather communion-table, a stately cloth of gold; the bishop useth the new red embroidered cope which is wrought full of stars, like one I have seen worn in St. Dennis in Fraunce; there are here other two rich copes, all which are shaped like unto long cloaks reaching down to the ground, and which have round capes.[2]

The tradition of high ceremonial continued here throughout the century, so that when Joseph Taylor visited Durham in 1705, on a day of thanksgiving, he was able to enjoy its ecclesiastical grandeur to the full; and it is interesting to see that after the processions and the music it was the vestments which made the greatest impression upon him: 'Seaven Copes of Velvet and Silk, are us'd there in divine service at the Altar; they are most curiously wrought, and express the severall historys of the Bible, and other particular passages relating to our saviour, all in needlework: In these habits the priests look like Monarchs triumphant,

[1] ibid., 6-7.
[2] *Travels in Holland, the United Provinces, England, Scotland and Ireland, 1634-5*, (ed.) Edward Hawkins, Chetham Society, 1894, 83.

and since we are so happy as to have reform'd from Romish Idolatry, I could not forbear calling these relicts of their pride, Rich Raggs of the Whore of Babylon.'[1]

Second only to this ecclesiastical interest, and again entirely characteristic of the outlook of the seventeenth century, came an interest in all technical and scientific matters. The Fens now came into their own: for while they continued to fascinate the tourists as an alien and strange land full of barbaric, if not amphibious, creatures, a new aspect now contended with the old: the sight of the drainage and reclamation of vast areas of marshy waste, probably one of the greatest technological achievements of the age. The Fenmen themselves still remained a race apart, a species to whom the normal attributes of mankind did not really apply, and it was doubtless considerably to his satisfaction that at Ely Lieutenant Hammond found all his worst suspicions of them confirmed: 'They haue butt a turfy sent and Fenny posture about them, which smell I did not relish at all with any content.' From the top of the towers of Peterborough Cathedral almost the entire Fenland lay spread at his feet, and his eyes roved over the countryside which bred such extraordinary native beings: 'This little kingdome of Marisches and Fenns, wherein were quarter'd many Regiments of Cattell; and her 2. old neighbouring, watry and phlegmaticke Sisters, Crowland and Ely, with their tatter'd and ragg'd blew Azure Mantles about them, which Time and Age made soe decreppit.' But everywhere the 'shaking Quagmires and rotten Fennes' were being reduced to fertile pastures and good farming land by the skill of the Dutch engineer Vermuyden and his minions: 'a numerous Company of lusty, stout, sweating Pioneers hard at worke, digging, deluing, casting up and quartering out new streames and Rivers, to gaine ground, and to make that large Continent of vast, foggie, miry, rotten, and unfruitfull Soyle, vsefull, fruitfull, and beneficiall, and for the aduantage of the Commonwealth'.[2] Sir William Dugdale's account of his travels through the Fens in 1657 was a long saga of rides beside great dykes, and across wide fenny flats recently drained; of sluices and drains newly made by the Adventurers; of deep channels cut with tremendous cost and labour; of banks built to defend

[1] *A Journey to Edenborough in Scotland in the Yeare 1705*, (ed.) William Cowan, Edinburgh, 1903, 78–9.
[2] *Short Survey of the Western Counties*, 1635, 89–92.

the country from flooding at times of high tide; of Willingham mere drained by diverting the Ouse, and banks raised eight or nine feet high beside the new river. The land on each side of the way towards Outwell had been drained by a multitude of ditches with the earth from them raised into ridges, so that the country-side was patterned by ditches and banks and marked by sluices, with between them rich fields of cultivation, fine plantations of fruit trees, cole-seed and corn. At Salter's Lode near Earith he was told that there were no less than eleven thousand men employed on the work at a time, and certainly it was a most remarkable achievement.[1]

Industry, and above all mining, had also about it something of the same character of scientific advance which attracted the tourists in the engineering feats of the Fen drainage. Sir William Brereton turned aside on his way from Newcastle to Tynemouth because here he could visit the salt-works, 'wherein is more salt made than in any part of England that I know, and all the salt here is made of salt-water; these pans are not to be numbered, placed in the river-mouth, and wrought with coals brought by water from the Newcastle pits. A most dainty new salt-work here erected, which is absolutely the most complete work that I ever saw . . .' and he went on to speak with well-informed enthusiasm of furnaces and pans, lumps of hard black salt, the measurements of cauldrons, and so on, following each successive stage of the manufacture with intense interest, in spite of 'such a cloud of smoke as amongst these works you cannot see to walk'.[2] Thomas and Edward Browne seemed to find it completely natural to turn from visiting churches in King's Lynn to seeing any local manufacture, and they were disappointed that when they visited the glass-works they were unable to see it in the making as the furnace was out.

The Lieutenant, as befitted a military man, took a great interest in his country's fortifications and defences, and as he made his way slowly along the south coast he missed no opportunity of inspecting every fort that lay within his path, taking immense pride in the thought that 'no daring approaching Enemies can pass these Chanells, without thundring Gun-shot from those

[1] *Things Observable in our Itinerarie begun from London 19 May 1657*, B. M. Lans. MS.
[2] *Travels in Holland . . . 1634-5, 88-9.*

commaunding castles'. He rejoiced when he saw Dover and
Corfe in a state of good repair, well guarded with strong walls
and ordnance, and he was even more greatly pleased with what he
found at Carisbrooke:

> It is mounted on a hill, with long deepe Ditches round about the
> walls, where-into I was suddenly admitted by a braue old Blade
> (the residing Deputy Governor thereof) ouer a stately large Bridge,
> through a stronglie-built Gatehouse. . . . As I march'd with my
> old keeper the Round upon the walls, I view'd the large Chambers
> and Lodgings; the Platforms, Counter-Scarffs, Casemates,
> Bulwarkes, and Trenches, without the walls, whereupon were
> mounted many Peeces of Ordnance; I found it well guarded with
> Armes, though not with Men; for in the Armory which is ouer
> against the Chappell in one Roome were 500. good Corselettes;
> And in another Roome by the other 7. or 8. Muskets.[1]

Standing on the walls of Portsmouth, watching an exchange
between the fort and two passing ships, his patriotic pride in
England's martial strength was obvious as he wrote:

> The stately Ship, the Swallow, tooke her flight close by vs, with
> swift wing and full Sayle, and 206. men in her: when she was right
> against the Fort, she vayl'd her Topsayle, and discharg'd halfe a
> dozen great Guns for her parting Salute; the officers straightway
> from the Fort requited her with three Peeces of Ordinance for a
> like parting volley; at the same time there pass'd another goodly
> ship, The Harry, soone after the other, with the like vayling
> Posture, and receiuing the like farewell Salute from the Fort of
> her Foy.[2]

This spontaneous interest and enthusiasm carried the tourists
into exploration of every possible aspect of the England they were
travelling: recent feats of engineering or proud military outposts,
the splendours of medieval architecture or the intricacies of
modern salt-workings, all were pursued with a vigorous and
whole-hearted enjoyment. Sometimes, indeed, this appetite for
information and experience of every sort tended to run to absurd
lengths. Dugdale, for example, could not help breaking off from
his painstaking antiquarian researches in tracing the Icknield
Way or measuring Lincoln Cathedral to record the fact that:
'10 May last 3 swarmes of Bees one after another lighted upon our

---

[1] *Short Survey of the Western Counties*, 1635, 57–8.
[2] ibid., 40.

goodman Turner's wife (who lived in Fordham parish on Mr Edmund Skipworth's lands) one on her Brest, ye 3rd under Clothes & crept up to her belly (people following after) wch frightened her so, she stript of her clothes, & ran home naked.' Nor did the Lieutenant seem to find it at all incongruous to turn from an inspection of cathedral architecture and vestments to examine such unorthodox possessions as the skeleton preserved in Exeter Cathedral library: 'A Rarity, which is a real Anatomy of a Man, who (for his Delinquency) ended his Life at the heauvy Tree: all his severall Bones, 248, his Teeth 28 &c. all fix'd and plac'd in their proper places, which was dissected by a skilful Italian Doctor with the approbation of the right-reverend-learned Lord Bishop of this Diocese, and with his leave here appointed to be kept.'[1] For this was essentially an age of unsophisticated touring, of uncritical and all-embracing enthusiasms, in which the canons of aesthetic and antiquarian taste had not yet been laid down; the cult of the Picturesque had not yet claimed its disciples; the romantic approach to industry had not yet been definitely formulated; nor had the tour of country houses developed into a stereotyped round. So indeed the seventeenth-century tourist, more than the tourist of any other age, was likely to produce a *Speculum Britanniae*, a description which mirrored his country in every variety of mood and aspect.

[1] ibid., 76.

34

4

A PLANTED GARDEN

Celia Fiennes and Daniel Defoe

N 1685 an intrepid young woman called Celia Fiennes set out to tour Britain, and by 1705 had covered more or less the whole length of the country. Twenty years later, in 1725, a hack journalist, Daniel Defoe, began to write a series of letters, the product of three general tours and seventeen large circuits he had made over the previous years. At first glance it would seem hard to find two writers more dissimilar. Defoe's letters were the distillation of notes taken on journeys over a long period of time and included lengthy digressions, economic discourses and moralizings. Celia Fiennes wrote a vivid day-to-day account of her travels, allowing her readers to follow her into all the varied adventures in which she continually found herself. Unlike Defoe she was not in anyone's pay; she travelled purely for pleasure, she would never write of anything she had not actually seen herself, and, apart from one passing reference to Camden, she was clearly oblivious of the writings of any earlier topographical authors. The differences between the two are immediately obvious from the actual quality of their writing. In her foreword Celia Fiennes warned her readers, though without seriously apologizing for it, that she wrote with a certain freedom and easiness, and that they must not expect 'exactness or politeness in this book, tho' such embellishments might have adorned the descriptions and suited the nicer taste'. The cascades of words pouring forth breathlessly with little regard for punctuation constitute at once the charm and the difficulty of her style, and contribute in no small measure to the impression she gives of a naive, childlike enthusiasm and enjoyment. Defoe in contrast writes a straightforward narrative prose, cold, critical and meassured, scorning to indulge in the hyperboles with which her work is adorned.

Yet they have a surprising amount in common, their greatest bond being a strong determination to see *contemporary* England. Neither felt any great interest in antiquities, and the frequency with which they condemned buildings as mean or old would have bewildered Leland or Stukeley as much as their regret at leaving busy industrial towns for lakes and mountains would have amazed the Rev. William Gilpin and those who cultivated the Picturesque. Taken together the two are at once a splendid foil and complement to each other, and between them they bring to life the England they found. Celia Fiennes is generally the more vivid because of the immediacy of her observation and because her woman's eye so often caught the intimate details of what she saw; Defoe brings a trained mind and a critical judgement to bear which could assess the importance of what he found and recognize its significance. Thus, while Celia Fiennes missed no opportunity of giving details of any local delicacy she especially enjoyed at her inn, Defoe would write of the growth of specialization in supplying the increasing needs of the metropolis. When she wrote with enthusiasm of the fine furnishings in the country houses she visited, or commented on the designs of their Dutch formal gardens, Defoe had something to say on the state of contemporary society which produced the wealth to make such building possible. Again, while both were impressed by the rapid growth of towns, Celia Fiennes' interests were aroused by such matters as sanitation and reasonable living conditions, and it would be left to Defoe to comment on the role they played in their immediate local economy.

'If novelty pleases here is the present state of the country described', announced Defoe, and Celia Fiennes protested her determination to portray the modern scene, hoping that others would be encouraged to follow her example and inform themselves of the nature of the land and the genius of its inhabitants so that trade and manufacture might thereby be improved. It was a rich, populous and thriving country that they set out to explore, a land at peace, after religious and political dissension, in which a growing population, expanding commerce and developing industry were, as Defoe said, opening new scenes every day and making England show a new and different face in many places, new discoveries, new undertakings, new inventions, new manufactures, 'in a nation pushing and improving as we are'.[1] As he stood on Bushey Heath surveying the rolling ground spread at his feet his feelings were well summed up for him by two foreign visitors who looked at each other and then turning their eyes in every direction said in voices of wonder that 'England was not like other's countrys, but it was all a planted garden'.[2]

Cultivated England, and, above all, scenes of industrial activity, called forth their passages of warmest praise; natural landscape on the whole left them unmoved. As he left the Lancashire towns and made his way north towards the Lake District, Defoe felt that he had come to the end of the pleasant part of England and was entering a land of unhospitable terror, barren and bleak, with high and impassable hills, of no use or advantage to either man or beast.[3] There was little of the romantic in him as he made that snowy August journey along the eight miles from Blackstone Edge to Halifax, mounting to the clouds and descending to the level again about eight times and all the while praying for the sight of the valley and a Christian country.[4] Celia Fiennes admittedly was delighted with the waterfalls of the Lake District and enjoyed the noise and violence of their passage down the rocks, but she was really only too thankful to leave those deserted and barren hills, and rejoiced that she had not ventured into Cumberland where 'I should have found more such and they tell me farr worse for height and stony-nesse'.[5]

The richness and variety of English agriculture, however, pleased them both greatly, for, though they were in no way as critical and scientific as later eighteenth-century agrarian writers,

[1] D. Defoe, *A Tour through England and Wales*, (ed.) G. D. H. Cole, London, 1928, II, *133*.
[2] Defoe, II, *8*.
[3] Defoe, II, *269*.
[4] Defoe, II, *193*.
[5] *The Journeys of Celia Fiennes*, (ed.) Christopher Morris, London, 1949, *195*, *198*.

they were immensely interested in all they saw. Leaving London
for the south through Kent the traveller came almost immediately
upon the Garden of England, where hop-yards and orchards of
cherry and apple stretched for mile after mile. Another countryside of gardens and fruit-farming was Worcestershire, Herefordshire and the Vale of Evesham, astounding Defoe that so close to
the barren hills of Wales there could be a land so pleasant and so
fertile that even the hedgerows were of apple and pear trees and
the passers-by could gather what fruit they pleased as they rode
past.[1] A contrast, though equally fine in its way, was pastoral
England, that land of downs which Defoe reflected as he passed
over Salisbury Plain must be amongst the most charming that
could be found anywhere.[2] Here he admired the great numbers
of sheep in flocks of four or five thousand, and then later was
impressed by the vast numbers he saw in Lincolnshire and
Leicestershire, providing an inexhaustible source for all the
manufacturing counties in which cloth was made.[3] About half
the arable land of the country was still held in open field strips,
mainly in that great belt stretching across from the Hampshire
downs through the Midlands to Yorkshire. Yet even here there
were many small scattered areas of enclosure, though it was mainly
in the south-west that the traveller rode through a landscape of
small fields with their surrounding hedges. Celia Fiennes found
quicksets in Devon and hazel and holly hedges in Cornwall, and
she had particular praise for smooth green banks, as well kept as in
any garden, between which she rode on her way to Manchester.[4]
She had little to say about the use to which arable land was put,
and it is Defoe who supplies information about the farming
methods he saw. The impression he gives is of widespread enterprise and experiment. Sheep and black cattle were being fattened
on turnips in Suffolk; in Essex and Suffolk underground drainage
had been introduced; on Salisbury Plain sheep were being folded
on the newly ploughed lands, which, as a result, were producing
excellent crops of wheat; experiments were already being made in
breeding; marl was being dug in Norfolk from the underlying
beds to mix with the sandy topsoil. Care about fertilizers, the

[1] Defoe, II, 43.
[2] Defoe, I, 187.
[3] Defoe, II, 194.
[4] C. Fiennes, 260, 244, 222.

introduction of turnips and clover, experiments in drainage or in breeding—here is a picture of agricultural improvement long before the days of Coke and Bakewell.[1]

Every village and small town naturally had its local craftsmen, miller, baker, cobbler, brewer and tanner, supplying the needs of those employed on the land. But there were also more specialized rural industries, and amongst these the manufacture of cloth still held pride of place as it had done for centuries. There was a marked contrast between the cloth making carried on in East Anglia or the south-west where the weavers and spinners worked for some master clothier, and that of the West Riding where every man was his own master, working in his own house with the help of his wife and family, and then carrying his finished piece of cloth to market. As Defoe rode through Yorkshire he noticed a tenter outside almost every home with a piece of cloth laid out to dry, and knocking on one such door he found a house full of lusty fellows, some at the dye-vat, some dressing the cloths, others at the loom, some at one thing and some at another, but all hard at work upon their own particular business.[2] It was typical of their respective interests that the best description of the actual manufacture should come from Celia Fiennes, while Defoe was more concerned with its marketing. At the Exeter serge market Celia Fiennes saw great packs of serges sold under the stone pillars of the market house and this so aroused her curiosity that she was not satisfied until she had followed the whole process of its manufacture at every stage from the loom through the fulling, burling, pressing and dyeing. She wrote with her peculiar zest in discovering how things worked of the fulling and scouring operations:

They lay them[3] in soack in urine then they soape them and soe put them into the fulling-mills and soe worke them in the mills drye till they are thick enough, then they turne water into them and soe scower them, the mill does draw out and gather in the serges, its a pretty divertion to see it, a sort of huge notch'd timbers like great teeth, one would thinke it should injure the serges but it

[1] Defoe, II, *58, 224, 285.* For an assessment of Defoe's comments on agriculture see T. S. Ashton, *Economic History of England. England in the Eighteenth Century,* London, 1955, *32–3.*
[2] Defoe, II, *195.*
[3] i.e. the serges which have just been brought from the loom.

does not, the mills draws in with such a great violence that if one stands neere it, and it catch a bitt of your garments it would be ready to draw in the person even in a trice.[1]

The cloth market at Leeds was a most remarkable sight, which Defoe thought a prodigy of its kind and not to be equalled in the world. When the market bell was rung at about 7 a.m. the clothiers would leave their inns or shops, each bearing his own cloth like some regiment drawn up in line, and would place it upon the trestles set up along the streets. The merchants and buyers then walked up and down viewing the cloths laid out for display, carrying out any transaction in whispers so that their neighbour might not hear, and the successful seller would then carry his piece on his shoulder to the merchant's house. When at 8.30 a.m. the bell rang again the market was over. Yet in little more than an hour between £10,000 and £20,000 worth of goods might have changed hands, all in a profound silence.[2]

The sight of mines filled Celia Fiennes with excitement and she excelled in writing of them. She described with real enjoyment the use of gunpowder in a mine at Buxton and the violent heat and fierce flames of the tin-mines she saw in Cornwall. She compared the coking-coal at Kingswood with the fine cannel-coal from Wigan which could be polished up to look like marble; she found that Derbyshire pit-coal burnt like a candle and made white ash similar to that of Nottinghamshire, and declared that the coal from the Malvern Hills was almost as good as sea-coal. At Beaudesert she saw coal being drawn up in a windlass; she watched the lead-miners at Buxton, pale and yellow from their life underground, being let down with a rope and pulley, and saw iron being smelted for bells and guns in the Weald. She admired the water-engines used to drain the tin-mines in Cornwall, which did three times as much as those turned by horses, and later watched the ore being blown in a stamping-mill, flung into a furnace so that it burnt together and made a violent heat and flame. The copperas works at Brownsea particularly fascinated her: 'They place iron spikes in the panns full of branches and so as the liquor boyles to a candy it hangs on those branches: I saw some taken up it look't like a vast bunch of grapes, the coullour of

[1] C. Fiennes, 246.
[2] Defoe, II, 204.

40

the Copperace not being much differing it looks cleare like sugar-candy.'[1]

The success of this varied economy depended to a large extent upon the handling of the local goods by the markets, fairs and ports which studded the travellers' way. Transport was improving, not only with the coming of the turnpike trusts to reform the state of the roads but also because developments in river navigation were making the Thames and Severn great arteries of trade connected to a whole network of lesser tributaries. Almost every small country town had established a reputation for its peculiar marketing: Welsh flannel at Wrexham, sheep at Newbury, cheese at Chipping Sodbury, corn at Warminster, cloth at Devizes and so on. Much of this produce went to London, for, as Defoe was never tired of insisting, the metropolis was coming to play an almost overwhelming role in the country's economic life. In the more remote corners of the kingdom, it is true, primitive means of transport were still in use, but this, as Celia Fiennes remarked acidly, was as much due to the hold of outdated custom over the local people as to the state of roads themselves.[2] But in general roads and rivers were full of heavy traffic, whether it was the Suffolk poultry being driven in their vast flocks to London, the Essex carriers and drovers taking cattle and provisions to the metropolis, the hundreds of waggons pouring into Farnham on a market day, the barges plying the Severn or the water traffic moving between Taunton and Exeter. Even at so small a place as Uppingham the landlord of the local inn would be prepared to put up 100 horses on a normal market day.

On their arrival at any of these provincial towns the first thing that both set out to discover was the particular staple commodity of the place. Leicester and Nottingham were renowned for their stockings; Bedford famous for its hats and bone-lace; silk-weaving was carried on at Canterbury; the making of tammies and ribbons at Coventry; and Newcastle had a great reputation for its pottery. Within a comparatively small area of the West Midlands, Birmingham specialized in guns, buttons and buckles, Walsall in bits and bridles, Dudley in nails, Wolverhampton in locks. But while Defoe investigated trade and manufacture, Celia Fiennes would notice whether the streets were paved and the houses well built,

[1] C. Fiennes, 10.
[2] C. Fiennes, 265.

and if there had been any progress in sanitation. She had little time for the merely Picturesque. She felt that the Rows at Chester only darkened the streets and spoilt the town, and she had no hesitation in dismissing such a place as Stafford as nothing but an old town built of timber and plaster with high gabled roofs. She warmly approved of building in brick, and some of her favourite adjectives for houses she liked were 'flat', 'neat' or 'even'. But while the pitching and paving of streets and the provision of running water in pipes and conduits were becoming increasingly common in such large towns as Liverpool or Newcastle, it could by no means be taken for granted in a place the size of Ely:

> The dirtyest place I ever saw, not a bitt of pitching in the streetes so its a perfect quagmire the whole Citty, only just about the Palace and Churches the streetes are well enough for breadth but for want of pitching it seemes only a harbour to breed and nest vermin in, of which there is plenty enough, so that tho' my chamber was near 20 stepps up I had froggs and slow-worms and snailes in my room . . . its true were the least care taken to pitch their streetes it would make it looke more properly an habitation for human beings, and not a cage or nest of unclean creatures.[1]

She was keenly interested in living conditions, and her sympathetic woman's eye noted that the poor at Swanage burnt only stones (with a strong offensive smell) for their heat and light, and that there were piles of cow-dung outside the cottage doors at Peterborough drying for use as fuel. The extreme poverty of the Lake District distressed her, sad little huts of dry stone walling without plaster or chimneys, though she had little patience with the poor conditions in the Lowlands which she attributed to the sloth of its inhabitants, and which she thought compared unfavourably with the simple Cornish cottages which, even though they looked like barns, were at least clean and plastered.

The years in which she was travelling were important for the emergence of a new phenomenon amongst English towns, the development of spas as centres of fashionable resort. The earliest springs such as Bath and Buxton had long been frequented; the early seventeenth century saw the growth of Epsom and Tunbridge Wells, but the real impetus came after the Civil War with the discovery and promotion of more than 100 mineral springs

[1] C. Fiennes, 155-6.

whose claims were set forth in a stream of pseudo-medical literature. In making the round of spas, however, Celia Fiennes was
more than a mere disciple of prevailing fashion. She approached
the whole subject in a thoroughly scientific frame of mind, comparing the diaretic waters with the sulphurous, and analysing
the amount of alum, steel or sulphur contained in each—an
exercise which must have demanded a very considerable degree
of stamina. At Harrogate her horse was probably wiser than she
in refusing to go anywhere near the well of the sulphur or stinking
spa which was furred with a white scum and both smelt and
tasted of sulphur with extreme offensiveness. It had, however,
a great reputation as a quick purger and good for 'all scurlutick
humours', and many of its visitors were prepared to drink two
quarts a day, though Celia Fiennes could manage no more than
one, and that only by holding her breath. At Barnet, having
looked at the source of the waters, she confessed that she had
little stomach to drink them, for they were full of leaves and dirt,
and every dip further troubled them. It was her sense of pro-
priety, however, which prevented her trying St. Winifred's Well.
'Its a cold water and cleare and runs off very quick so that it would
be a pleasant refreshment in summer to washe ones self in it, but
its shallow not up to the waste so its not easye to dive and washe
in; but I thinke I could not have been persuaded to have gone in
unless might have had curtains to have drawn about some part of
it have shelter'd from the streete, for the wett garments are no
covering to the body.'[1]

In many cases the accommodation provided was still very
primitive—at Alford non-existent, 'the Country people being a
clounish rude people', though here she drank the waters with
pleasure since they were said to be a quick purger and good for
all sharp humours and obstructions. Few could endure the dis-
comforts of Buxton for more than two or three nights, for its
lodgings were notoriously bad, with often as many as four beds
in a room, so that visitors might find themselves sharing a room
with total strangers, or even lying with strange bedfellows since
it was by no means uncommon to sleep three to a bed.[2] But it is
scarcely fair to judge the spas by such extreme examples. At
Tunbridge Wells Celia Fiennes met with good lodging houses, a

[1] C. Fiennes, *181*.
[2] C. Fiennes, *103*.

newly built chapel, shops selling fine wares, bowling greens, coffee houses and rooms for lottery and hazard. So successful, indeed, were its attempts to attract the *beau monde* that twenty-five years later Defoe was complaining that company and diversion were the main business of the place and it was overrun with fops, fools, beaux and the like. Bath, of course, held a place of special pre-eminence which no other spa could ever seriously hope to rival, however hard it might exploit its attractions. Defoe gave a colourful picture of a typical day there:

> In the morning you (supposing you to be a young lady) are fetch'd in a close chair, dress'd in your bathing cloths, that is stript to the smock, to the Cross-Bath. There the musick plays you into the bath, and the women that tend you present you with a little floating wooden dish, like a bason; in which the lady puts a handkerchief, and a nosegay, of late the snuff-box is added, and some patches; tho' the bath occasioning a little perspiration, the patches do not stick so kindly as they should. Here the ladies and gentlemen pretend to keep some distance, and each to their proper side, but frequently mingle . . . and the place being but narrow, they converse freely and talk, rally, make vows, and sometimes love; and having thus amus'd themselves an hour or two, they call their chairs and return to their lodgings.[1]

Celia Fiennes added rather more intimate details to this account:

> The Ladye goes into the bath with garments made of a fine yellow canvas, which is stiff and made large with great sleeves like a parsons gown, the water fills it up so that its borne off that your shape is not seen, it does not cling close as other linning, the Gentlemen have drawers and waistcoates of the same sort of canvas, that is the best linning, for the bath water will change any other yellow; when you go out of the bath you go within a doore that leads to steps which you ascend by degrees, that are in the water, then the doore is shut which shutts down into the ways a good way, so you are in a private place, where you still ascend severall more steps, and let your canvass drop of by degrees into the water, which your women guides takes off and the meanetyme your maide flings a garment of flannell made like a nightgown with great sleeves over your head, and the guides take the taile and so pulls it on you just as you rise the steps, and your other garments drop off so you are wrapped up in the flannell and your nightgown on top.[2]

[1] Defoe, II, *34*.
[2] C. Fiennes, *19*.

Defoe's determination not to be led astray from his avowed purpose of studying the present day into the delightful view of antiquity, has deprived us of what would undoubtedly have been refreshingly sane and balanced descriptions. For whenever he does remark upon them he is both critical and caustic, qualities found all too rarely amongst writers on antiquities. He was quite prepared to dismiss Arthur's Round Table at Winchcombe as no better than a fib, and to pour scorn upon the attribution of the dyke between Sheffield and Rotherham to the devil, as though he had more leisure for such undertakings than a whole army of men. But that he could also feel on occasion a certain sympathy for what he called the 'looking back into remote things' is clear from the reluctance with which he dragged himself away from the Roman Wall.

The trophies, the buildings, the religious as well as the military remains, as well of the Britains, as of the Romans, Saxons, and Normans, are but, as we may say, like a wound hastily healed up . . . yet they are beautiful, even in their decay, and the venerable face of antiquity has something so pleasing, so surprizing, so satisfactory in it, especially to those who have with any attention read the histories of pass'd ages, that I know nothing renders travelling more pleasant and more agreeable.[1]

Celia Fiennes by contrast was completely uncritical, and never sceptical of any remnant of antiquity or natural wonder. She was intrigued by any curiosity, and would always go out of her way to see such extraordinary objects as the stuffed bodies in the Barber Surgeons Hall at Newcastle, the rattlesnake and the shark's jaw at Chatham Hospital, or the Eskimo with his canoe preserved at Hull.

All his Cloths Cap and a large Bag behind him wherein his fish and provision were, these were all made of the skin of fishes and were the same which he wore when taken, the forme of his face is only added and just resemble the Wildman that they took, for so the Inscription calls him or the Bonny Boatesman; he was taken by Captain Baker and there are his oars and spear that was with him— this is all written on the boate to perpetuate the memory of it—he would not speake any language or word to them that took him nor would he eate, so in a few days died.[2]

[1] Defoe, II, 254.
[2] C. Fiennes, 88-9.

She was equally prepared to try her hand at anything which caught her fancy, particularly any mechanical device. While she was in York watching the minting of coins she begged to be allowed to stamp one half-crown herself, and she recorded with great pride that in the Sheldonian she had been allowed to print her name several times. If she could actually carry off some trophy she was even better pleased, and knowing her weakness Sir Charles Shuckburgh, her host near Daventry, ordered one of his daughters to get her an unusual stone dug locally which was like the mullet in armorial bearings. She left Buxton with some lead just brought up out of one of the mines and so bright that it looked like silver, and in a Cornish stamping-mill had a piece poured out and made cold to take away with her.

ROMANS AND GOTHS

William Stukeley and the Antiquarians

'WHAT Regions boast of more Antiquity and genuine Reliques of it of all sorts? What Earth throws up so many Roman Coyns, Medals, Urns &c that one would think Rome it selfe was transplanted in to Great Brittain?'[1] demanded the youthful William Stukeley at the end of a successful expedition made in 1710 with seven companions who constituted themselves an 'Itinerant Society'. For Stukeley this was only the first of a dozen such tours, made either alone or with one friend, during the next fifteen years. His major and overwhelming passion was the search for antiquities, an interest which he pursued with a whole-hearted enthusiasm. He was not only a most learned antiquary but also a keen practical archaeologist, always prepared to stop and do a little field-work wherever a site seemed promising; pacing, measuring and investigating as thoroughly as he might without actually undertaking a major excavation. His greatest love of all was for Roman Britain, and it was therefore only fitting that his final and longest tour should take the form of a pilgrimage to the Roman Wall. But he also showed a very considerable interest in prehistoric remains, particularly on the two expeditions he made

[1] 'Iter Oxiense', May 1730, B.M. Lans. MSS. 688, f. 16. This original text of Stukeley's first tour varies in certain respects from that which he printed in his *Itinerarium Curiosum* fifteen years later, notably in his omission of various passages in which enthusiasm verges on exuberance.

in 1723, the *Iter Dumooniense* and the *Iter Septimum Antonini Aug*. Here his pages are full of descriptions and speculations upon Celtic fields and Belgic dykes, earthworks and amphitheatres, forts and barrows. Although he tended to be a little confused in his dating, calling much that was prehistoric, including Maiden Castle, Roman, yet he does show some grasp of historical perspective beyond the Romans and even beyond the Belgae, as when, for example, he designated stone circles pre-Belgic.

In attributing the series of great banks and dykes in Dorset and Wiltshire to successive stages in the Belgic occupation of Wessex he was, as Stuart Piggott points out, showing a perception of basic archaeological principles: he recognized a long pre-Roman period over which these antiquities were to be distributed, and he allowed for successive waves of prehistoric invasion and immigration from the continent.[1]

Wessex pleased him above all, a countryside well planted with stout camps, which provided a veritable feast of hill forts and tumuli. He wrote of them vividly, revealing his essential romanticism as he did so, as when he described the Iron Age camp at Oldbury on the Cotswold scarp: 'The precipice on those two sides is altogether inaccessible, falling down in narrow cavitys or ribs as it were the great roots of a tree, with an odd and tremendous aspect . . . one would imagine they had been spew'd out of the hardning chalk at the creation, as extreneous bodys, tho' of greater specific gravity than it self.'[2] Standing stones brought forth even more colourful writing, and the young Stukeley exclaimed with wonder at the sight of the Rollright Stones on that first tour: ' 'Tis a very Noble Rustic Sight, and Strikes an Odd Terrour into the Spectators, and Admiration of the designers of 'em. It is no small part of the Curiosity to see how these that are left are Coroded like Worm Eaten wood by the harsh Jaws of time . . . But how these unpolished people could get such prodigious stones together I know not, however they very well deserve the most serious Inspection and Consideration of any Curious Traveller.'[3] In 1712 he set out for Wales on his *Iter Cimbricum*, likening himself to Caesar in making some small

---

[1] *William Stukeley, an eighteenth century antiquary*, Oxford, 1950, *68–70*.

[2] *Itinerarium Curiosum, or, an Account of the Antiquitys and Remarkable Curiositys in Nature or Art, Observ'd in Travels thro' Great Britain*, London, 1724, *133*.

[3] B.M. Lans. MSS. 688, f. 12.

TUNBRIDGE WELLS IN 1718.

By Johannes Kipp.

inroads into that country. Here his aim was not so much the pursuit of objects of antiquity themselves as the chance to hear the Welsh language spoken, for, as he explained in his prefatory dedication: 'I had conceiv'd great notions of the old *Britons* betimes, and long'd to hear at least a language spoke soon after the deluge.'[1]

But although he dabbled with the prehistoric and Celtic past his great concern was with Roman Britain. Following wherever possible the Roman roads, he visited Roman towns and forts, impressed wherever he went both by their artistic triumphs and their engineering skill, and writing of the Roman achievement in tones of the deepest admiration. He made his fifth tour, the *Iter Romanum*, almost entirely along 500 miles of Roman road, travelling the four great highways and stopping wherever there was a Roman station (he managed to include thirty-five) or any other Roman foundation, to measure and record. As he went he could not help commenting time and again on the excellence of the Romans' road construction which he felt reflected both their natural genius and their powers of organization. He had followed Watling Street a year or so before. 'It is laid very broad and deep with gravel not yet worn out, where it goes over commons and moores. It is rais'd a good height above the soil, and so strait that upon an eminence you may see it ten or twelve miles before you, and as much behind, over many hill-tops answering one the other as a visto of trees.'[2]

'In their roads they have exceeded themselves', he philosophized:

Nothing but the highest pitch of good sense and public spirit could prompt 'em to so immense a labor. 'tis altogether astonishing to consider how they begirt the whole globe, as it were, with new meridians and great circles all manner of ways. . . . they study'd eternity in all their works, just opposite to our present narrow souls who say it will serve our time well enough, for that reason they made few bridges, as liable to decay, but fords were laid out with great skill and labor, many of which remains firm to this day without any reparation.[3]

He naturally took a great interest in the techniques of Roman building. At Verulamium he noted that in general their bricks

[1] *Iter. Cur. 48.*
[2] ibid., *57.*
[3] ibid., *72.*

were eighteen inches long and when he found certain of a greater length and thickness he concluded that they must be intended for use in the hypocausts. At the station called *Ad Pontem* near Newark he traced the foundations of walls and houses, and discovered that they were made of stones set edgewise in clay over which liquid mortar had been poured, with short oak posts or piles placed at intervals—a number of which he pulled out with his hands in the course of his investigation, a procedure which he seemed to regard as perfectly justified.[1] Faced with the magnificent gateway at Lincoln he set about taking a most accurate survey of it: the vast semicircle of large stones laid without mortar, and held together by their cuneiform shape; the arch itself sixteen feet in diameter, the stones four feet thick at the base; horizontal stones of ten or twelve feet laid towards the upper parts to take off the side pressure; the posterns or foot passages at the bottom of similar stones. Well might Stukeley praise it for its noble simplicity and declare it something to delight any lover of architecture.[2] He was much excited by Car Dyke, the vast artificial canal running for fifty miles through the Fens and opening up a great waterway for inland traffic to avoid the hazardous voyage by coast. He regarded it as essentially a product of Roman industry and judgement, one more example of the greatness of thought peculiar to that wise people. Amphitheatres captured his imagination not only because of the splendour of their ruins but because of the scenes of past grandeur they conjured up for him. At Silchester he examined the terraces and circular walks, picking out the form which was still scarcely obscured, and after surveying the whole, found himself calling to mind such Roman magnificence as the planting of huge trees in circuses and camps, *pro tempore* to imitate the forests in which they hunted beasts.[3] At Maumbury Rings he felt strong indignation at the sight of the plough encroaching every year and corn growing in this noble concavity where once the *gens togata* and the majesty of imperial Rome used to show itself.[4]

In every Roman town that he visited Stukeley was not only able to trace its foundations and the general pattern of its layout,

[1] ibid., *110, 100*.
[2] ibid., *83–4*.
[3] ibid., *171*.
[4] ibid., *155–68*.

WILLIAM STUKELEY AND THE ANTIQUARIANS

but found himself confronted by a wealth of lesser objects lying about in a casual profusion that is quite startling to modern eyes. At Alchester on his first journey he described a scene which was to be only too frequently repeated elsewhere. The local farmers were constantly breaking their ploughs on foundations of hewn stone; a shower of rain sometimes produced great numbers of coins which were soon dispersed throughout the adjacent villages; pieces of pot, vessels, brickwork, even brass images and *lares* were lying scattered about for anyone to put in their pockets. He was able to pick up several pieces of pot and coloured vessels, two or three coins of Tetricus junior, and would have taken more except that they were strewn so thickly over the fields that they were to be found at almost every step. He stopped here to do a piece of field-work on an artificial hill just outside the town. He considered it carefully and was able to trace its circuit quite plainly, a square of 200 feet, because he noticed that its edges stood out from the meadow by the different colour of the grass, one grey, the other green—a remarkably perspicacious fore-shadowing of the techniques employed by aerial photography in archaeology today. Although he speculated about it and decided that it was probably some considerable building, a temple or a pretorium, more could not be ascertained without digging, and he left it hoping that some curious person might feel impelled to excavate, for, he concluded regretfully, anyone at the expense of digging would find it well worth while.[1] When he visited Ariconium, the Birmingham of Roman Britain which handled the rich iron ore produced in the Forest of Dean, he found he could still quite easily follow the walls, though they were becoming overgrown with hedges and trees. A very fine mosaic floor in perfect condition had been discovered a few years previously, but it had soon been torn to pieces, and Stukeley clearly felt no compunction in hastening its disintegration by taking up a few of the remaining stones of different colours and adding them to some bits of fine red pottery he had already gleaned from the site.[2] But, naturally enough, considering its importance in Roman Britain, Cirencester was the richest town of all, where Roman remains were being frequently brought to light and as quickly dispersed or destroyed. 'They dig up antiquities here every day',

[1] ibid., *39–40*.
[2] ibid., *66*.

he wrote, though again in no particular tone of surprise; large quantities of carved stones were carried off yearly in carts to mend the highways or to be used in local building; rings, coins and intaglios were found in great quantities, even mosaics and pavements might be dug up. A fortunate local inhabitant, a certain Richard Bishop, had adorned the front of his house with pillars which must have been the foundation of a Roman temple and had installed an entire mosaic pavement in his privy vault. Stukeley himself went off with a little head which had been broken off from a *basso relievo* which by its curious tiara he thought must have been the genius of a city or one of the *deae matres*. He failed, however, to get hold of a small brass image recently found by a gardener which was probably one of the *lares*, because after a diligent search it appeared that it had been 'played away' by his children.[1] For where they were not to be had for the asking (or taking) antiquities might be bought quite easily, and the amateur collector would find it no difficult matter to assemble a number of mementos of his travels. Stukeley was lucky on many occasions, as at Pillbridge near Yeovil, where, after buying a number of Roman coins from a gardener, he found that he had arrived just in time to join in the dismemberment of a tesselated pavement discovered only two days before and by now reduced to a great parcel of little stones by the crowds of people who had come out of curiosity and torn it to pieces.[2]

His last great tour, made in 1725 with his fellow antiquary Roger Gale, was an *Iter Boreale*, an expedition to the Roman Wall. Together the two of them travelled the length of this supreme example of Roman military virtue. They visited all the garrisons so admirably disposed along it, wrestling with in-scriptions and trying to interpret curiously carved stones, all the while paying homage to the knowledge of military affairs it displayed. They recalled its success in holding at bay the North Britons, that bold and daring race, 'redundant in numbers, strong and hardy in body, fierce in manners, who refused sub-jection and a polite life'. Even when he had turned south again and was making his way homeward through Durham and York its spell was still upon him, and he dwelt with pleasure upon the thought of this stupendous achievement of the people he so

[1] ibid., *62–3*.
[2] ibid., *147*.

greatly admired: 'I hold myself obliged to preserve as well as I can the memory of such things as I saw; which, added to what future time will discover, will revive the Roman glory among us, and may serve to invite noble minds to endeavour at that merit and public-spiritedness which shine through all their actions. This tribute at least we owe them, and they deserve it at our hands, to preserve their remains.'[1]

This was in fact not only the last of his tours but the climax of them all. It might also be considered the end of his career as a serious antiquary, for his latter years were to be devoted to those Druidic studies which, as they became increasingly extravagant and far-fetched, sat so strangely upon the shoulders of an Anglican country parson. We shall take leave of him at this point as he stands a little larger than life amongst his fellow antiquaries of the eighteenth century. Many searchers for antiquities, it is true, took their expeditions as seriously as Stukeley, but most were considerably more amateur than he, lacking both his technical skill in investigating sites and his imaginative understanding of the past. Nevertheless, many saw their primary purpose, as the Rev. William Gilpin expressed it, 'to perform the due rites of antiquities by pacing the dimensions and counting the stones'. Bishop Pococke, for example, traced a camp he saw outside Chichester and marked it out along the ground,[2] while on the very first page of his journal Sir Joseph Banks told how he went in search of a barrow that he had been told of by the Bishop of Carlisle, and having measured it most carefully was anxious to have it opened there and then.[3] He was to have frequent cause to wish this a number of times during his travels, but it was all too rarely possible, and he had to console himself with speculating upon the character and purpose of the camps and forts he saw.

Speculation was all too frequently the common alternative to scientific examination, but while with a number of antiquaries this had at least some basis in probability if not in fact, with the less well informed it was simply a chance to let their imaginations run riot. Antiquities such as standing stones were all too likely to

---

[1] *Iter Boreale, Itinerarium Curiosum, Centuria II*, London, 1776, 55, 76–7.
[2] *Travels through England . . . during 1750, 1751 and later years*, (ed.) J. J. Cartwright, Camden Society, 1889, II, 87.
[3] Camb. Univ. Lib. MSS. 6294, f. 1b, 4.

produce romantic reveries of an extreme kind. 'My ideas wandered in the fields of imagination', wrote William Hutchinson:

> I reflected on the trembling enthusiastic multitudes who here perhaps had assembled to hear the priestly dictates touching government and moral conduct; to learn the druids, arrogant philosophy and superstitions, and cherish an implicit faith of the immortality of man's intellectual spirit, tho' in transmigration to reptiles and beasts of prey. Perhaps here Princes submissively have stood to hear the haughty druid exclaiming
>
>> 'Thou art a King, a sovereign o'er frail men;
>> I am a druid, servant of the Gods;
>> Such service is above such sovereignty.'[1]

Gothic lent itself to even greater flights of fancy, above all the Gothic of ruined abbeys, and many an eighteenth-century tourist indulged a luxurious melancholy amidst crumbling arches and spring ivy. Arthur Young enjoyed himself in Fountains Abbey just because the falling walls and imperfect arches impressed his mind with a kind of religious gloom and allowed his imagination free scope in which to range and to sketch in ideas beyond the boldest limits of reality.[2] Mrs. Radcliffe was in her element in such a situation, and at Furness Abbey settled down opposite the east window and allowed the images and manners of times past to present themselves vividly before her.

> The midnight procession of monks, clothed in white and bearing lighted tapers, appeared to the mind's eye issuing to the choir through the very door-case, by which such processions were wont to pass from the cloisters to perform the matin service, when, at the moment of their entering the church the deep chanting of voices was heard, and the organ swelled a solemn peal. To fancy, the strain still echoed feebly along the arcades and died in the breeze among the woods, the rustling leaves mingling with them close.[3]

But Gothic might also be approached in a sterner frame of mind. The round of abbeys and cathedrals also attracted those who prided themselves upon their knowledge of architecture and

---

[1] *An Excursion to the Lakes in Westmorland and Cumberland August 1773*, London, 1774, *98–9*.

[2] *Northern Tour*, London, 1770, II, *323–5*.

[3] *A Journey made in the Summer of 1794*, London, 1795, *49–51*.

their aesthetic appreciation. Their chief concern was with Gothic in its later and more elaborate manifestations: Saxon they dismissed as heavy and coarse, nothing more than Roman degenerating into barbarism, and Norman was placed in much the same category. Thus those cathedrals which were predominantly Norman received scant attention. John Dodd dismissed Chester laconically as excessively mean, built of country stone which was little better than petrified mud; and Mawman agreed that it was no more than a rough, heavy pile. Carlisle to the Rev. William Gilpin's eye seemed a heavy Saxon pile entirely lacking in any beauty, and even the interior of Durham struck Mawman as very clumsy with its vast cylindrical pillars. The only exception was the Norman nave at Gloucester which was occasionally admitted to possess some little merit. Any sense of the historic development of architecture was almost wholly lacking, and comparisons with European architecture of the same period were never attempted. It was not until the building of the time of Henry II, when 'an airy lightness' began to prevail over the Saxon heaviness, the short clumsy pillars to cluster and the windows to increase in elegance, 'trailed over with beautiful scrawl-work', that the tourists could write with any real enthusiasm. The choir and east window of Gloucester, famous for their height and size, were greatly admired, and they also muchly approved the front of Wells 'adorned in good Gothick taste', the symmetry of the nave of Salisbury and its spire, easily the highest in England. But it was York minster which was held to be the queen of Gothic buildings, the glory of all other Gothic churches. 'Admirable for its size, style and ornaments, and probably the finest model of gothic architecture in the world', exclaimed Mawman. 'Standing under the steeple, and looking round us, we were filled with astonishment and rapture, by the union of magnificence and elegance, which so eminently distinguished this structure. Here the windows, being entirely of painted glass, diffuse over the whole cathedral a soothing "dim, religious light", a rich and awful grandeur, exceeding perhaps the effect of any other place of worship in England.'[1] Its chapter house impressed Arthur Young as 'perhaps the most peculiar *Gothic* building in the world', and he praised

[1] *An Excursion to the Highlands of Scotland and the English Lakes 1805*, London, 1805, *40–1*.

it for its elegance and proportion. 'No person can enter this room without being struck with the justness and harmony of the proportion. Seven of the divisions are large windows, and there is a small gallery that runs round the whole, which I should have mentioned, but it is observable the projection of it is so well and skilfully contrived, as not in the least to offend the eye.'[1]

As he wandered round Chester cathedral looking at its monuments Sir Joseph Banks noticed that one of the tombs, said to be that of some pre-Conquest Emperor of Germany's son, had been recently opened to reveal the bones in an excellent state of preservation. As he helped himself to one he congratulated himself that he would not often have the chance of procuring a bone of such age—and clearly did not think for one moment that there was anything unusual or reprehensible in such behaviour.[2] Indeed, all tourists recounted the triumphs they enjoyed in securing trophies on their travels, whether they came by them by honest means, by craft or by outright theft. At Lincoln the Rev. John Skinner bought several Roman coins from a surveyor of the highways who had some hundred in his possession, and it was generally gardeners or surveyors who did the largest trade in such small objects. It was considered perfectly natural for all antiquarian tourists to see what plunder they could secure from the sites they visited. Thus one anonymous tourist at Caerwent immediately set to work to make enquiries throughout the village for Roman tiles and coins, and was successful to the extent of managing to get hold of thirteen small pieces of tile ornamented with antique figures and Roman inscriptions. R. J. Sullivan was in fact very seriously alarmed that the Caerwent pavement would soon disappear altogether, since there was nothing at all to prevent idle people from picking up little bits as matters of curiosity. The Hon. John Byng's particular interest was collecting stained glass and monumental brasses wherever this was possible. He grumbled that at Boston most of the brasses had been carefully removed, and the few that remained were all too firmly fixed. He coveted most earnestly those magnificent ones he saw at South Kyme with painted labels issuing from their mouths, but he felt himself inhibited by the presence of a local gentleman and a farmer, and so concluded bitterly: 'I look'd around me; but

[1] *Northern Tour*, I, 201–2.
[2] Camb. Univ. Lib. MSS. 6294, f. 64.

dared not plunder.' At Tattersall he clearly made an honest deal, though smaller than he would have liked, since, as the plates of arms were in the keeping of the clerk, he could get possession only of one—though one which was in fact probably that of the Cromwell family. Again at Upwood the deal was honest but rather more profitable, for he was able to fill his pockets with fragments of glass from the church which he bought for sixpence in a glazier's shop.[1]

Perhaps the only moment at which these tourists paused to reflect upon their actions was when they found that their fellow antiquarians had stolen a march upon them and there was nothing left to despoil. At Haddon, where the east window of the chapel was famous for its curious painting and had formed a great attraction for visitors, John Byng reaped the fruits of such vandalism: 'One of my brethren (antiquaries) (a sad dog!) lately cut out five of the Saints faces.'[2] The view of posterity may well echo him. Perhaps our first debt of gratitude to these eighteenth-century tourists should be for the amount of monumental remains they had the grace to leave *in situ* for succeeding generations.

[1] *The Torrington Diaries*, (ed.) C. Bruyn Andrews, abridged Fanny Andrews, London, 1954, *265, 349, 350, 334, 254.*
[2] ibid., *180.*

STATELY HOMES

The Round of Country Houses

HE publicity which has attended the opening of their homes to sightseers by the aristocracy might lead one to believe that this was some new departure on their part. In fact, since snobbery is inbred in the English nation, the aristocracy have always exercised a lure for other members of society, and their wealth, taste and material possessions have aroused an interest which is by no means confined to the mid-twentieth century. Seeing round country houses has long been a popular English pastime (though one which, in the eighteenth century, was confined to those who might call themselves gentlemen), and a ring at the bell of some stately home, the purchase of a catalogue if one were on sale, a conducted tour by the house-keeper, were as familiar to the eighteenth-century tourist as they are to the visitors of today.

Some houses were open one or two days a week in the eighteenth century, though most might be seen at any time, irrespective of day or hour. 'We arrived there about nine o'clock', said Edward Harley of his visit to Wilton in 1738. 'My Lord was not there, we were admitted to see the house and gardens; nobody is denied though my Lord be there.'[1] At Chatsworth the Duke of Devonshire kept two public days a week; Woburn might be seen only on Mondays, Wanstead on Saturdays, and so on. As he rode

[1] 'Journeys in England', Hist. MSS. Comm., VI, *176*.

through Derby in 1778 R. J. Sullivan and his companion were warned that if they wished to see Kedleston they must make haste, as it was then noon and visitors were admitted only from twelve to two.[1] Having extolled the delights of Fonthill, the Rev. Richard Warner had then to warn his readers that this dazzling scene could be viewed only between the hours of twelve and four.[2] A rather different technique was employed at Hafod House in Cardiganshire where tourists who wished to see the house had first to obtain a ticket from the local inn, which would then admit them from twelve until two.

At one or two houses the tourist might find the door shut in his face, and he could then do nothing but call down curses upon the head of the unco-operative owner who practised such churlish tricks. The Hon. John Byng had set out to see Wroxton, the seat of Lord Guilford, but unluckily for him his lordship was just arrived from London and denied him admittance. 'Very rude this, and unlike an old courtly earl! Let him either forbid his place entirely; open it allways; or else fix a day of admission; but, for shame, don't refuse travellers who may have come 20 miles out of their way for a sight of this place.' And then, only three days later, the same thing happened again, when after a tedious sultry ride of sixteen miles over much nasty country to see Sherborne Castle, Lord Macclesfield summarily refused him permission. 'Let people proclaim their great houses are not to be viewed', cried Byng in anger and disappointment at this second rebuff.[3] It was not quite so surprising that Sullivan should find Lord Shrewsbury's seat, Heythrop House, temporarily closed for improvements, though in fact even this was by no means general, for watching building operations in progress was extremely popular, and tourists felt no hesitation in taking such an opportunity to pass judgement upon the improvements intended by the noble owner and his architect.

In certain houses the tourist was allowed to spend a leisurely two or three hours wandering through the place at will, catalogue in hand, unharassed by attendants and free to inspect everything from the kitchens to the chapel. Houghton or Wilton, which

[1] R. J. Sullivan, *Observations made during a Tour through Parts of England, Scotland and Wales in a Series of Letters*, London, 1780, 69.
[2] *Excursions from Bath, 1800*, London, 1801, 127.
[3] 'A Ride Taken in 1785', *The Torrington Diaries*, (ed.) C. Bruyn Andrews, abridged Fanny Andrews, London, 1954, 103, 106.

housed important collections of pictures and antiquities, would naturally have printed catalogues. The *Copious and Comprehensive Catalogue of the Curiosities of Wilton-House* ran to 150 pages; it impressed the Rev. Richard Warner by its intimate acquaintance with the classics, though he complained that much of the interest and entertainment it might otherwise have possessed was wanting because the compilers confined themselves to dry mythological and historical details in their account of the statues and busts, and did not give any description of the peculiar beauties and costumes of each.[1] Craven Ord found the 'house catalogue', which was offered to visitors at Holkham, written in a confused and incorrect manner, and not of much service, while that at Houghton dealt with the pictures in a 'critical order' which was different from the order in which they were hung in the rooms.[2]

The most inadequate catalogue, however, was generally preferable to being shown over a house by an illiterate and ill-informed housekeeper or servant. Most tourists agreed that servants were both ignorant and insolent, and housekeepers proved so full of pretentious and wholly unreliable information that John Dodd could only conclude that it was a 'Laudable Custome of England that they should be unacquainted with what they were showing'.[3] Men like Horace Walpole or John Byng were unlikely to be amused when Cleopatra and Lucretia were called by one housekeeper the two mistresses of Charles II, and another, pointing to a portrait of the Duke of Buckingham, called him that villain Felton, finely confusing the murderer with his victim. Lady Beauchamp Proctor, describing her Norfolk tour of 1771 in a series of letters to her cousin Agneta Yorke, told her how extremely distasteful she had found it to be taken over Lord Buckingham's house by a very dirty housemaid with a duster in her hands, or to see Raynham in the company of 'an old *witch*, and a great Dog, that attended us all over the House, and saluted every corner that was convenient for his purposes'.[4] But probably the worst hazards of these conducted tours befell the tourist when he was forced to join a large party to see the house. Sir Harbottle

[1] *Excursions* . . . *1800*, 153-4.
[2] 'Journal of Tours in the Counties of Norfolk and Suffolk, commenced in 1781 and continued until 1797', B.M. Add. MSS. 14,823.
[3] 'Journal of a Tour through England 1735', B.M. Add. MSS. 5957.
[4] I am indebted to Mr. Gerald Yorke for permission to see these letters which are among the papers of Mary Yorke in his possession.

Grimston felt quite unable to do justice to Blenheim in 1769 from the crowd of all kinds that was ushered into that noble mansion, the pride of England, and Mrs. Morgan later complained that not only was she dragged round what would take a week to survey properly, but she was obliged to follow a party 'whose numerous absurd questions to the person who conducts you prevents even the agreeable ideas you might have in that short stay'.[1] At Holkham Lady Beauchamp Proctor had to wait in a vestibule while another party was going over the house, shut up with a whole tribe of people until the housekeeper was free. 'Nothing could be more disagreeable than this situation: we all stared at one another, and not a creature opened their mouths. Some of the Masters amused themselves with trying to throw their hats upon the heads of the busts, whilst the Misses scrutinized one another's dresses.'

Byng would vent his feelings at such treatment in the pages of his diary, storming at 'being dragged about by a foolish housekeeper of very drunken, dawdling appearance'. 'No-one shou'd suffer his place to be visited, but with intention to make those visitors happy', he wrote after a particularly unfortunate visit to Hagley in 1781, 'and shou'd equip his servants with attention and civility.' The final insult, of course, was that these servants expected to be tipped handsomely for their trouble. Conducted round Grimsthorpe by the Duke of Ancaster, whom he found a sufficiently tedious guide, Byng could at least congratulate himself that he had seen no servants and had thus escaped tipping. The Blenheim servants had a great reputation for being very attentive in gleaning money from rich travellers, while a visit to Chatsworth was generally reckoned to prove expensive because of the numbers of porters and gardeners ready to demonstrate the water-works by letting loose cascades and setting the fountains flowing. After seeing Hafod the Rev. James Plumptre pressed half a crown into the housekeeper's hands, to be met with the retort that she never took less than five shillings, to which he replied that he had often given a shilling at a gentleman's house and never more than half a crown, and if she was dissatisfied he would take it back again. 'The house does not take much time in seeing', he continued. 'If I was 20 minutes in it I am sure it was the utmost. At a place like Burleigh or Keddleston, where a

[1] *Tour to Milford Haven 1791*, London, 1795, 69.

profusion of fine paintings are to be seen and the housekeeper is detained for perhaps nearly two hours there may seem some plea for a donation.'[1] An Irish cleric, probably expressing himself considerably more forcibly than his fellow English tourists, declared that he found himself with but a few pieces of Irish currency in his purse after a 'Strict Search & Curious Examination into all ye Antiquities & Rareties of Bristol, Bath, Oxford & Blenheim wch views & Reviews whosoever passes is sure to pay for thro' ye Nose, & must Rest Contented to have his Pocket picked toties quoties so that all ye senses of a curious Traveller seem contracted & Reduced to two only: those of ye sight and touch.' He even complained that he was scarcely able to pay his reckoning at his inn after seeing Blenheim, 'having our Pockets Egregiously picked by those Beggarly & Rascally Conductors not only Here but in all ye Places of Public Resort where strangers in England Generally go to Gratifie their Curiosity'.[2]

But it was unusual for tourists to sound such a jaundiced note. Arthur Young found most agreeable treatment at Wentworth, and praised the politeness of Lady Strafford who retired from her apartment for them to see it; Plumptre could hardly sing the praises of the housekeeper at Kedleston too highly, the most obliging and intelligent he had met with in any nobleman's house, who seemed to take a delight in her business and was willing to answer questions and careful to show the best lights for viewing pictures and setting off the furniture.[3] Visits often ended with some appropriate entertainment, or tourists might be sent away with spoils from the garden. The Rev. Jeremiah Milles finished his tour of Kimbolton in 1735 in the Duke of Manchester's cellars, where the butler produced a glass of some good strong beer fourteen years old, of mellow and pleasant taste.[4] At Wolterton, although the family were not yet down, Lady Beauchamp Proctor was offered wine by a very dirty French cook and the party left Felbrigge with a fine nosegay of orange flowers and geraniums which they carried with them for the rest

[1] 'A Pedestrian Journey through Yorkshire, Durham and Northumberland 1799', Camb. Univ. Lib. Add. MSS. 5816, ff. 161–2.
[2] 'Travel diary August–October 1761 and August–September 1772', B.M. Add. MSS. 27,951.
[3] 'A Tour into Derbyshire, 1793', Camb. Univ. Lib. Add. MSS. 5804, ff. 8–9.
[4] 'Journals of Travels in different parts of England and Wales, 1735 and 1743', B.M. Add. MSS. 15,776.

of their tour. The visit to Holkham ended more favourably than it had begun, for they were conducted a second time to the vestibule, poured libations of chocolate upon the altar of the statue of Jupiter there and received entertainment in the best Leicester style.

Thus the tourists descended like vultures upon their prey, sweeping through house and gardens, relentlessly determined to see everything, to speculate upon its cost and pass judgement upon the taste of the noble owners. They recorded their verdicts in journals and diaries, in which they compared one house with another and gave painstaking accounts of even the most minute details of furnishing and decoration. No one could begin to think himself a connoisseur in these matters until he had seen Blenheim, Wilton, Houghton and Holkham, with Kedleston, Castle Howard and Hardwick high on the list of those of second rank. Any medieval building aroused little or no enthusiasm, and there was small appreciation of either Elizabethan or Jacobean. Berkeley was admired, if it was admired at all, for its antiquity, but any quality of beauty was denied it. 'Not in its first design either elegant or grand', declared R. J. Sullivan, expressing the general view. 'It is now destitute of even the commonest pretension to magnificence.'[1] Southam, which he dated to the time of Henry IV, Shaw found merely a very obscure and undistinguished mansion; Sir Harbottle Grimston could say of Ingestre only that it was a very ancient fabric, 'both inconvenient and inelegant';[2] Haddon appeared quite simply barbaric to Walpole: 'It is said to be built in the reign of King John. It is low & can never have been a tolerable House, the gallery is the only good room. Within the court in a corner is a strange confusion of half arches & beams, that imply the greatest ignorance in the art.'[3] An exception, however, was made for Longleat, which was sufficiently imposing to impress the visitor and to cause speculation upon the origin of its form. 'All here is on the great scale', exclaimed Warner:

> and everything around recalls the remembrance of ancient English magnificence. . . . We survey a mansion of stone . . . not indeed of Gothic or classical architecture but vestiges of the declining Gothic may be traced in the vast projecting windows . . . and attempts at the Grecian discover themselves in the pilasters . . . .

[1] *Observations*, 1780, *III*.
[2] Hist. MSS. Comm., Verulam, *273*.
[3] *Journal of Visits to Country Seats*, (ed.) P. Toynbee, Walpole Society, 1928, XVI, *29*.

This singular mixture of styles ... was the effect of that struggle between the expiring Gothic, which our national architects endeavoured to keep alive, and the classical style imported from Italy by the foreign artists who flocked hither in the sixteenth century.[1]

'We are amused with looking into these mansions of antiquity as objects of curiosity', concluded the Rev. William Gilpin pompously after his visit there, 'but should never think of comparing them in point of convenience with the great houses of modern taste in which the hall and the saloon fill the eye on our entrance; are notable reservoirs of air; and grand antechambers to the several rooms of state that divide on each hand from them. Longleat has nothing of the Grecian grandeur to recommend it. The whole is certainly a grand pile; but it has little beauty and I should suppose less convenience.'[2] Of an early seventeenth-century house in Ipswich an anonymous tourist of 1741 said laconically: 'I can't think there's any beauty in it. It shows a very frantick taste in the architect.'[3]

It is a little more surprising to find that the works of Vanbrugh, Hawksmoor and their contemporaries were greeted with almost universal contempt. 'Execrable within, without, almost all round', was Walpole's view of Blenheim in 1769. Warner poured scorn on Vanbrugh's work at King's Weston:

It bears testimony to the truth of the satire on his style in this epigrammatic epitaph:

> 'Lie light upon him, Earth, though he
> Laid many a heavy load on thee!'

disgusting the eye, both within and without, by its weight and clumsiness. Had Sir John tried his art in castles and pyramids, edifices which were to resist the shocks of military operations and structures that should endure as long as time itself, he probably would have succeeded; but he certainly mistook the path to fame when his taste led him to design domestic mansions in which, instead of massiveness and ponderosity, we only look for lightness and elegance, just proportion and convenience.[4]

[1] *Excursions . . . 1800, 42–3.*
[2] *Observations on the Western Parts of England*, London, 1798, *125–8.*
[3] 'Itinerary of a Journey from Cambridge to Suffolk, Norfolk, Lincolnshire and Yorkshire', B.M. Add. MSS. 38,488.
[4] *Excursions . . . 1800, 279–80.*

WORTH GATE, CANTERBURY.

NEWPORT GATE, LINCOLN.

Both from William Stukeley's *Itinerarium Curiosum*, Centuria I, 1776.

ÆDES WALPOLIANÆ:

OR, A

DESCRIPTION

OF THE

Collection of Pictures

AT

Houghton-Hall in *Norfolk*,

The Seat of the Right Honourable

Sir *ROBERT WALPOLE,*

EARL of ORFORD.

The Second Edition with Additions.

Artists and Plans reliev'd my solemn Hours;
I founded Palaces, and planted Bow'rs.
Prior's *Solomon.*

LONDON:

Printed in the Year MDCCLII.

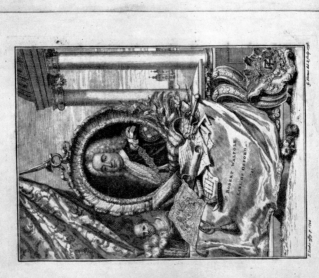

ROBERT WALPOLE
LORD OF ORFORD

There was little in Castle Howard to please Arthur Young; he felt it lacked grandeur as well as the beauty that ought to attend so large and expensive a building, since its parts had no sense of unity or of connection with each other. The Duke of Argyll's house at Adderbury was scarcely worth comment, dismissed as in as bad taste as something by Vanbrugh, while Flitcroft's work at Wentworth was regarded as wanting in any taste at all. But sometimes the sheer magnificence of Blenheim or Castle Howard would overcome the tourist. Even Walpole found himself bound to confess that the latter was the grandest scene of real magnificence that he had ever seen, while Shaw, forgetting for the moment that any house of Vanbrugh's building must of necessity be a monument of the vilest taste, could only gaze at this 'princely fabric with sublime veneration'. Blenheim indeed stood apart from the ordinary run of country houses: 'It bars all words & cuts all description short', as John Dodd put it, 'for its beauties & absurdities are so blendid that while you are expatiating on one, you are check'd by the intervening ideas of the other.'[1] Gilpin admitted that its heaviness and enormity had been greatly criticized, but he felt bound to allow that here Vanbrugh had created a magnificent whole which was invested with an air of grandeur seldom seen in a more regular style of building.[2] 'It must be recognized as the most magnificent pile of architecture in this kingdom', one anonymous tourist stated categorically in 1791, and Vanbrugh should be duly honoured 'in a pile intended to remain a lasting monument of British valour and British generosity'.[3]

'It is well for the county of Norfolk that three or four Noblemen etc. have done so much to their Places, else very few strangers would visit a Country that has so few natural Beautys to attract them', wrote Charles Lyttelton to Sanderson Miller in 1758.[4] The concentration here of those six great houses, Houghton, Holkham, Raynham, Blickling, Narford and Wolterton, drew a constant stream of tourists throughout the eighteenth century, and made the 'Tour of Norfolk' one of the most popular of

[1] B.M. Add. MSS. 5957.

[2] *Observations Relative Chiefly to Picturesque Beauty Made in the Year 1772, on several Parts of England; particularly the Mountains and Lakes of Cumberland and Westmorland*, London, 1786, I, 27–8.

[3] *A Tour throughout the South of England, Wales and part of Ireland, made during the Summer of 1791*, By a Gentleman, London, 1792, 387–8.

[4] L. Dickins and M. Stanton, *An Eighteenth-Century Correspondence*, London, 1910, 397.

pilgrimages. 'To a man of your taste no part of England is so
well worth a visit, at least none that I have seen', wrote Sir George
Lyttelton to Miller. 'Lord Leicester's alone would pay you the
trouble and expense of your journey.'[1] Holkham and Houghton
were rivals for first place in popular esteem. Houghton, begun for
Sir Robert Walpole by Colen Campbell in 1722, was completed
fifteen years later, with internal decorations by William Kent
in 1726–31. Almost without exception it received the warmest
acclaim, not only for its exterior, with its fine colonnades and
superb stables, but for its rich furniture and decorations, particularly the doors and window-cases of mahogany and gilt.
'We scarce observed any instances of littleness or affectation',
concluded one tourist in tones of deep satisfaction.[2] Only Harley
dissented, though here possibly political spleen influenced his
artistic judgement. 'This house at Houghton has made a great
deal of noise', he complained after seeing it in 1722, 'but I think
it is not deserving of it. Some admire it because it belongs to the
first Minister; others envy it because it is his, and consequently
rail at it . . . I think it is neither magnificent or beautiful. There
is a very great expense without either judgement or taste . . . I
dare say had the money which has been laid out here, nay and
much less, been put into the hands of a man of taste and understanding there would have been a much finer house, and better
rooms and greater.'[3] The other Norfolk houses were like lesser
luminaries around the great planets. Raynham, which was universally believed to be the work of Inigo Jones, was always popular,
and the Rev. Jeremiah Milles described it in 1735 as furnished
in the neatest manner and with the most elegant taste; though
there was nothing particularly magnificent in the rooms, yet at
the same time there was nothing that was not perfectly agreeable.
Narford, although not specially distinguished, was always pleasing,
and the comments of an anonymous tourist in 1758 were typical:
'tho' the house is but small, & it's Outside seems to promise
nothing extraordinary, yet there are many things in it worth seeing.
The Staircase is very handsome, & adorned with some fine
Antique Bustos. The Hall is a very good Room, the Walls of it are

[1] I owe this reference to R. W. Ketton-Cremer, *Norfolk Assembly*, London,
1957, *171–203*.
[2] W. Gilpin, *Observations on several Parts of the Counties of Cambridge,
Norfolk, Suffolk, and Essex, 1769 and 1773*, London, 1809, *42*.
[3] Harley, 'Journeys in England', Hist. MSS. Comm., VI, *161*.

painted by La Guerre. There is an Inconveniency in seeing this Place, & that is, the Want of an Inn to put the Horses in.'[1]

A great part of the pleasure of touring houses lay in passing judgement upon the architecture and criticizing the internal décor, and the tourists felt little compunction in stating their views roundly. Woburn generally came off badly, damned with faint praise as large and commodious with nothing particularly grand or magnificent about it. Wrest was summarily dismissed by Milles as very old and bad, and Chatsworth was scarcely worth more than a casual aside as in no way striking except in being in the wilds of Derbyshire. But at most houses the tourists settled down to examine and assess, exploring critically to their hearts' content. 'A superb and is esteemed an elegant pile', Gilpin began cautiously, as he stood before Wentworth Woodhouse, but then continued, getting into his stride:

> yet there seems to be a want of simplicity about it. The front appears broken into too many parts; and the inside, incumbered. A simple plan has certainly more dignity. The gallery is what they call a *shelf*. For myself, I saw nothing offensive in it, though it is undoubtedly a more masterly contrivance to raise a gallery *upon* a wall than to affix one to it. The long gallery is a noble apartment; and the interception of a breakfast-room from it by pillars, and an occasional curtain gives a pleasant idea of retirement . . . on the whole, I was not much pleased with anything I saw here.[2]

Arthur Young also spent a long time here weighing up its merits and defects.

> This portico is lightness and elegance itself; the projection is bold, and when viewed aslant from one side, admits the light through the pillars at the ends, which has a most happy effect, and adds surprizingly to the lightness of the edifice. The bases of the pillars rest on pedestals, in a line upon the rustics, which by some criticks has been objected to by asserting that the pedestal of a column ought to be fixed on the ground alone but without enquiring into the propriety of such strict rules, let me remark that the effect of breaking them is to my eye a beauty. . . . In this portico, the ballustrade extending from pedestal to pedestal, the shafts are seen complete, and the unity of the view not in the least destroyed.[3]

---

[1] 'Tour thro' Part of England, 1758', Bodleian MS. Top. gen. e. 52, ff. 35–6.
[2] *Cumberland and Westmorland, 1772*, II, *220*.
[3] *A Six Months Tour through the North of England*, London, 1770, I, *278–9*.

The most enthusiastic praise was reserved for anything which could be said to answer the ideals of 'beautifull & regular Architecture', which in fact meant any work of the brothers Adam. Kedleston was probably the most consistently admired of any house in the country. 'A composition of elegance and grandeur', wrote Gilpin with warm approval. Only two of the four wings were completed when Walpole saw it in 1768 but he was still delighted with all he found. 'Magnificently finished & furnished all designed by Adam in the best taste . . . the sash frames are gilt without like Chatsworth . . . the Ceilings by him are light.'[1] 'One of the best, if not the very best in the kingdom, uniting comfort with grandeur', wrote William Gray after his visit there in 1811:

> The hall a most noble room supported by twenty Alabaster corinthian columns. The statues cast from most of the celebrated antiques. . . . The Saloon a circular one, the ceilings beautifully painted with Roman Antiquities by Hamilton & I think in watercolours. Some curious deceptions here & in other rooms in chiaro obscuro. The corridors light & elegant, one of them embellished with capital engravings. The drawing room & other rooms just of ye scale & size one would have wished them. . . .[2]

Only Dr. Johnson held himself aloof from any such eulogies: 'Very costly but ill contrived. The hall is very stately, lighted by three sky lights: it has two rows of marble pillars, dug, as I hear from Langley, in a quarry of Northamptonshire. The pillars are very large and massy, and take up too much room. They were better away. Behind the hall is a circular salon, useless, and therefore ill contrived . . . There seemed in the whole more cost than judgement.'[3] Twelve years later Sullivan became almost lyrical in his attempts to describe his delight here:

> On your first entrance into the house you get into a most superb hall, the side and ceilings of which are most beautifully ornamented, and the whole supported by four and twenty massive pillars of variegated alabaster finely fluted. Here indeed the senses become astonished. The alabaster pillars have a wonderful appearance; the other ornaments, likewise, carry their intrinsic proportion of

[1] *Journal of Visits, 64.*
[2] 'Tour to York, Bath, Derbyshire etc. 1811', York Public Library MS. T/5.
[3] *Diary of a Journey into North Wales in the Year 1774*, (ed.) R. Duppa, London, 1816, *14–16.*

elegance. In one word, the whole strikes you as if it were designed for more than mortal residence.[1]

Adam's interior decorations impressed Lady Beauchamp Proctor when she visited Osterley which he was remodelling for Robert Child in 1772. Although it was still unfinished several rooms were already open, and she admired the gallery hung with pea-green paper, the lemon and blue of the breakfast-room, and, above all, the 'profusion of rich China and Japan that I could fancy myself in Pekin'.

Fonthill, the extravaganza built by James Wyatt for William Beckford, was popular with all those who indulged a taste for the byways of Gothic fantasy. An anonymous tourist who saw it when it was still unfinished in 1766 declared that Beckford clearly intended it to be as magnificent as anything in England, and this was the note struck by all who visited it. The richness of its furnishings caught the imagination and even while they felt that it verged on the vulgar they could not help being dazzled by the wealth it represented. 'Abundance of splendor', wrote Gilpin, 'not without a little dash of vanity and ostentation. What is wanting in taste is made up in finery. Never house was so bedecked with all the pride of upholstery. The very plate-glass in one room cost fifteen hundred pounds.'[2] Having enjoyed all its decorations and furnishings with great enthusiasm, Bishop Pococke could scarcely contain his delight and excitement at finding a very fine large organ in the hall which played thirty tunes without a hand, and cost about £1500.[3] Warner wrote of the place in tones of awe as one of the most splendid mansions in the kingdom 'where expence has reached its utmost limits in furniture and ornaments; where every room is a gold mine, and every apartment a picture gallery, where in fact every thing bespeaks the presence of unbounded wealth and expensive ideas'.[4]

Lesser follies, however, were dealt with rather more severely. Sullivan called a house recently built in the form of a tower on Durdham Downs a 'preposterous building which seemed to have been erected in the extravagance of caprice, its use nothing but as a monument of the imbecility of human nature'. Walpole

[1] *Observations*, 1780, *144*.
[2] Gilpin, *Observations on the Western Parts*, 1798, *117*.
[3] *The Travels through England of Dr. Richard Pococke, during 1750, 1751 and later years*, (ed.) J. J. Cartwright, Camden Society, 1888 and 1889, II, 47.
[4] *Excursions . . . 1800, 119–20*.

expressed himself even more strongly in his condemnation of Payne's Hill near Cobham. 'It is taken from Batty Langley's book (which does not contain a single design of true or good Gothic) & is made worse by pendent ornaments in the arches, & by being enclosed on two sides at bottom, with cheeks that bear no relation to Gothic. The whole is an unmeaning edifice.'[1] Lord Egmont had been building himself a castle at Enmore in Somerset, and Gilpin, having crossed its moat by a drawbridge and entered the main courtyard which housed the apartments, expressed himself strongly at this example of aristocratic foolishness:

> It is called whimsical; and no doubt there is something whimsical in the idea of a man's inclosing himself, in the reign of George the Second, in a fortress that would have suited the times of King Stephen. The situation of the stables seems the most whimsical. You enter them through a subterraneous passage, on the right of the great gate. . . . The towers, which occupy the corners and middle of the curtains are all of equal height, which gives the whole an unpleasing appearance . . . . The old baronial castle, in its ancient state, even before it had received from time the beauties of ruin, was certainly a more pleasing object than we have in this imitation of it. . . . As it obtains no *particular convenience* from its castle-form it might perhaps have been as well if the noble founder had built, like other people, on a modern plan.[2]

Sarah Haslam would not allow herself to be amused by James Wyatt's fantasies at High Wycombe and wrote in severely puritanical tones of what she saw there.

> The Architect is exercising his *Shreds* of Gothic Genius in every possible quimp & Crank of wanton & extravagent foolery—the rooms are of different heights, some too low, others too Lofty, the Passages are immensely broad in proportion to the Rooms which are in general too narrow, the Chimney Pieces are very low & very small for the size of the rooms. Mr W.'s Object is an imitation of Ancient Times, which accord very indifferently with Modern Customs. . . . Mr W. hopes to finish it in four years from this time, when if POOR Lord Carrington survive—and Mr W. has transfer'd Lord C's fortune into his own coffers, I should recommend it to be Call'd Rag Man's Castle.[3]

[1] *Journal of Visits*, 35.
[2] Gilpin, *Observations on the Western Parts*, *1798*, *157–60*.
[3] 'Travel Journal, August–October 1802', Edward Hall Collection, Wigan Public Library, M 696 EHC 177.

Taken in tow by the housekeeper at Chatsworth, Byng found himself forced to admire all the interior decorations and furnishings of French tables, gilt chairs and uneasy sofas which he privately regarded as mere affectation imposed upon the house by its Duchess. 'All the foolish glare, uncomfortable rooms, and frippery French furniture of this vile house', he complained sadly, and to make matters worse all had to be viewed at imminent peril of his life, since to complete the French atmosphere the oaken floors of the great apartments were all waxed until they were like ice and every step taken upon them seemed dangerous to life and limb.[1] But what really interested the tourists inside the houses was not so much furniture as pictures. The most important collections were well hung and catalogued, but in a suprisingly large number of houses the visitor was quite likely to find valuable treasures in a state of neglect and decay. 'The wasteful, idle nobility do not know what they possess', exclaimed Byng with fury at Haddon where he found many extremely good pictures lying forgotten in this abandoned house, while at Althorp he saw several fine portraits 'tumbled about the house', in the housekeeper's room and elsewhere. Pennant had been particularly anxious at Castle Ashby to see the portraits of John Talbot, first Earl of Shrewsbury, and his wife, and when the attendant there denied all knowledge of them he searched the house and was rewarded by unearthing them in an attic. At Belvoir the Duke of Rutland had 'laid about him like a Dragon to buy Pictures' and had built up a most magnificent collection, but when Byng saw it in 1789 it was all in a state of great confusion, many still not hung, others left lying about the house, so that the place looked like an auctioneer's room, filled with fine paintings piled about in every corner. A peculiar idiosyncrasy of the Duke of Somerset was to hang some of his best pictures on the back stairs at Petworth, where the Rev. Jeremiah Milles discovered 'an incomparable piece representing five or six of ye Apostles (as I take them to be) in conference together; & pointing to a Golden vase that stands on an altar at a little distance. I could not learn ye name of ye Painter nor ye history; ye former I am told ye Duke studiously conceals as he does that of most of his pictures out of an unusual & ridiculous whimsy.'

Those who found their greatest pleasure in seeing pictures

[1] 'A Tour in the Midlands, 1789', *The Torrington Diaries*, 177.

generally managed to combine pure aesthetic enjoyment with moral edification, so that they enjoyed them from an ethical as well as an artistic point of view. Thomas Pennant's great passion was for what he called in an apt phrase 'the instructive furniture of pictures', and his visits to any portrait gallery became the occasion for anecdotes, reminiscences and moralizings. 'They now undergo a posthumous trial', he would say, a note of macabre satisfaction in his voice as he stood on the threshold of Woburn, 'and, like the *Egyptians* of old, receive censure or praise according to their respective merits.'[1] At Arundel he was pleased by a portrait of the current Duke in the character of Solomon, seated in an elevated state, holding a jovial cup over his head in his right hand, and with his left inviting the Queen of Sheba, who sat at a table, to partake of a fine collation.[2] More rewarding, however, are the accounts and comments of those whose main interest lay with the Rubens and Van Dycks, the Romneys, Reynolds and Gainsboroughs, and the endless succession of Salvator Rosas, Carlo Dolcis, Luca Giordanos and Carlo Marattis. Walpole's splendidly succinct descriptions can hardly be excelled. He would list dispassionately portraits, biblical and classical scenes, with a short note on each, as at Althorp:

> Daedalus & Icarus, half length by Vandyke; fine surly impatience in the young Man & his body, good. Holy family, Rubens, coarse. Descent on the isle of Rhee, neat. Several good Spagnolets, particularly Job & his Wife. St Luke painting the Virgin, large Albano, very Indifferent. Lady Southampton in blue, in the clouds, with a globe, whole length by Vandyke; she was mad. Henry Howard, third sone of the Earl of Arundel, in black satten, by Lely; the carnations too pale, but a fine picture.[3]

Craven Ord had rather more to say of the pictures at Houghton, expressing artistic and moral judgements with a refreshingly forthright common sense, and showing a keen sense of enjoyment of the subject-matter.

> The stoning of St. Stephen, a capital picture of Le Sœur. It contains 19 figures. St. Stephen is just sunk to the ground; by a considerable anachronism, but a very common one among the Roman Catholics, he is drest in the rich habit of a modern Priest

[1] *A Journey from Chester to London*, London, 1782, 347.
[2] *A Journey from London to the Isle of Wight*, London, 1801, II, 99.
[3] *Journal of Visits*, 32.

at high mass. . . . A sleeping Bacchus; he appears as usual pale &
sickly. . . . King Charles Ist a whole length in armour by Vandyke.
I observed in this picture Sr ANT. VANDIKE; if this is the
painter's own mark, & he knew how to spell his own name, why
does not Mr Walpole follow him . . . Moses striking the rock by
Nicholas Poussin; there is a great fault in it, Moses is by no means
the principal figure, nor is he striking the rock angrily, and with a
great air, but seems rather to be scraping out the water. . . . The
Holy Family, a most celebrated picture of Vandyke, the chief part
of it is a dance of boy angels painted in the highest manner, the
Virgin seems to have been a portrait and is not handsome, it is too
much crowded with fruits, flowers, & birds . . . a great ugly
sunflower close to the Virgin. I have not taste enough to like this
picture.[1]

This was unusual, for in general Van Dyck was much admired,
and above all for what Harley called his 'transcendent picture' of
the Pembroke family at Wilton, which was commonly agreed to
be one of his masterpieces. Charlbury, the seat of the Earl of
Clarendon, was famous because here, as John Dodd put it,
'Vandyke has truly Eterniz'd himself and the many Great heroes
that still seem to breathe Courage and Loyalty here'.

One of the pleasures of viewing the pictures at Houghton was
that of differing from Walpole's remarks in the printed catalogue.
'Mine I hope will not be thought too severe', Gilpin apologized
with a note of satisfaction before launching his attack, 'though
there are very few pictures in this noble collection which *intirely*
pleased me. "The Stoning of St. Stephen by Le Sœur!" I have
heard called one of the capital pieces in this collection. I am sorry
to say it did not please me. There is an awkwardness in the figures,
particularly in the principal one, which is very displeasing, and
it has besides so many offensive parts that no beauties (and it has
many) could atone for them in my eyes.' The room with twenty
Carlo Marattis he dismissed as 'unpleasant pictures. There seems
to be a deficiency both in the *colouring* and in the *execution*—the
colouring is gaudy. A glare which hurts the eye runs through every
picture. There is no sobriety in the tints; no harmony; no balance.
Instead of a whole you have only a splendid piece of splendid
patch-work.' Although he would allow that Salvator Rosa had
painted the prodigal son with his usual spirit, freedom and force,
he thought that:

[1] B.M. Add. MSS. 14,823.

the character of the prodigal is ill preserved. Instead of a melancholy posture, brooding over his misery . . . he is presented in a cold, unanimated attitude. . . . His garb is tattered, but his face wears the hue of plenty. The muscles of his arms and legs are full-fed. . . . But of all the disagreeable parts in this picture, the cow which runs athwart the prodigal, and cuts him at right angles, is the most displeasing.[1]

Salvator Rosa, however, was generally popular, and the highlight of any visit to Raynham was the sight of his 'Belisaurus'. 'A most wonderful performance', wrote Craven Ord with pleasure:

> He leans a little against a pillar behind him with his face towards the ground in a kind of melancholy holy musing, his arms & withered hands, his hair and beard are most admirable done; they appear entangled and quite matted together through neglect . . . the old shattered tree at his right hand is I suppose intended to be expressive of the reduced warrior, it is rather a dark piece, and hangs in so indifferent a light that it cannot be seen to perfection but when the sun shines, this I had the good luck to have for almost half the hour which I took to view it.[2]

'Not a favourite master of mine', declared Byng vigorously after seeing the numerous works of Rubens which hung at Blenheim. 'All his male figures are coarse, and his women wet nurses.' Such a verdict was echoed time and time again, and perhaps no other painter received such universal condemnation. 'A vast, glaring, disgusting object and ill-suited to the company it appears in', said Gilpin of a cartoon of Meliager and Atalanta at Houghton, and although allowing that the head of an old woman was good, added, 'the drapery and every thing else is disagreeable'. Mrs. Morgan found a very large Bacchanalian piece by Rubens almost too shocking to be looked at, and yet it was so striking at the same time that she could hardly take her eyes from it. 'It consists of numerous groups of men and women, bigger than life . . . the most digusting objects are the females: they have beauty, but it is so much obscured by the disagreeable situations into which their intoxication has thrown them. They expose their persons without repugnance or shame. . . .'[3]

But pictures were by no means the only *objets d'art* to be seen

[1] *Observations on Several Parts of the Counties of Cambridge, Norfolk, Suffolk and Essex, 1769 and 1773*, London, 1809, *42–59*.
[2] B.M. Add. MSS. 14,823.
[3] *Tour to Milford Haven 1791*, London, 1795, *70–1*.

and discussed; most houses could boast a very considerable collection of urns, busts, bronzes, statues and bas-reliefs. The treasures at Wilton remained unrivalled, one great room alone containing, according to Harley who saw it in 1738, 170 busts, more than seventy statues, as well as inscriptions, bas-reliefs, urns, sarcophagi, pillars of granite, three tables of Egyptian marble, two whole columns of granite, two tables of granite and one of lapis lazuli. 'To describe this Place wd be to write the Greek and Roman History', said John Dodd in despair. But fortunately such a task was not necessary, since all the objects had been carefully arranged to be seen to the best advantage and listed in a catalogue, which by the end of the century had swollen to a very sizeable volume. Castle Howard also had its museum: 'Every room that will admit it is filled with antique busts, urns, vases, mosaic pavement, Roman tiles, and every curiosity that could possibly be procured by the late Lord Carlisle, Indian chests and cabinets, the most rich, in which ornament rather than convenience has been consulted', wrote Sir Harbottle Grimston in admiration. Holkham was famous for its fine antique busts and statues, and Craven Ord was especially delighted by the 'many beautiful female busts, their hair in general very bushy and high curled; equal to the excess of modern fashion, *edificare caput*, hardly a hyperbole!' Narford was exceptional in housing a great collection of fine china. 'A most wretched place', grumbled the querulous Harley, 'set out upon shelves, like a shop, no old china, a mere baby room.' George Vertue, however, who visited it a few years later, described it with rather more justice as 'a most rare cabinet of earthenware, painted, gilded, and adorned with great beauty and variety . . . and arranged in the most elegant order that could be imagined'.[1] Craven Ord was dissatisfied with the display, not because he disliked it, but because he was not allowed to do it full justice. 'The closet which contains the old enamel and famous earthenware of Raphael is shut up; and you view the curiosities thro' a large plate of glass in the door; the pieces are numerous, and of different shapes, some large as dishes, jars, cisterns, &c, none of the figures are well distinguishable; so that the curiosity is sharpened without being satisfied.' But that many tourists merited such treatment is clear from the state of affairs at Blenheim where the Dresden china presented to the Duke in return for a

[1] I owe this reference to R. W. Ketton-Cremer, *op. cit., 184.*

pack of staghounds sent to the King of Poland was no longer exhibited by the end of the century, as many pieces had been dropped or smashed by rough handling by visitors. Moreover, many small articles had been secreted in pockets and carried off, including some of the miniature paintings in the palace, particularly one valuable one by which the Duke lost 500 guineas.

The smaller country houses offered their own peculiar attractions. The Rev. William Gilpin stopped at Norbury Park in Surrey to see a closet filled with heads, hands, feet, trunks and other parts of the human body, a collection which, though it consisted chiefly of casts, contained some genuine antiques, particularly a discabolus which turned on a pivot and was thus able to exhibit itself 'on every side in the justest proportions and the most pleasing attitudes'. The statue gallery at Newby Hall near Boroughbridge, however, caused another parson, the Rev. James Plumptre, to reflect that though anyone having viewed some of the choicest remains of the sculpture of ancient Greece and Rome and modern Britain would be accused of prudery if he were to object to the naked figures of a Venus, Hercules or Bacchus, yet he could not forbear saying that he should not wish such things to be amongst the decorations of a house where he hoped that modesty would be its principal ornament.[1]

Viewing such collections could land the tourist in awkward situations, as Sir Joseph Banks found to his chagrin at a house belonging to a Mr. Green near Lichfield. 'Saw a Very Bad Collection of Shells, a worse of Fossills & a Collection of woods worthy to be imitated from their method of arrangement, the subjects however were more to be Laugh'd at especially two specimens both inlayd with plates of silver upon one which was wrote Shakespeares Mulberry on the other Royal Oak meaning that in which Charles the 2nd was concealed from his Pursuers.' A little later he was subjected to the treasures of a Mr. Newton recently returned from the East Indies. 'I was obliged to admire drawers full of Indian weapons, Fly flappa pictures of the nabob & his Court, Letters from him to Mrs. Newton in Indian Language & Closets full of China defend me I say from a Nabobs collection unless half an hour is Given me to use as I list Mem: never again to Capitulate unless such terms are before agreed upon.'[2]

[1] Camb. Univ. Lib. Add. MSS. 5814, f. 40.
[2] Camb. Univ. Lib. Add. MSS. 6294.

THE PURSUIT OF
A TERRESTRIAL PARADISE

The Round of Gardens

'ᴏᴜ must know, sir, that I look upon the pleasure which
we take in a garden as one of the most innocent delights
in human life. . . . It is naturally apt to fill the mind
with calmness and tranquillity . . . and suggests
innumerable subjects for contemplation.'[1] The attraction which
gardens held for eighteenth-century tourists did not derive merely
from the visual satisfaction to be gained from fine planting and
successful landscaping but from the stimulus to the imagination
and the literary and philosophical ideas they were expected to
evoke. Thus they criticized the actual design of the gardens, and
then, if they found it aesthetically satisfying, settled down to
enjoy the beautiful or the sublime effect produced by the associa-
tion of ideas it aroused. As the century progressed landscape
gardening drew increasingly closer to the principles of painting
and the direct copying of nature until the natural wilderness was
encouraged to come up to the very doors of the house. Those
tourists who had learnt their lesson well and now sought only
nature untrammelled by art were harsh in their judgements upon
anything which they felt fell below the strict canons which the
modern taste demanded.

[1] *The Spectator*, No. 477, quoted H. F. Clark, 'Eighteenth-Century Elysiums',
Journal of the Warburg and Courtauld Institutes, 1943, VI, *165*.

The few houses which still retained their old Dutch formal gardens were looked upon as objects of purely academic interest, 'relicks of those sorts of antiquities', as Stebbing Shaw put it after visiting Holme Lacy in Herefordshire, where he found all laid out 'in King William's style of fortifications surrounded with yew hedges, cut in variety of forms, according to the style of that time'.[1] 'The gardens are very curious having been kept up in their original stile since the time of Charles II', wrote Mrs. Cobbold after seeing Levens near Windermere in 1795. 'They are in that formal false Taste which Addison so justly ridiculed; Parterres formed by eddyings of Box into Stars, Scrolls, and Labyrinths, which at every turning are decorated with Yews clipt and trimmed into the most fantastick shapes: Pyramids, Columns, Globes, Vases, Temples, nay even Animals. There is one in particular which resembles a Peacock with its wings and Tail expanded.'[2] Joseph Budworth agreed with her and dismissed them as 'too formal to be interesting'; and the only redeeming feature which gave him any pleasure at all was a tree 'whose trunk is cut off a foot from the earth, and whose branches were engrafted or rather inoculated into another tree; it was in full foliage, and seemed alive to the bottom of the Trunk'.[3] A house belonging to a Mrs. Lambe near Fairford called forth from R. J. Sullivan tones of the deepest horror: 'The aera of ill taste is discernible throughout. On the one side a row of methodistical yews, starched and prim as the enlightened Whitfieldites, and on the other a sluggish stream tortured into the resemblance of an inverted T.'[4] None could resist going to see the gardens at Chatsworth, but few could afterwards say anything in their favour. 'The strait canal, basons, terrace and deal walls certainly must be destroyed', wrote Sullivan. 'While they remain grandeur of view can never be expected. The spouting horses, Naiads, and other little matters must likewise be removed for without this they can never hope to rise to a modern degree of reputation.'[5] 'A curious specimen of the

---

[1] Stebbing Shaw, *A Tour to the West of England in 1788*, London, 1789, 174.

[2] 'A Tour in the Lake District 1795', B.M. Add. MSS. 19,203, f. 105.

[3] Joseph Budworth, *A Fortnight's Ramble to the Lakes in Westmorland, Lancashire and Cumberland*, London, 1795, 29–30.

[4] R. J. Sullivan, *Observations made during a Tour through parts of England, Scotland and Wales in a Series of Letters*, London, 1780, 116.

[5] ibid., *172*.

old taste' was all that Plumptre would allow, and then proceeded, with youthful censoriousness, to condemn them more or less out of hand:

The waterworks are worth seeing once, and that I think is the utmost to be said of them. Those who have never seen anything of the kind before, curiosity tempts them to see, and is perhaps scarcely gratified when it has. The devices are many of them Childish, and, as the water is only set playing at particular times, you do not see them in their best state at once, but have to wait for them to be set going. There is a large stone temple with many flights of steps up to it, when you get there the man turns the cocks, and water gushes from all parts of it and falls down this formal flight of steps. It is a trick sometimes play'd I believe to get a person into this temple, when water spirts up from beneath and wets him completely. There is also a tin-tree, which, as you approach it, the leaves spit out water.[1]

The main attraction of visiting gardens lay, in fact, in watching the transformation from such formal designs to the natural landscapes, and to see a garden whose potentialities lay unexploited would cause any sensitive tourist acute pain. 'In passing through the grounds of Lord Weymouth', wrote Sullivan after seeing Longleat in 1780:

one is surprized at the vast capabilities which they possess. Very little is required: Nature has done her share, not indeed in the wildest or grandest style, but in such a way as will make Longleath beautiful if it is properly attended to. Trees indeed in clumps are already planting, and in time it is probable the old canals, the most glaring vestiges of exploded taste, will be either turned into more natural forms or be entirely filled up.[2]

For most owners were already at work on their grounds, though their efforts were by no means always greeted with approval by their critical visitors. Lady Beauchamp Proctor was particularly scornful of what Walpole had been doing at Houghton when she saw it in 1771. 'There is an artificiall knoll in the park, which is so ill made and formal that it looks like a plum cake just drawn out of the oven. Here is no water, except a small bason near the stables, which has swallowed up an immense sum and after all

---

[1] 'A Journal of a Tour into Derbyshire in the year 1793', Camb. Univ. Lib. MSS. 5804, ff. 30-1.
[2] *Observations*, 1780, 61-2.

looks like a watering pond, and I believe is used as such.'[1] Water was, of course, vitally important for any successful landscaping, and the trials and expenses of bringing it into dry ground were a source of great interest, and often of considerable amusement, to the tourists. John Dodd recounted the notorious episode of the Duke of Marlborough at Blenheim with enormous relish after his visit there in 1735:

> The view from the house of the Bridge, Obelisk & Theatre is inexpressibly beautifull but who can help Laughing to think that this prodigeous large Bridge (whose Arch is 101 feet wide) was first built & then a monstrous Sume of money expended to fetch water to run under it, which is but very scanty, and in no proportion to the Bridge—when there was none under it some passenger wrote the following Epigram on the top of it
>
> > 'The Arch above his Wide Ambition Shows
> > His Bounty like the water under flows'
>
> which if it be truly said throws a Shade over all the Virtues & great Actions of this Hero . . .[2]

The process of redemption was by no means complete at Studley Park, seat of Mr. Aislabie near Ripon, when Sullivan visited it: 'Here you receive a shock at the formality of a large bason of water, nor are you much better pleased, on a little further progress, at the regular embankation of a pretty little rivulet.' But his account ended on a note of praise for its more 'artless and rural aspects', the hanging woods overshadowing the rivers, the rocks romantically showing themselves in natural wildness, and the succession of 'artless vistos' opening at every turn until the visitor eventually discovered himself amongst 'a beautiful assemblage of new objects most elegantly diversified; the banqueting-house, cold bath, rotunda, and a small pavilion just peering above the trees'.[3]

But by the middle years of the century a greater number of gardens were well calculated to rejoice the heart of the connoisseur, and call forth almost lyrical praises. Hagley, the Leasowes, Persfield, Mount Edgcumbe, Stowe, Stourhead—all these were amongst the finest creations of the gardener's art, and as such drew countless pilgrims in search of a terrestrial paradise. Some were always open, others might be visited on one or two

---

[1] Yorke papers, Forthampton Court.
[2] 'Journal of a Tour through England, 1735', B.M. Add. MSS. 5957.
[3] *Observations*, 1780, *190–1*.

WILTON HOUSE.
By Richard Wilson.

days of the week only, such as Persfield which could be seen on
Tuesdays and Fridays. Procedure was quite simple: 'the only
ceremony required being that of setting down your name and
address in a book kept for that purpose at the Porters Lodge. Then
you are permitted to stroll through the park and grounds.'[1]
Mount Edgcumbe announced to its visitors that the park and
pleasure gardens might be seen on application on any day and 'the
Flower-Garden may be seen occasionally, during the summer,
by a particular ticket, granted only to parties not exceeding six
persons'. This was one of the gardens which made surprisingly
modern provision for its tourists in a cottage in the middle of the
park 'for the accomodation of strangers, where hot water for
making tea and other conveniences may be procured, since those
who make this pleasant excursion generally furnish themselves
with a hamper of provisions'.[2] At Rokeby, the seat of Sir Thomas
Robinson, there was also a tea-room, situated 'on the rocky banks
of the *Greta* raging like a torrent over the rocks, and tumbling
in a romantic manner under the windows'.[3] Printed guides were
available at some gardens, with plans and illustrations which set
out the vistas in the order in which they should be viewed so
as to gain the greatest possible aesthetic satisfaction. *A Walk
round Mount Edgcumbe*, for example, conducted the tourist
either along the Great Tour of four and a quarter miles, or along
the lesser of one and a quarter, of pleasure gardens only, describing the prospects and drawing attention to the most advantageous
points of view. It was intended, as its introduction explained, for
the 'many persons of real taste and curiosity', and the Rev.
Richard Warner commended it warmly to his readers: 'written
with neatness and elegance . . . in which its interesting parts are
taken in the best succession . . . embracing by this arrangement
the whole routine of its multifarious scenes and diversified
objects'.[4]

*A Description of the House and Gardens of the most noble and
puissant Richard Grenville Nugent Chandos Temple, Marquess of
Buckingham*, published in the early nineteenth century, included
prints and plans for its great flood of tourists, for Stowe retained

[1] D. C. Webb, *Observations and Remarks during Four Excursions*, London,
1812, *92*.
[2] ibid., *92–3*.
[3] Arthur Young, *Northern Tour*, London, 1770, II, *186*.
[4] *Tour through Cornwall in the Autumn of 1808*, London, 1809, *73*.

its position of pre-eminent popularity among English, and indeed among European, gardens. Here, with the aid of such men as Vanbrugh, Kent and Gibbs, Lord Cobham had filled 400 acres with vistas, trees and prospects, a serpentine lake and no less than thirty-eight temples, On the threshold of 'these Elysian fields' Sir Harbottle Grimston stood enraptured, delighted with the distant prospect of the house and enthralled by the immediate beauties on either hand. 'The walk round is computed five miles, but the variety of pleasing objects, particularly of Temples, Obelisks, Pavilions, etc. etc. takes off the tedium so much that it appears to be much less. The buildings, which are most dedicated to the heathen gods, or to some of his departed friends, have each of them their inscription, which shews in their application the good taste of the person who chose them.'[1] The park and grounds of Wentworth impressed Arthur Young far more than the house itself, and his description was almost ecstatic as he found himself torn between the great variety of viewpoints, many of them still in the actual course of creation when he saw them.

> A part of this design was the cutting away a large part of that hill, which projected too much before the front of the house; a vast design but not yet compleated, although his lordship has already moved from it upwards of one hundred and forty thousand square yards of earth. . . . Which way soever you approach, very magnificent woods, spreading waters, and elegant temples break upon the eye at every angle. . . . The woods stretching away above, below, and to the right and left with inconceivable magnificence; from the pyramid on one side, which rises from the bosom of a great wood, quite around to your left hand, where they join one of above an hundred acres hanging on the side of a vast hill, and forming altogether an ampitheatrical prospect, the beauties of which are much easier imagined than described. In one place the rustic temple crowns the point of a waving hill, and in another the ionic one appears with a lightness that decorates the surrounding groves. . . . The pyramids and temples are finely scattered over the scene, and give it just the air of liveliness which is consistent with the grandeur of the extent.[2]

'Nothing here is forced, nothing formal', wrote one tourist in 1791 of Mount Edgcumbe, finding there everything which the

[1] 'A Tour in Wales 1769', Hist. MSS. Comm., Verulam, 244.
[2] Arthur Young, Northern Tour, 1770, II, 298–301.

modern taste demanded. 'Nature reigns supreme, wild, simple, and frequently contracting her features to a frown, assumes an appearance grand, sublime, and awful.'[1] Amongst the other gardens which received such enthusiastic praise were Hagley and the Leasowes. Hagley, near Stourbridge, was the seat of Lord Lyttelton, its gardens a reflection of his Italian travels, literary interests and his connection with Pope, Thomson and Shenstone. Sullivan was moved to flights of lyrical prose as he attempted to recapture for his readers the beauties of this 'terrestrial paradise'.

> Conceive to yourself a beautiful enamelled lawn, swelled in all the elegancy of art and nature, for a distance of about four miles; while hill, dale and grove, delightfully interspersed, render it as perfect an elysium as possibly can be conceived. The tender fawn here finds a brow for play, and the little lambkin skips about with joy. The church, which is the nearest object to the house, is totally concealed from it; a close embowering wood shades it entirely from the sight. . . . At the other side of the lawn is a truly charming spot. A lovely ivy twines its tendrils round the body of an antient oak, the oldest of the place. The woods surround it, water in murmurs wanders at its side, and carefully formed vistos present a happy disposition of pavilions. Here the poet could sit him down and think. Wildness predominates everywhere . . .[2]

The Leasowes, the work of Lyttelton's neighbour, the poet and landscape gardener William Shenstone, attracted possibly even more attention. Though it lacked the temples with which his more prosperous contemporaries could adorn their estates, Shenstone had filled his walks with urns, inscriptions painted on boards and judiciously placed seats which commanded carefully arranged vistas. Its 'wild and coquettish' studied negligence particularly pleased J. Grant, as he wandered among its dark Gothic alcoves, admired its small bridge built of tree-trunks, and paid homage at the 'rustic temple to Pan, formed of rough stone, with a trophy of the Tibia and Syrinx'. But he gained his keenest enjoyment from the melancholy induced by a stroll along the Lovers' Walk.

> The silent gloominess diffused over it prepares the mind for the beautiful and pathetic inscription on the urn, to the memory of

[1] *A Tour through the South of England, Wales and part of Ireland, made during the Summer of 1791*, London, 1792, 55.
[2] *Observations*, 1780, 136.

Miss Maria Dolman, the daughter of a clergyman near Kidder-
minster, and a cousin of Mr Shenstone's, who died of the small
pox about twenty one years of age.

> Ah! Maria!
> Puella elegantissima,
> Vale!
> Heu quanto minus est
> Cum reliquis versari
> Quam tui
> Meminisse.[1]

The wealth of the banker Hoare had been poured out upon the
gardens at Stourhead until the tourists' eyes must have been
dazzled by the galaxy of obelisks, statues, pillars and pavilions;
a cavern of Neptune; a temple to Flora and another to Apollo;
'the venerable remains of a mouldering arch'; a Druid's cell
formed from roots and branches of old trees; a Pantheon, the
exact model of that at Rome, rising from the banks of a winding
river. 'No expence has been spared it seems to have been lavish'd
to adorn them', exclaimed one tourist in 1766, as he wandered
through these three miles of grounds, following a shady walk
past a figure of Belvedere Apollo to a Chinese pavilion, and then,
on coming through a grove, finding a 'beautifull gloomy path
by the side of a Lake', passing under a rude arch or rock to enter:

> one of the most beautifull Grottos that can be imagined—the
> Sides are form'd of Petrifactions. The noise of the falling Water
> and the gloominess of the scene are very striking—under a
> beautifull Arch of this rock work lies the statue of a sleeping
> Venus, she rests upon a kind of Tablet of rock work, from whence
> the Water falls in pleasing murmurs, at her feet is the following
> Inscription—

> > Nymph of the Grot, these sacred Springs I keep,
> > And to the murmurs of these waters sleep.
> > Oh! spare my slumbers, gently tread the cave,
> > And drink in silence, or in silence lave.[2]

The fame of Persfield rested less on such grottos and pavilions
in themselves than on the succession of carefully contrived vistas

---

[1] *Journal of a Three Weeks Tour in 1797 through Derbyshire to the Lakes*,
Mavor, *British Tourists*, London, 1809, IV, *223–9*.
[2] 'Notes of a Tour in Nottinghamshire, Derbyshire etc. in 1766', B.M. Add.
MSS. 6767.

opening from them, designed to present the tourist with unex-
pected and variegated panoramas. 'You get involved in the serpentine windings of the wood', wrote Sullivan:

> and continue so until you come to a grotto in an artificial hill, from
> whence you have a most romantic view of Land-caught cliff, the
> rivers Severn and Wye. Still proceeding in the shrubbery you
> next ascend a small eminence which opens an enchanting prospect
> of Land-caught. Next you come to a spot which affords a wild and
> extensive view—on the one side Land-caught village with a
> beautiful ascent from the river Wye, rearing its little head with
> the cliff of the same name serving as the background to the picture.
> On the other, Chepstow, with its ivy-mantled towers, the lordly
> Severn receiving its tributary rivulets, and the distant but fertile
> regions of Gloucestershire and Somerset.[1]

The fact that many of these gardens had been designed by
their owners themselves and not by professionals undoubtedly
added considerably to their interest for the tourists, who looked
upon them with the practised eye of men themselves engaged
upon similar tasks. The work of one professional, however,
Lancelot Brown, was always the subject of special interest. His
greatest achievement was held to be the grounds at Blenheim,
where, as one tourist put it, could be seen 'the effect of polished
taste and the sublime in design in one continual series of charming
prospects and agreeably diversified scenes'. The gardens occupied
more than 200 acres, with carefully contrived intersecting walks,
temples and other artificial objects 'at once elegant and neat'. A
Chinese bridge thrown over the lake led to a large tract of hill
enclosed and elegantly laid out with grottos so naturally introduced, 'that art scarcely appears', and the water, under his guiding
hands, had been 'taught to wind according to the designs of taste,
to fall in broken murmurs over the rough cascade, and again to
smooth its bosom and move imperceptibly along'.[2] At Wrest
Walpole rejoiced to find him reshaping the formal gardens: 'The
Gardens were fine & ugly in the old fashioned manner with high
hedges & canals, at the End of the principal one of which is a
frightful Temple designed by Mr. Archer the groomporter. Mr.
Brown has much corrected this garden, & built a hermitage &

[1] *Observations*, 1780, *27–8*.
[2] ibid., *394–6*.

cold bath in bold good taste.'[1] At Combe Abbey on the other hand Byng felt that his faith in him had been betrayed: 'Mean is the entrance into Coombe-Abbey Park; a place of which I had heard much, and where my friend Capability Brown was allow'd to act, so modern taste, join'd to antiquity, I hoped wou'd produce great things: but Brown here sadly deceived me; for he has ruined old avenues, and not planted in their place, half enough; the water is stagnate, and there is no inequality of the ground.'[2] When Brown thus failed his critics it was generally because he did not design as a painter or observe the rules of picturesque composition, a weakness for which he was being satirized as early as 1775 as Mr. Layout, 'introducing the same objects at the same distances in most of our largest gardens'.[3]

Far more entertaining, even if not so aesthetically satisfying as Brown's careful compositions, were the pleasure gardens, follies and menageries, in which the individual owners indulged their eccentricities and idiosyncrasies. Arthur Young proves himself an excellent guide here, for he was always ready to turn aside from the consideration of sainfoin, ploughs or turnips, to see some newly built ruin, grotto or temple. He held very definite ideas on the construction of an artificial ruin, demanding that it should always be in exact imitation of a real one. 'For this reason it should never serve a double purpose, that of an object, and a banqueting or tea-room; because the contrast between the out and the inside is apparently too great and dissonant. The one is an image of melancholy; the other a temple of festivity.'[4] Among the more curious items in his collection are Mrs. Henley's hermitage at Docking, its bedroom walled with oyster shells and its parlour frescoed 'with scrolls and festoons of sea-weed, deal-shavings, and painted ropes, in a gothic but neat taste', and the grotto made of two halves of a boat at Snettisham, 'stuck full of spar, shells, sea-weed, coral, glass, ore, &c, all disposed with taste. The front pretty, but too regular, and not rustic enough.'[5] Even his

[1] *Journals of Visits to Country Seats*, (ed.) P. Toynbee, Walpole Society, 1928, XVI, 71.
[2] John Byng, 'A Ride Taken in 1785', *The Torrington Diaries*, (ed.) C. Bruyn Andrews, abridged Fanny Andrews, London, 1954, *106*.
[3] Rev. James Craddock, *Village Memoirs, an Epistolary Novel*, London, 1775, *143*.
[4] *Northern Tour*, 1770, II, *235*.
[5] I owe these examples to R. W. Ketton-Cremer, *Norfolk Assembly*, London, 1957, *197*.

accustomed eye was startled when at Clifton, after entering a grotto underground, and passing through a dark arched passage, he entered a den to be greeted by the statue of a lion. 'Pleasing objects are generally wished for in a sequestered grot; but the owner of this is more pleased with that of terror.'[1] Bishop Pococke described a much more conventional rustic folly which he found at Hagley: 'A very well designed sylvan hexagon temple; the sides are open, and it is built on pillars made of the trunks of oaks, between which lathes are fix'd, to which the rods of ivy are nail'd on the inside and outside. Before the ends of the rafters little clumps of wood are fix'd, which resemble a rustick frieze, and above it is a projection as for the base of the cornish, all made in like manner with rods of ivie.'[2] He approved of the Gothic additions made by the Earl of Darlington to Raby Castle, 'a bath, an alcove seat, a farm house and dog-house'.[3] He took an almost boyish pleasure in Sanderson Miller's Gothic rotunda at Wroxton 'in which he has practis'd curtains, that by turning screws let down so as to afford shelter which ever way you please. This commands a most delightful view of the head that supports the great body of water I have mentioned cover'd with shrubs and a cascade falls down twenty feet from it, and forms the serpentine river which runs by a chinese summer house.'[4] But Plumptre, visiting Wimpole in 1800, brought the melancholy reminder that such elegant fantasies might all too soon become scenes of ruin and desolation. The pavilion there, built twenty-five years before at a cost he estimated of about £1500, was when he first saw it:

one of the most elegant buildings I ever remember. The Tea room was simple and elegant; the little room on the side was a rare specimen of painting, of Etruscan figures in colours. It was done by Stewart and cost £700. What the inside is now we could not see, we could discern from the outside that the blinds were falling to pieces. The pillars which supported the centre were rotting away, and the building supported by rough props. . . . The stucco which covered the outside and gave it the appearance

[1] Arthur Young, *Southern Tour*, London, 1768, *187*.
[2] *Travels through England during 1750, 1751 and later years*, (ed.) J. J. Cartwright, Camden Society, 1888 and 1889, II, *234-5*.
[3] *Northern Journey 1760*, Surtees Society, 1915, CXXIV, *204*.
[4] *Travels through England*, 1750, II, *240*.

of stone, was everywhere falling off. I brought away a piece of it . . .[1]

Another source of pleasure to the tourists were the menageries with which many owners adorned their grounds. The main attraction for John Dodd on his visit to Goodwood in 1735 lay in the Duke of Richmond's large collection of foreign birds and beasts, for the house he dismissed summarily as old, and the park he found 'merely pleasant'.[2] In 1743, however, when the Rev. Jeremiah Milles saw it, the Duke had disposed of all his beasts, and nothing remained except a monument of Portland stone in the garden marking the burial place of one of the lionesses.[3] Similarly at Longleat, where the aviary had once been famed as among the largest and best-stocked in the country, the Rev. Richard Warner in 1800 found that it had been 'neglected for some years and exhibits at present nothing curious, except a male and female Kangaroo, brought from Botany Bay and presented by their Majesties to the Dowager Marchioness of Bath. They are the only animals of the kind in the kingdom.'[4] At Wentworth, however, every care had been taken of the menagerie, and it was housed in 'a little light *Chinese* building of a very pleasing design; it is stocked with *Canary* and other foreign birds, which are kept alive in winter by means of hot walls at the back of the building; the front is open net-work in compartments';[5] and at Bulstrode Pococke followed a canal covered with wild duck which led to the dairy and menagerie where 'several sorts of birds and fowls are kept and bred of both kinds. The dairy is adorn'd with a Chinese front, as a sort of open summer-house, and about it are some pieces of water for the different water poultry.'[6] At Shugborough in Staffordshire, the seat of Lord Anson, Sir Joseph Banks found many of the more unusual animals, which interested him greatly:

> Two animals which were new to me. The first was the Persian Cat which differs from the Common Cat in nothing but the extreme length of her hair which is Lank & the thickness of her

[1] 'A Tour to the Source of the Cam in 1800', Camb. Univ. Lib. MSS. 5819, ff. 115–16.
[2] *op. cit.*, B.M. Add. MSS. 5957.
[3] B.M. Add. MSS. 15,776.
[4] *Excursions from Bath . . . 1800*, London, 1801, *82*.
[5] Arthur Young, *Northern Tour*, 1770, I, *297–8*.
[6] Pococke, *Travels . . . 1750*, II, *259–60*.

tail which is twice as thick. The other, Corsican deer or goat, is certainly mentioned by Strabo—the head small & Conical the muzzel whiteish the horns are strong but small bending back & forming about one third of a Circle . . . the Chin has no Beard, but the neck & breasts are Covered with Long Hair. The tail is remarkably short & triangular . . . . on each side of the belly is a whiteish spot the Belly underneath is white as are the Leggs below . . .[1]

Most tourists, however, lacked such a technical appreciation and were content to enjoy exotic creatures, particularly birds, simply for the gaiety of their colour and their decorative shape. At Kimbolton, the house built for Sarah Duchess of Marlborough, Horace Walpole rejoiced at the sight of a toucan: 'a bird almost as large as a pheasant, black body, whitish tail, the bill yellow, red, blue & salmon colour, most beautifull', while at Holkham Lady Beauchamp Proctor was delighted with 'one uncommon bird, which came from Barbary, coal black with a yellow bill and frizzld crown, about the size of a goose. It made such a doleful noise, I can liken it to nothing but the humming of a bass string of a violoncello, and so loud withal that you could not avoid hearing it the whole time you were in the garden.' Houghton possessed a particularly fine collection of rare animals and strange birds which pleased Walpole when he went there.

In the Menagerie which is a little wood, very prettily disposed with many basons of gold fish, are several curious birds & beasts. Storks; Raccoons that breed there much, & I believe the first that have bred here; a very large Strong Eagle, another with a white head; two hogs from the Havannah with navels on their backs; two young Tigers; two uncommon Martins; doves from the Guadaloupe, brown with blue heads, & a milk white streak crossing their cheeks; a kind of Ermine, Sandy with many spots all over the body and tail.[2]

Among eighteenth-century gardens, the grounds of Hawkestone fulfilled all the canons demanded by the purists of landscape and exhibited such an exuberant display of follies and conceits that they had become a veritable pleasure ground of every imaginable delight. They earned the praises of Dr. Johnson for their

striking scenes and terrific grandeur. We were always on the brink of a precipice, or at the foot of a lofty rock; but the steeps

[1] 'Journals of Excursions to Eastbury etc. 1767–8', Camb. Univ. Lib. Add. MSS. 6294, ff. 115–16.
[2] *Journals of Visits*, 27–8.

were seldom naked; in many places, oaks of uncommon magnitude
shot up from the crannies of stone; and where there were not tall
trees, there were underwoods and bushes. Round the rocks is a
narrow path, cut upon the stone, which is very frequently hewn
into steps; but art has proceeded no further than to make the
succession of wonders accessible . . . [1]

In 1802 when Jonathan Gray saw it there were a number of new
attractions:

We were shown an Otaheitan Cottage, fitted up in a very appropriate
stile. A summer house called Neptune's Whim, near which is an
enormous statue of that deity. Near this place a most sumptuous
Egyptian tent is pitched; & what renders it more interesting is
that it was brought over from Egypt last year by Colonel Hill
and that it belonged to Murad Bey; from whom it was taken by
the French; & came into possession of the English on the
surrender of Cairo.[2]

After amusing himself in a pleasure boat, and listening to a small
band of musicians stationed in a grove, the visitor might make his
way towards a 'cottage ornamented with coloured prints, chiefly
of a humorous kind, and intended for the temporary refreshment
of visitors, with rustic chairs for their accommodation'; then
following a walk with picturesque views opening out on either
hand he would suddenly be startled by the appearance of an
attendant in the guise of a Druid, with a hoary and laurelled head
made to look yet more awesome by the light thrown on his face
from a pale green glass. The *pièce de résistance*, 'which must
produce a powerful effect on the minds of women & children',
said Gray with a note of distinct satisfaction in his voice, came
when the tourist found himself standing outside a hermitage.
The emaciated figure of a hermit sitting at a table would then
rise with difficulty, and in a hollow tremulous voice repeat
'*Memento mori*' or some other suitable monitory phrase, meanwhile lifting a hand supposedly rotted with age and showing
two bloody stumps—a sight which more than one tourist found
altogether too unnatural and disgusting.[3]

[1] July 1774, *Boswell's Life of Johnson*, (ed.) G. E. Hill, revised L. F· Powell,
Oxford, 1934–50, V, *433*.
[2] 'Tour in the Western Counties and South Wales, 1802', York Public Library
MSS. T/14.
[3] E. Butcher, *An Excursion from Sidmouth to Chester in the Summer of 1803*,
London, 1805, *173–80*.

HORRID AND SUBLIME

Mills, Mines and Furnaces

'To have been at Newcastle, and men of curiosity too, without seeing a coal-pit, would have been a sin of the most unpardonable nature.'[1] The motives of the tourist who wrote this in 1780 were at the same time romantic, economic, aesthetic and practical. A patriotism which delighted in the sight of the country's manufacturing and engineering achievements went hand in hand with an imagination which was nurtured on discussions of the distinction between romantic and picturesque, and sought for gloom and terror as conducive to true emotion, anxious to experience that sense of vastness and power which Burke had taught to be the essence of the sublime. Thus the traveller to the Lakes would turn aside to descend the Cheshire salt-mines or visit the Lancashire cotton-mills; expeditions to Devon or Cornwall to make the round of the tin- and copper-mines were almost as popular as journeys to Snowdonia; and after visiting the great country houses of the Midlands, the potteries or the Derby silk-mills proved almost equally rewarding.

'This mood of enchantment', as Klingender calls it,[2] with its union between art and science, its delight in industry and its enthusiasm for technical advance, had been caught by Joseph

[1] R. J. Sullivan, *Observations made during a Tour through parts of England, Scotland and Wales in a series of Letters*, London, 1780, *199.*
[2] F. G. Klingender, *Art and the Industrial Revolution*, London, 1947.

Wright, Erasmus Darwin and countless other topographical poets, engravers and draughtsmen who found a roaring furnace or a coal-pit blazing on a heath sources of inspiration for their art. The strictly economic aspects of industrial undertakings had, of course, interested Celia Fiennes and Daniel Defoe early in the eighteenth century, as they were to form the main attraction later for men such as Arthur Young or William Cobbett, who travelled to study agrarian progress. These more dilettante tourists, however, also frequently displayed considerable knowledge of technical processes and industrial development, and showed an indomitable determination to descend every pit, to enter subterranean canals, to spend hours in mines crawling along on hands and knees or wading knee-deep in water. Being lowered 200 feet in a bucket into a Northwich salt-mine seemed an extraordinarily easy and agreeable means of descent to a tourist of 1791 after the hazards he had encountered elsewhere from 'broken ladders, slippery precipices, horrid chasms, dismal dungeons, where one half of our bodies was soaked in water, and the other exposed to the suffocating fumes of sulphur'.

In preparation for his expedition below ground the tourist had to don miner's clothing: flannel trousers and jacket, woollen shirt, a night-cap, with possibly an old broad-brimmed hat on top to shield the face from droppings, and equip himself with a candle in one hand and a supply of half a pound more suspended round his neck. 'It requires a good strong stomach, and a large portion of curiosity to go through with this', wrote this same tourist as he got ready to go down a Cornish tin-mine, 'for beside the fatigue and toil in the mine, the cloaths they give you are as greasy as sweat can make them, smell abominably, and are often stocked with a republic of creepers.'[1] In many mines guides were waiting to conduct tourists along a carefully planned route. At a Staffordshire lead-mine R. J. Sullivan climbed down 107 steps under the direction of the steward to the river where a boat awaited them.

Holding our candles therefore, and entrusting ourselves to this second Charon, off pushed the boat, when, by sticks placed on either side in the rocks, at the distance of about six feet from each other, he shoved us along for a considerable distance. Tremendous as this subterranean navigation was, the whole was exceeding

[1] *A Tour through the South of England, Wales, and part of Ireland, made during the Summer of 1791*, London, 1793, 359.

awful and sublime. The air rustled along in dreadful majesty; the place was dark, saving the lights of our tapers; all was quietness in the boat, and the imagination at work, fancied everything that was grand. In this way, coasting it with a degree of pleasure that we had not in any of our excursions tasted . . . at length, having traversed between 16 and 18,000 feet, we came to the end, where we found three hale and cheerful men busied at their occupations.[1]

When he visited the Holywell lead-mine the Rev. Richard Warner was navigated for the first part of his journey in a long, narrow, flat boat which was forced along the subterranean canal, cut through the solid rock of the mountain, by workmen propelling it with their hands against the sides. A thousand yards from the entrance he reached a large natural cavern, entering it through 'a elegant gothick arch (thrown accidentally into this form) hewn thro' a vast bed of quartz, which reflecting and refracting the rays of our tapers, and being beautifully variegated with the tinges of sulphur and other minerals, displayed a specimen of natural architecture that exceeded all the efforts of art'. The main objective of the expedition was heralded by the sound of blasts of gunpowder, and he next began to ascend several shafts to watch the miners at work. This involved first climbing a rough stairway, then struggling up a vertical pit four feet square, often with no more support than pieces of wood fixed in the rock at distances of two feet, so that he complained that he constantly found himself with legs and arms stretched out to the utmost in a position as though extended on a Greek cross.[2] Few things could daunt the Rev. James Plumptre, and he was quite prepared to be let down a hundred yards, tied by a chain fastened to a rope, at Bedlam mine near Ironbridge, or to descend the Heaton colliery near Gateshead in a basket in which the coals were drawn up, though here there was only room for him and his guide if each sat with one leg in and the other out.

He held with his right arm round the chain and directed us with his left; my left was round his right, and I held fast to the chain with my right. I shut my eyes till we reached the bottom, when we stopped suddenly, and I was held by a collier who led me to a seat, I was quite bewildered with the quickness and the novelty

[1] *Observations*, 1780, *158–9*.
[2] *A Second Walk through Wales, in August and September 1798*, Bath, 1799, *211–17*.

of the motion, and possibly some little apprehension, and the darkness of the place, the dim light of the lamps, and the grim figures of the colliers had a very strange effect.[1]

In other mines, less important or not so frequently visited, the tourist would be left to make his own way as best he could. The Rev. W. Bingley visited the Llanberis copper-mine in 1798 and seeing a loaded waggon being brought out of the level seized the opportunity of returning in an empty one, which was dragged by three miners for 200 yards into the interior of the mine along bad wooden rails.[2] The Cornish mines were the most primitive of all, and here the tourists were lowered in buckets, let down by a rope tied round their thighs or forced to clamber down ladders where to miss a hold would precipitate a fall to the very bottom of the mine. Among the hazards of these smaller mines was the frequent necessity of descending into the shaft in which the steam-engine was actually working, where, as Maton complained, 'the noise arising from its movements, together with the horrible appearance of the rod when lifted over his head, occasions the most uneasy sensations imaginable'.[3] The conditions in the Mendip lead-mines were scarcely any better, and Maton found that after a quarter of an hour in one gallery 'of such length and so confined that amidst the fumes of gunpowder (used for splitting the rock) the breath of three or four people huddled close together, and the oily *effluvia* of the candles, I had nearly sunk with suffocation'.[4] Plumptre gave a most vivid account of the lead-mine he visited in 1792. At first navigation was along the river, with the tourists sitting in chairs placed on the boat. They then walked along planks placed upon rafters for 200 yards, stooping all the way. After this, being warned that many turned back at this point, they climbed for ten yards up the face of the rock by rails fixed into the sides, sometimes as much as a yard apart. 'Here our Guides again asked us if we would proceed, telling us it was forty yards climbing up the same manner till we got to the shaft they worked

---

[1] *A Narrative of a Pedestrian Journey through some parts of Yorkshire, Durham and Northumberland*, 1799, Camb. Univ. Lib. MSS. 5814, f. 38.

[2] *A Tour round North Wales during the summer of 1798*, London, 1804, I, 231–4.

[3] W. G. Maton, *Observations relative chiefly to the Natural History, Picturesque Scenery, and Antiquities of the Western Counties of England, made in the years 1794 and 1796*, Salisbury, 1797, I, 164–5.

[4] ibid., II, 133–4.

at. They looked in our faces (as they told us afterwards) to see if we were frightened, but we were determined to go on; and with much labour and difficulty got to the end of our scrambling, which was sometimes through holes in rock just big enough to admit the body.' Here they refreshed themselves with brandy while the miners explained the whole mining process to them. 'The air here was unpleasant, the smell of smoaking and gunpowder used in blasting the rock being not yet gone off.' Only on their return did they dare look back along the way they had come.

> The sight was dreadful. A candle, forty yards above us, appeared like a star, and afforded a dim light, just sufficient to give an idea of the danger we had braved. The Cavern was shaped like a Beehive, the way to the top was by stakes fixed into the sides sloping inwards, sometimes by ladders, many of the steps of which were worn nearly through, and only a slight ballustrade, so that one false step, or the breaking of a rail, had dashed us lifeless to the bottom. But all danger was now passed, and we congratulated ourselves that we had escaped it. . . . We returned to the Boat, and set forward again for daylight in high spirits, singing 'God Save the King', 'Rule Britannia', and a variety of songs in which we all joined.[1]

The intrepid Mrs. Morgan, who toured South Wales in her one-horse chaise in 1791, had resolved to go down a coal-pit, but her courage began to fail her when she heard that someone had quite recently been suffocated in the very mine she planned to see. 'I confess I did not like the idea of being arrested by death so suddenly, particularly in taking a view of the infernal regions; this would have been paying too dear for my curiosity.'[2] But in this she was not typical of her fellow tourists. Such dangers deterred so few that the complaint found far more frequently upon their lips was that, as one of them put it, they visited so many pits and mines that they found themselves at the end of their tour 'entirely satiated with subterranean scenery'.

The popularity of the copper-mines at Pary's Mountain in North Wales, however, may have been in part due to the fact that here the awe and horror of mining operations could be

---

[1] 'A Journal of a Tour into Derbyshire in the year 1793', Camb. Univ. Lib. MSS. 5804, ff. 26–8.
[2] *A Tour to Milford Haven in the year 1791*, London, 1795, *228–9*.

enjoyed to the utmost without hazardous descents into the very bowels of the earth. Standing on the edge of the excavations the tourist found below him 'an awful range of huge caverns, profound hollows, stupendous arches, gloomy passages and enormous masses of rock'. The perpetual echo of blasts of gunpowder, the shattered fragments tumbling down after an explosion, the rise and fall of the innumerable baskets bringing up the ore, together with the incessant movement of crowds of men, brought dramatic human elements into the scene, and induced philosophical speculations upon the relations of man with nature. Warner was particularly moved at the sight of the miners:

> engaged in their curious but perilous occupations. Some sticking to the sides of the rock, or seated on the narrow ledges of precipices, which gape beneath them to the depth of one or two hundred feet, tearing the ore from the mountain and breaking it into smaller masses; others boring the rock in order to blast it; whilst a third party are literally *hanging* over the abyss below them, drawing up and lowering down the ore buckets, supported only by a frame of wood-work, which quivers like an aspen leaf with the operations carrying on upon it.[1]

Bingley found here an incomparable feast for his romantic imagination.

> I found myself standing on the verge of a vast and tremendous chasm. I stepped on one of the stages suspended over the edge of the steep, and the prospect was dreadful. The number of caverns at different heights along the sides; the broken and irregular masses of rock which everywhere presented themselves; the multitudes of men at work in different parts, and apparently in the most perilous situations; the motions of the whimsies and the raising and lowering of the buckets to draw out the ore and the rubbish; the noise of picking the ore from the rock, and of hammering the wadding when it was about to be blasted; with at intervals the roar of the blasts in distant parts of the mine, altogether excited the most sublime ideas, intermixed however with sensations of Terror.[2]

'The Flaming Labyrinths', as Robert Clutterbuck called the smelting houses and blast-furnaces which dealt with the ore from the mines, were almost equally dramatic, and their first sight of

[1] *Second Walk . . . 1798, 288–9.*
[2] *Tour round North Wales . . . 1798,* I, *309–10.*

PARYS COPPER MINES, *c.* 1785.
By J. C. Ibbetson.

industrial South Wales generally made a great impression upon the tourists. They admired the copper-works at Llanelly, 'sending up a volume of smoke, which curling in spiral wreaths above the summits of the mountains, adds no inconsiderable object to the rest of the scenery', and enjoyed the smelting houses at Swansea seen through heavy rain on a dark night which 'displayed such a glorious light, and so many beautiful colours from their ashes which lay on each side of the road, that I should not have regretted being wet through, if it was for the pleasure of seeing these alone'.[1] Even John Byng who had once maintained that he 'abominated the sight of mines, and miners, as unproductive of pleasure' was moved to quote *Paradise Lost* after venturing to inspect an iron-furnace in the Forest of Dean.

> I enter'd therein, and was well receiv'd by the devils who can bear the infernal heat, which soon drove me forth: they shewed me the iron smelting, and the immense bellows moved by water, eternally keeping alive the monstrous fire: for they work day and night, and make about 4 tons in the 24 hours.

> > Yet from these flames
> > No light, but rather darkness visible
> > Serv'd only to discover sights of woe.[2]

'The Pandemonium of Milton!' exclaimed Henry Kett as he travelled the road from Walsall to Birmingham by night, surrounded by coal- and iron-works, alternately flaring and pouring forth vast clouds of illuminated smoke.[3] But although classical allusions or quotations from Milton or Dante sprang naturally to mind, the tourists combined this literary and romantic approach with an accurate appreciation of the technical processes involved, and their sense of awe was derived as much from pride in human achievement as from the purely aesthetic enjoyment of a pictorially pleasing scene. 'Here we contemplate with astonishment the operations of machines of which before we had no idea', wrote the Rev. Richard Warner after seeing the tin-plate works at Inysgerwn. 'Rollers of such immense power as reduced bars of iron two inches deep to the thickness of a crown-piece, by passing

---

[1] *Tour through the South of England . . . 1791*, 202–3, 210–11.
[2] 'Tour to the West, 1781', *The Torrington Diaries*, abridged by F. Andrews, London, 1954, 37.
[3] 'A Tour to the Lakes of Cumberland and Westmorland in August 1798', W. Mavor, *British Tourists*, London, 1809, V, 119.

them a certain number of times through their revolving cylinders; and scissors cutting plates and bars in sunder of half an inch thick with the same ease that a fair sempstress would divide a wrist-band.' At Melincourt near Neath where he was impressed by the sight of a blast-furnace and finery 'upon an improved and stupendous plan' his admiration seems to have gained not a little from the sense of imminent peril he felt on watching it at work. 'The great wheel exhibits a periphery of 120 feet, and the bellows of new construction, may be considered as another wonder of modern mechanism. They are easily regulated, but still some care is necessary in the management of them, since their action may be increased to such a degree as to threaten the destruction of the whole building.'[1] The tourists who travelled down the Wye in search of the Picturesque under the inspiration of the Rev. William Gilpin would turn from Tintern Abbey to visit the nearby iron-works, and Gray found it completely natural at Sizergh to leave the contemplation of two waterfalls to watch an iron-forge with its thumping hammers with 'the daemons at work by the light of their own fires'.[2]

Shropshire, and, above all, the area near Coalbrookdale, offered a rich field to the tourist, for here, set amidst scenery of the greatest natural beauty, were all those industrial prospects most calculated to rejoice the heart. 'The approach to Iron Bridge presents a singular scene', wrote Plumptre with warm approval. 'To the right are limekilns burning close to the water's edge, whilst above them a hill rises with a swift ascent, covered with wood to the top: at the foot of this runs the Severn crowded with masts of vessels, on the shore are large piles of coals; the bridge in front with the river, boats, furnaces and houses all intermingling with trees; the horse at the windlass drawing up the load added life to the scene, & a blast from one of the mouths spoke like thunder.'[3] Sir Joseph Banks spent two days at Coalbrookdale and wrote of the processes he watched there in a typical amalgam of technical and romantic terms.

> While the Piggs are casting the Bellows are sufferd to go but gently, but the small wind they occasion finding vent at the hole in

[1] *Second Walk . . . 1798, 100–2.*
[2] 'Journal in a Letter to Dr. Wharton, October 1769', West, *Guide to the Lakes*, 2nd ed., London, 1780, *216.*
[3] Camb. Univ. Lib. MSS. 5811, f. 69.

the Furnace made for the dross to run over fills the room almost intirely full of sparks making a most beautifull appearance. The waste of the cinder before casting affords an appearance which gives the Idea of rivers of Lava running down the sides of a volcano in an irruption. Streams of Liquid Fire issuing out from thence & dispersing different ways still run slower as they become cooler.[1]

The complex impression which such scenes made upon the tourist is seen in Webb's description of Ferreday's iron-works at Bilston.

Plain narrative is inadequate to convey what I felt at this wonderful combination of the ingenious productions of man! I was not only astonished by the works of art, but Nature had also contributed to add terror to the scene, by the earth smoking at different places; in consequence of the burning coal-pits, by which these works are surrounded. . . . The roaring of the furnaces, the clanking of iron-chains and machinery reminded the traveller of the poetical descriptions given us of the infernal regions. . . . The awfulness of the scene reminded me of the description of the Cyclops forging thunder for Jupiter. The men here only work two hours at a time, which is quite sufficient for the great heat they are compelled to endure. Their appearance, covered with dirt, together with the reflection of the fire, their quick movements, the violent agitation of the machinery, the heat of the pavement on which you stand, contributes to inspire the mind with terror. Here are three or four smelting houses, and as many mills for rolling and slitting. A sight of this concussion of wind, fire and water, exceeds all ancient or modern descriptions I have heretofore read of as much as reality does imagination.[2]

The latter half of the eighteenth century had not yet seen the worst of that straggle of ill-built housing or that rash of ugly red-brick mills which was later to bring squalor and desolation to miles of the northern countryside. Something therefore of the charm of seeing the industrial districts of Lancashire or the Midlands lay in the fact that manufacture was still conducted in rural surroundings, and that the introduction of machinery meant no more than the addition of 'noise, bustle and appearance of business' to 'a deep glen with well-wooded banks on each side . . . which may be called a *picturesque* scene'. The tourists' main

[1] 'Journals of Excursions to Eastbury etc. 1767–8', Camb. Univ. Lib. MSS. 6294, ff. 121–2.
[2] D. C. Webb, *Observations and Remarks during Four Excursions made to various parts of Great Britain in the years 1810 and 1811*, London, 1812, 186–90.

concern, however, was to make a really close survey of the machinery, and they could expect at every mill, almost without exception, to be allowed a full sight of the manufacture in progress. 'A stupendous piece of mechanism', wrote Warner after watching an improved cotton machine at Holywell, 'the first view of which irresistibly impresses the mind with the idea of magick; here thirty or forty thousand wheels and spindles are seen moving in the most rapid manner, without any perceptible cause, spontaneously performing operations of the most curious nature, and in the most systematick manner. Nothing that we had seen indeed before gave us so exalted a notion of human ingenuity as the work before us.' The sight of 200 people employed in the cloth industry at Wotton-under-Edge in the Stroud Valley created a much greater impression on him than his visit to the Roman pavement at Woodchester. 'Curious complicated machines above, moving with a velocity that defies the nicest vision to detect their motions; and ponderous engines below, astonishing the mind in an equal degree by their simplicity and gigantic powers.'[1] 'Truly a most usefull Curiosity', commented John Dodd in the silk-mills at Derby in 1735 where he found a machine which contained 26,586 wheels and made 97,746 movements. 'All receive their motion from one water wheel, and may any of them be stopped separately. They work day and night, 73,728 yards of silk every time the said Wheel goes round or 221,184 yards a minute.'[2] The epithet 'curious' was in fact the favourite adjective of those tourists who lacked either the fertile pen of the Rev. Richard Warner or the grasp of intricacies of detail shown by John Dodd. 'Very curious and surprising', commented William Phillips after watching the machines for the manufacture of cotton at Ashton-under-Lyne.[3] 'To attempt a description of a piece of mechanism so curious and complicated would be vain', one tourist apologized to his readers on visiting Arkwright's cotton mills at Cromford. 'I can only say that the whole process of cleaning, carding, combing, twisting, and compleating the yarn for the loom seems to be done almost without human aid.'[4]

[1] *Excursions from Bath . . . 1800*, London, 1801, *334*.
[2] 'Journal of a Tour through England, 1735', B.M. Add. MSS. 5957.
[3] *Account of a Journey made by William Phillips of Broadway to Manchester and Liverpool and back, May 1798*, B.M. Add. MSS. 30,173.
[4] *A Tour in England and Scotland in 1785, By an English Gentleman*, London, 1788, *29*.

Among all the factories and workshops of the Midlands it was always Etruria, the factory of Josiah Wedgwood, which called forth their highest praises. The room in which the black and the 'new discovered blue' were made was never shown, but the rest of the works were open to the public and the tourists could enjoy the gratifying sight of 300 people employed in the production of this very finest china. 'Here we have a colony raised in a desert,' exclaimed Walker in 1791, 'where clay-built man subsists on clay, and where he seems to want nothing but the power of Prometheus to copy himself in that material.'[1] Birmingham was extremely popular for the great variety of manufactures it offered, and, after seeing there the making of hardware, whips, painted glass and a whole series of knick-knacks, J. Grant called it with some justification 'the grand toy shop of Europe'.[2] Boulton's factory at Soho, of course, held pride of place and was visited first, but the rest received their due attention and were examined in careful detail. Lombes' silk-mills at Derby were another great attraction. Robert Clutterbuck making his tour through the mills and following every stage of the manufacture with care found himself most particularly impressed by the water-wheel.

Of large circumference it is the primum Mobile of this curious complication of Mechanism. The axle of it passes through the side of the building like the Wheel of a common Water Mill, round which a smaller one furnished with Wooden Teeth revolves with it. These Teeth fit into the Cogs of a horizontal Wheel which communicates motion to the rest of the Mechanical powers And is distributed by them over every part of the building. . . . To regulate & equal the motion of this Wheel a Stick projects horizontally from the Circumference which when the Wheel has made a complete revolution Strikes a bell, by looking at a Clock on the opposite side of the room, the Person who attends it is enabled to know the revolutions are performed at proper intervals, and either accelerate or retard the motion by letting down more or less Water upon the Wheel.[3]

[1] A. Walker, *Observations, Natural, Oeconomical and Literary made in a Tour from London to the Lakes in the Summer of 1791*, London, 1792, 19.

[2] 'A London Journal of a Three Weeks Tour in 1797 through Derbyshire to the Lakes,' W. Mavor, *British Tourists*, London, 1809, IV, 219-92.

[3] *Journal of a Tour from Cardiff, Glamorganshire through South & North Wales in the summer of 1794*, Cardiff Public Library MS. 3.277, ff. 130-1.

Worcester was a particular favourite with the women tourists, who felt themselves peculiarly qualified to speak with authority here, and to let feminine judgement assess the fineness of the porcelain. Mrs. Selwyn followed the whole process at the Royal China works at Flight and Bar's and was greatly impressed to discover that every piece of painted china went through forty hands.[1] Lucy Wright visited the works in 1806 when they were engaged in making a beautiful service for the King's use.

> The whole process of this art is curious, the composition of the clay is a secret known only to the partners who prepare it themselves before they give it to the workmen; the principal ingredient is a sort of rock, but which is quite soft and you can crumble it with your fingers; it comes from Cornwall & the whole of it is purchased by Flight and Bar for the use of their factory; the factory is situate on the Severn as well for the convenience of the water nearby as the shipping of their goods; from their Quay you have a view of the Malvern Hills which prospect forms one of the principal beauties of Worcester.[2]

And so the descriptions continue. Sir Joseph Banks was clearly delighted with the 'ingenious manufacture' he saw at Burslem.

> Plates & dishes are made on a mould of Alabaster burnt or what we call Plaster on this the patterns are formd but they are afterwards before they are burnt Polish'd & compleated by Lathes & sharp tools which the Clay is very soon firm enough to bear. Handles of Cupps Teapots &c: are made by a box in the Bottom of which is a hole properly Shapd to answer the pattern intended the top of this is moveable & by the Power of a strong screw presses the Clay that is in the Box through the Hole which consequently takes the impressions its shape & size has given to it.[3]

At Blackburn the pleasure he derived from his observation of the alum works was as much aesthetic as technical. 'It is attended by the striker whose business is a profound secret by him it is Causd to shoot into small Chrystals which are taken out washed & again disolved in as small proportion of water & pourd into Large casks to the sides of which it fixes itself in Large Chrystals.

---

[1] *Journal of Excursions thro' the most interesting parts of England, Wales and Scotland, during the Summers and Autumns of 1819-23*, London, 1824, 8o.

[2] *Notebook of a Tour through Wales to the South Coast, 1806*, Edward Hall Collection, Wigan Public Library, M 842 EHC 73.

[3] Camb. Univ. Lib. MSS. 6294, f. 84.

. . . The inside of a Cask when the head is first struck out is the most beautiful sight imaginable resembling a Cavern filld with Large Chrystals pointing all ways at this time more than semi transparent & in all the different positions that can be conceived.'[1] Arthur Young recommended all travellers who passed through Sheffield to see all the mills in the town, and was specially anxious that they should not miss the tilting-mill, 'which is a blacksmith's immense hammer in constant motion on an anvil, worked by water-wheels, and by the same power the bellows of a forge adjoining kept regularly blown: the force of this mechanism is prodigious; so great, that you cannot lay your hand upon a gate a three perch distance, without feeling a strong trembling motion, which is communicated to all the earth around'.[2] The coming of the steam-engine was the crowning mechanical development, and when Webb wrote, after seeing a cotton-mill at Manchester in 1810, that 'it appeared like magic to see weaving thus performed so regularly without hands',[3] he was expressing that sense of awe which forms the one constant note underlying all these accounts.

The Cheshire salt-mines lured aside many a romantic traveller on his way to Wales or the Lakes, and even that experienced tourist R. J. Sullivan allowed that 'of all subterranean curiosities in this island they are the best worth seeing'. Dressed in miners' caps and jackets the tourists were lowered 200 feet or more in a bucket through a perpendicular shaft leading into the heart of the mine. Here the most cynical and hardened sightseer could not help being startled by the sheer size and amazing beauty of the scene before him. The almost transparent salt had been cut into 'a vast glittering cavern' supported by monstrous pillars which had been left in the course of working the mine, colonnades forty-five feet high and eighteen feet thick supporting a roof rising to a dome. Sullivan could only suggest that his readers turn to Oriental fantasy to gain any impression of the wonders of the sight. 'Seize, therefore, upon the Arabian Nights Entertainments, and pick out the dazzling palace of some Genii, and there transport yourself in imagination: this will give you some idea of it; inadequate perhaps, but sufficient in some degree to answer the

---

[1] ibid., f. 97.
[2] *A Six Months Tour through the North of England*, London, 1770, I, 134–5.
[3] *Four Excursions . . . 1810 and 1811, 195.*

impression I am desirous you should receive.'[1] The Rev. William Gilpin could only say that while novels might be written about enchanted castles here was 'an inchanted cathedral'.

> For what purpose designed, or by what art of man contrived, and thus erected in the bowels of the earth, you are at a loss to conceive. The largest cathedral compared to it is a mole-hill near a mountain. Its arched roof is formed of splendid crystal; and is supported by innumerable rows of pillars composed of the same rich materials. The pavement glitters like glass. Windows it can have none, so deep below the surface. But windows are unnecessary; it is illumined with various lights hung up among the pillars, which being reflected from bright surfaces in every direction, are multiplied into thousands. One may almost speak of them in the language of poetry:
>
>> 'From the arched roof
>> Pendent by subtil magic, many a row
>> Of starry lamps, and blazing crescents, fed
>> With naptha, and asphaltus, yielded light
>> As from a sky.'
>
> In some parts of this superb edifice the ornaments appear to be Gothic; in others, Grecian: but as you examine it nicely you find it cannot exactly be reduced to the rules of any order. In short, it appears to be an amazing piece of perspective, constructed in a mode of architecture wholly its own.[2]

Finally, canal scenery presented the tourists with a peculiarly attractive type of industrial landscape. 'Very interesting and rather singular', wrote Hassell after seeing the junction of the Braunston and Oxfordshire canals. 'The weighing engine on one side, and a lock-house on the other, are backed by a noble wood that ranges down the brow of the hill, and is met by another, of less consequence, on the opposite side of the canal. . . . The weighing-house, steam-engine, bridge, lock and other objects make up a pretty scene.'[3] A canal in the course of being built at Chirk with an aqueduct to carry the water across the valley and river made a most pleasing sight. 'All here is bustle and business;

---

[1] *Observations . . . 1780, 242–3.*

[2] *Observations on several parts of the Counties of Cambridge, Norfolk, Suffolk and Essex. Also on several parts of North Wales, 1769 and 1773*, London, 1809, 97–9.

[3] *Tour of the Grand Junction Canal*, London, 1792, 19.

in one spot are seen numerous parties of workmen driving on the course of the canal in spite of rock, mountain and every other obstacle which nature has thrown in their way. At a little distance the builders of the aqueduct are employed in their stupendous labour. And immediately upon the canal several miners perforate the mountain and follow up a rich vein of coal lately discovered, which from its happy situation, must prove the certain source of future fortune.'[1] At Stonefield, near Derby, Walker launched into flowery prose to hymn 'that magnificent entreprize the canal for the junction of the eastern and western oceans . . . our aspiring genius scoffs at obstructions, and difficulties serve but to whet our ardor: our aqueducts pass over our once-admired rivers, now despised for the purpose of navigation: we fill vallies, we penetrate mountains. How would the prophet have been treated who, forty years ago, should have predicted that a vessel of seventy five tons would be seen sailing over Stonefield?'[2] Although Manchester itself impressed Sir Harbottle Grimston, it was the Duke of Bridgewater's canal which he accounted the most remarkable thing he saw. 'This work would be justly called one of the wonders of the world, exceeding in magnificence, use and grandeur every work of that kind, and proving indisputably the judgement, caution and courage in making the attempt, of the noble con-triver.'[3]

A full appreciation of everything that the canals offered to the tourist was possible only after making a journey by water. Boats were available on the canal between Manchester and Liverpool, and William Phillips took a naive delight in the journey he made in 1792. He started at eight in the morning, and breakfast was served after four or five miles.

A very fine Morning and Pleasant riding. Between Manchester and London Bridge the Place where we got out is 21 Miles and we went under 23 Bridges & over 9 or 10, theres a River Mersey runs under it, and several Roads and Brooks goes under it. There was a Gentleman went under in a Pheaton and pair, Just at the time we were going over him in the Boat, Horsemen Waggons and Carts we see in other places go under. This was a very great undertaking of the Duke's and must cost an amazing sum of Money, got to London

---

[1] R. Warner, *A Walk through Wales in August 1797*, Bath, 1799, *189*.
[2] *Tour to the Lakes . . . 1791, 50–4.*
[3] *A Northern Tour from St. Albans 1768*, Hist. MSS. Comm., Verulam, *232*.

Bridge about 1 o'clock. There is 4 Coaches stand ready every day
to take the Passengers on for Liverpool and other places.[1]

These were very definitely social boats, whose prices ranged
according to the accommodation provided and were 'so well
regulated by the Duke that no improper company can go in
them, as he has given orders to the boat-master to return them
their money, and to set them on shore provided any of the passengers are guilty of improper conduct'. When the Rev. John
Skinner travelled on the Manchester Canal in 1801 he was careful
to go in that part of the boat reserved for superior passengers and
provided with a stove, tables and convenient seats.[2] Conditions
on the passage-boat between Liverpool and Wigan were even
more luxurious, for there the front cabin had a large table in the
middle, with seats round it for the reception of sixty people, and
newspapers were provided for their amusement. The middle of
the barge was fitted up like the bar of an inn, with fireplace and
apparatus for cooking, and refreshment was available. Passengers
'of a lower description' were sent aft, but their journey cost them
half a crown instead of the 3s. 6d. demanded from their superiors.[3]

More in accord with the true traditions of industrial touring
was the expedition made by Walker along that first great canal
built by James Brindley for the Duke of Bridgewater to carry coal
from his mine at Worsley to Manchester.

We pushed up this subterraneous passage (just wide enough for
the boat) above a mile, when we arrive at the place where the colliers
are working. The rushing of water and clanking of chains realize
the fabulous Tartarus!—The ear is assaulted with such an
uncommon noise, that the stoutest heart finds itself under some dis-
may . . . several other passages lead from this principal one into
divers parts of the mountain, and recesses cut in the rock suffer
one boat to pass another. In this singular voyage it is almost
impossible to believe one's self in motion; the rocky passage,
arched with brick, seems to be flying from you, and makes the
head dizzy; and in returning the distant entrance looks like a
bright star.[4]

[1] 'Account of a Journey . . . from Broadway to Manchester and Liverpool, and
back; 13–31 May 1792', B.M. Add. MSS. 30,173.
[2] 'Tour to the Lakes, 1801', B.M. Add. MSS. 33,639, f. 136.
[3] *Four Excursions . . . 1810 and 1811*, 209–10.
[4] *Tour to the Lakes . . . 1791*, 28–9.

But this mood of enchantment was not to survive long into the nineteenth century. Mines and factories soon began to lose their novelty, mills built of ugly materials, using cheap brick and slate, sprawling with trails of shoddy houses across miles of the northern countryside, retained little that was pleasing to the eye. Moreover, the succession of Parliamentary Commissions on factories, the reports of Edwin Chadwick on urban sanitation, the 'condition of England' novels—all these made it impossible not to translate the industrial scene into terms of human suffering and misery. As soon as the workers in furnaces and mills came to be recognized as human beings capable of pain and not merely regarded as demons adding colour and movement to some scene of hell from Dante or Milton, industrial touring became impossible. The first hint of this new attitude is seen among the Clapham sect when, as part of his education, the young Henry Thornton was taken on a succession of visits from Buxton in 1806, with a distinctly moral end in view. 'We have gone together to see a variety of Manufacturers,' he reported, 'and have been learning to feel for those who dig in Mines, who toil in Quarries, perspire in Salt Works, wear out their Eyes in looking at Furnaces, or pass their morning noon and Even in the limited Employment of putting on the head of a Pin, or drawing over and over the same pattern on a piece of China. . . . I trust that seeing the world in this sense will prove very useful.'[1] An awakening nineteenth-century conscience revolted against the idle dilettantism which was all too easily content to see a new industrial world in purely aesthetic and romantic terms.

[1] E. M. Forster, *Marianne Thornton*, London, 1956, 53-4.

LANDSCAPE WITH FIGURES

Arthur Young and William Cobbett

N the opening pages of his *Northern Tour* Arthur Young
presented his credentials to his readers, and explained the
method and purpose of his writing: 'I have been a farmer
these many years, and that not in a single field or two, but
upon a tract of near three hundred acres, most part of the time;
and never less than one hundred. . . . I have always kept from the
first day I began a minute register of my business.'[1] His approach,
therefore, to the compilation of his tours was that of a practising
farmer, and his methods were entirely practical and businesslike.
He would advertise his intended journey and after receiving
replies send out notes to those who had invited him to visit their
farms. 'Registering minutes on the spot was a new undertaking,
having never been executed either in this or any other country
of *Europe*', he said, and claimed with pride that his books carried
'proof in every page of the time when they are written: the principal part is executed during the journey, recording intelligence
on the spot, and at the moment; or minuting at night the transactions of the day; indeed the method in which these journeys
are executed is so very simple, and have so little appearance of
authorcraft, or writing journeys in a garret; or engaging in the
expence and absence of journeys for profit'.[2] As a result, throughout

---

[1] *A Six Months Tour through the North of England*, 4 vols., London, 1770, I, x.
[2] *The Farmer's Tour through the East of England*, 4 vols., London, 1771,
preface.

the pages of his tours Young is continually introducing his readers to farmers and landlords, and describing the 'judicious and spirited designs' which they showed him. His England, therefore, is a country of farms and estates, of soil and implements, rent and wages, courses of crops and cost of provisions, with more particular attention to such vital topics as drainage, manure, the growth of turnips and the cultivation of grasses. The real theme of his books was *agricultural improvement*, the progress of enclosure, the disappearance of the old England of scattered strip-farming into the new land of compact square fields surrounded by post-and-rail fences and newly planted hedgerows. 'All the country from Holkham to Houghton was a wild sheep-walk before the spirit of improvement seized the inhabitants', he will write on finding a landscape which really rejoiced his heart, 'and this spirit has wrought amazing effects; for instead of boundless wilds, and uncultivated wastes, inhabited by scarcely anything but sheep; the country is all cut into enclosures, cultivated in a most husband-like manner, richly manured, well peopled, and yielding an hundred times the produce it did in its former state.'[1]

With this end in view he had little to say about nature in the raw, although every now and again, as when he left Barnard Castle, he might become carried away by the sheer magnificence of the view.

> I never yet travelled such a line of country so astonishingly fine, containing so noble a variety: It is a continued landscape, sufficient to captivate the most languid observer. A glorious range of black mountains, fertile valleys, beautiful inclosures, hanging woods, steep precipices, raging torrents, tremendous winding streams, and beautiful cascades—The whole line is a perpetual hill and dale, thickly strewed with all these romantic glories—you, literally speaking, do not move an hundred yards without being struck with continual waterfalls.—A morning's ride well worth a journey of a thousand miles to travel.—But to return to husbandry . . .[2]

Or again he would break off:

> I forgot to tell you that near *Horndon*, on the summit of a vast hill, one of the most astonishing prospects to be beheld, breaks almost at once upon one of the dark lanes. Such a prodigious valley

[1] *A Six Weeks Tour through the Southern Counties of England and Wales*, London, 1768, 3-4.
[2] *Northern Tour*, II, 201-2.

every where painted with the finest verdure, and intersected with numberless hedges and woods, appears beneath you, this is past description; the *Thames* winding through it, full of ships, and bounded by the hills of *Kent*. Nothing can exceed it, unless that which Hannibal exhibited to his disconsolate troops, when he had them behold the glories of the *Italian* plains! If ever a turnpike should lead through this country, I beg you will go and view this enchanting scene. I never beheld any thing equal to it in the West of England, that region of landscape.[1]

But in general he saw the countryside with the eye of the improver. As he crossed Salisbury Plain he complained:

in twenty miles I met with only one habitation, which was a hut. A little reflection will tell us, that such a vast tract of uncultivated land is a public nuisance. . . . What an amazing improvement would it be, to cut this vast plain into farms, by inclosure of quick hedges, with portions planted with such trees as best suit the soil! A very different aspect the country would present from what it does at present, without a hedge, tree or hut; and inhabited by only a few shepherds and their flocks.[2]

He found the great tracts of northern moorland particularly depressing, and blamed 'those indolent landlords who sleep in the paths of their predecessors, without ever opening their eyes to a meridian sun: they will possess the most improveable of wastes, but leave them in their most desart state, because they so received them: *What has been, may be*, is none of their motto; *but what has not been, shall not be*, is the drowsy guide of their actions'.[3] The sight which caused him the greatest pleasure was that of a newly enclosed farm, such as that belonging to John Symonds lying between Bury St. Edmunds and Stowmarket:

which is done in a very neat manner; the hedges are all of white thorn, and the banks regularly planted with several sorts of timber trees; the gates remarkably good and all painted. *Mr Symonds* has informed me that his method of preserving the excellence and beauty of the fences on this farm, after it got into a tenant's hands, was by making it an article of the lease, that he would keep them in repair, and accordingly he has always employed labourers in preserving and repairing them.[4]

[1] *Southern Tour*, 89.
[2] ibid., 193–7.
[3] *Northern Tour*, II, 216.
[4] *Southern Tour*, 38.

Hedges and fences were the symbols of the new England, bringing the end of the sweeping open fields of the medieval landscape and heralding changes in farming practice and technique. Young assessed them with an extremely critical eye. In Hertfordshire he wrote 'the fences throughout this country consist of plashed hedges, with scarcely any ditches; these are excellently worked; they have a most neat and husband-like appearance, and would, with the assistance of good ditches, form the most impenetrable fences'.[1] As he travelled between Alton and Farnham he cast an approving eye on the fences which ran along the side of the road: 'I never beheld any thing equal to them; the whitethorn hedges are of a most vigorous growth; a great number of them are regularly clipt and the hedges herdle work three feet or three feet six inches high; the stakes strong in the ground, and closely interlaced; and whenever you see young quick there is one on each side of it, and the white-thorn plants kept clean weeded. . . .'[2] In Yorkshire he particularly remarked that 'all the banks of hedges are paved with large coble stones, stuck into the earth, which they assert strengthens the fences greatly, and will, if well done, last one hundred years. Their ditches are mere nothings; the hedges grows out of a bank about a yard high, and two feet wide at the top.'[3]

From looking at the hedges he turned to consider the agriculture which was being practised in the new fields. He noted the planting of turnips, cabbages and carrots, 'one of the most profitable crops in the world'. He contrasted the correct turnip husbandry as practised in Norfolk, Suffolk and Essex with that of Wales or Salisbury. 'Of all crops none require hoeing so much; there is none that will pay so well for that operation, the value of them being very trifling without it. . . . A universal loss attending a bad culture of beans and turnips is the loss of a year for a poor crop; for nothing is a better preparation for corn, than these vegetables when kept perfectly clean, but none worse when managed in a slovenly manner.'[4] Near Ilford he found 'their potatoe-husbandry is admirable; they *dig* in the clover (and natural grass, when they break it up the same) about *February* and immediately dibble in

[1] *Eastern Tour*, I, 7.
[2] *Southern Tour*, 209.
[3] *Northern Tour*, II, 231.
[4] *Southern Tour*, 280-1.

potatoe setts four inches deep, and from eight to ten inches square. Before they come up, they hoe the ground perfectly clean; —after they appear, twice more. They dig them up with a three pronged fork, and generally before they are half grown.'[1] He compared the different practices of manures. Marl was dug at Earlham near Norwich, and was 'rather hard, and like chalk on the first digging, but it breaks in pieces easily, and on being thrown into water will dissolve in a quarter of an hour, and be soapy: if powdered, it effervesces immediately with vinegar: the colour is white, with a tinge of yellow. It destroys weeds almost at once, particularly ketlocks and poppies.'[2] He first saw manure made from paring and burning the surface of the ground in Gloucestershire.

> They find it extremely beneficial, if not practised too often; it cleans the soil greatly, and enriches it equally; nor do turnips, particularly, ever fail the year they pare and burn. This method would answer greatly in many parts of the Eastern counties, but they have no idea of it; except burning the sedgy turf and stubble in the *Isle of Ely*. It is beyond all doubt the best way of breaking up old and bad pastures, and fitting them for corn.[3]

He praised the Earl of Darlington at Raby Castle: 'his management respecting manure is much more masterly than that of his northern neighbours—principally by means of an excellently contrived farmyard, in which he fodders all his cattle in winter; making thereby a vast quantity of dung'.[4] But he reserved his real eulogy for Lord Rockingham, whose manures at Wentworth:

> are too curious to be overlooked. The composts are formed of all sorts of manures, particularly farm yard dung, and manures purchased at the neighbouring towns; such as soap-boiler's ashes, coal ashes, horn shavings, curriers shavings &c &c. And sometimes mole-hills, turf and lime are added, layers of these are formed one on another, and after remaining a few months are turned over; then the heap remains some time longer, after which it is mixed again, and so repeated until the substances are thoroughly rotted which takes with some no trifling time and pains, particularly horn shavings; one compost of which manure mixed with dung I observed was in so complete a state of corruption, that it cut like

[1] *Southern Tour*, 231–2.
[2] *Eastern Tour*, II, 102.
[3] *Southern Tour*, 297.
[4] *Northern Tour*, II, 476.

butter, and must undoubtedly be the richest manure in the world.[1]

He found striking differences in animal husbandry as he toured the country. The horses bred in Suffolk impressed him greatly:

> The breed of horses peculiar to this county is one of the greatest curiosities in it: I never yet saw any that are comparable to them in shape, or the amazing power they have in drawing. They are called the sorrel breed; the colour a bay sorrel. The form, that of a true round barrel, remarkably short, and the legs the same and lower over the forehand than in any part of the back; which they reckon here a point of consequence. . . . The work they will do is extraordinary. . . . They are all taught with very great care to draw in concert; and many farmers are so attentive to this point, that they have teams, every horse of which will fall on his knees at the word of command, in the full drawing attitude, and all at the same moment.[2]

He enjoyed the sight of Romney Marsh sheep without horns, 'admirably made, short legs, true round barrels, of a fine size, and their fleeces remarkably white'.[3] The fattening of oxen by Mr. Moody of Retford was a fine achievement, for, contrary to general opinion, he believed that the hotter they were kept the better they would fatten, and accordingly 'he kept them shut up, and, for some time, does not so much as let in any air through the holes in the doors; the breath of so many with the natural heat of their bodies, brings them soon to sweating prodigiously, and, when this is in its height, they fatten the best and quickest. After sweating a fortnight, the hair all peels off them, and a fresh coat comes, like that in *April* or *May*, and, after that, they sweat no more.'[4]

Traditions of ploughing also varied throughout the country, and while in Suffolk it required only a pair of horses and one man to plough one acre, in Hertfordshire farmers would use four horses and two men, and in Buckinghamshire five or often six. Young was always interested to see any new machinery at work, describing it in detail and illustrating it with careful diagrams and drawings. He was delighted to see the drill plough invented by Mr. Wilson at Ayton, 'upon the principle of the *Persian* wheel, lifting the seed up, and throwing it over into the tubes that

---

[1] *Northern Tour*, I, 334-5.
[2] *Eastern Tour*, II, 173-4.
[3] ibid., III, 331.
[4] ibid., I, 407.

convey it into the ground; it sows three rows at fourteen inches asunder, or six at seven'.[1] He illustrated Lord Rockingham's plough, commenting on it point by point, and finally approving it: 'This plough is an excellent one, for its simplicity and strength are such that it is never out of order; will bear the rough usage of country hands, and perform its work even in the strongest of soils; many have been invented with more powers, but then the complex mechanism is such as renders them little better than gimcracks.'[2] Experiments in cultivation were also studied with care and exactly recorded, and he obviously took great pride in the achievements of such enterprising farmers as Sir John Turner of Wells in Norfolk, who had been using sea-ooze as manure with heavy yields, Thomas Bevor, also of Norfolk, who flouted general opinion by turning his sows on to clover with success; or Anthony Warton, near Doncaster, whose cabbages were famous.[3]

And so, meeting the farmers and landowners, seeing their new machinery and discussing their experiments, Arthur Young toured the length and breadth of the country, and judged what he found by his own high standards, generous in praise when he saw an enterprising farmer, but unsparing in his condemnation of slovenly cultivation. He thought the management of sheep in Dorset, for example, inferior to the rest of England, and after writing a slating account of local methods could only recommend a complete change from a thoroughly 'vile husbandry'. He was appalled in the Fens: 'this husbandry is, upon the whole, as amazing a system of barbarism as I remember to have heard',[4] and as he rode between Aylesbury and Buckingham he exclaimed: 'In no part of the kingdom have I met with husbandry that requires greater amendment than this: such products are, their soil considered, contemptible.'[5] He listed the points on which he found the East Riding farmers particularly backward: their courses of crops and general management of their arable were very faulty; they had certainly introduced turnips, 'but their culture is so wretchedly defective, that I may, without paradox, assert, they had better have left it alone'; their beans were sown in great quantities but never hoed, 'execrably full of weeds; this is a most pernicious

[1] *Northern Tour*, II, 103.
[2] ibid., I, 317-20.
[3] ibid., II, 54, II, 117, I, 345.
[4] ibid., I, 483-4.
[5] ibid., I, 20.

practice, and cannot be too much condemned'; even the waggons were denounced as 'paltry insignificant things', holding only forty or fifty bushels while elsewhere farmers were changing to narrow wheels which would carry a hundred. 'This is remaining in the darkness and ignorance of five centuries ago.'[1]

To ride through land whose potentialities lay undeveloped grieved him most deeply of all. He could find no reason for letting the New Forest lie in its present melancholy state, and proceeded to outline a plan for its conversion into farms, down to the last detail of buildings and hedges. 'I shall never be deterred from offering such calculations; because none have yet been executed, or because the world is full of mean souls, who deem every noble undertaking of this sort visionary.'[2] Sedgmoor distressed him almost more:

> A flat black peat bog, but so rich, that some sensible farmers assured me it wanted nothing but draining to be made well worth from 20 shillings to 25 shillings an acre, on an average. But at present it is so encompassed by higher lands, that the water has no way to get off, but by evaporation; in winter it is a sea, and yields scarce any food, except in very dry summers. What a disgrace to the whole nation is it, to have 11,520 such acres to lie waste in a kingdom that is quarrelling about high prices of provisions! The present use made of this moor is not of the value of 2s 6d an acre.[3]

He was peculiarly saddened by the sight of farms where new methods were soon abandoned, or full advantage was not taken of enclosure. 'Gentlemen that try carrots have not acted with spirit', he commented in Nottinghamshire, 'they sow an acre, and, if they extend it to three, they plume themselves on doing great things';[4] and while in Yorkshire the recently enclosed land should have made a great show, in fact 'the white thorn plants in the new hedges were all full of weeds, and of a stinted growth'.[5]

Yet there were stretches of countryside which cheered his heart. He often saw fine crops and careful cultivation, and praised 'accuracy, expensive management, and unremitted industry'. He was pleased by special crops, such as hops and madder in Kent, and by peculiar practices, such as stacking in the Isle of Wight:

[1] *Northern Tour*, I, *251-2*.
[2] *Eastern Tour*, III, *233-4*.
[3] ibid., III, *193*.
[4] ibid., I, *431*.
[5] *Northern Tour*, I, *160*.

all their hay and cornstacks (and they have very little barn room on the largest farms) are round, drawn up as regularly as possible to a point, which is ornamented with a little knob of straw; the thatch regularly cut round, and the outside bound in circles one foot distant from each other with brambles. It is surprising with what exactness they build, and with what neatness they thatch them: they are really beautiful, nor can you easily imagine how much these stacks ornament the country.[1]

The rich and well-farmed grazing lands of Northamptonshire drew forth a paean of praise:

There cannot be a finer sight than the view of the closes throughout this country. . . . The quantity of great oxen and sheep is very noble; it is very common to see from forty to sixty oxen, and two hundred sheep in a single field; and the beasts are all of a fine large breed, well made, good skins and form altogether an appearance greatly striking. This effect is owing in no slight degree to the nature of the country, which is wholly composed of gentle hills, so that you look over many hundred acres at one stroke of the eye, and command all the cattle feeding in them in a manner nobly picturesque. Stock in a flat is lost; but to see numerous herds of fine beasts spread over the sides of waving hills, is a sight that cannot fail of delighting the spectator.[2]

The Vale of Bedford was rich in soil and excellently managed: 'The wheat and barley, and turnips, were very fine, and equal to any I ever saw, and the beans in point of height and thickness made a fine appearance, but I doubt can never turn out equal to the other crops for want of hoeing. . . .'[3] But at Woodbridge in Suffolk he found farming that excelled anything he knew elsewhere: 'Their crag husbandry, their culture of carrots, their breed of horses, are circumstances peculiar, no where else to be seen. Their management of the pea and bean crops, is much more masterly than anything met with in most parts of the kingdom. Their courses of crops are unexceptionable—in a word, they exert every effort of good husbandry to command success.—They enjoy it: and well deserve the fruit of their labours.'[4]

William Cobbett adds another side to Arthur Young's picture of rural England, for while Young delighted in modern techniques, new crops, improved machinery, and approved of the

[1] *Eastern Tour*, III, *193*.
[2] ibid., I, *53–4*.
[3] *Northern Tour*, I, *44–5*.
[4] *Eastern Tour*, II, *177–8*.

farmers he met in proportion to their understanding and use of such things, Cobbett hated anything that had about it the stamp of modernity, and did not care whether a man were a skilful mechanic or not. He cared about the countryside and country society as he found it, and he rode the shires of England to see the *people*, 'hearing what gentlemen, farmers, tradesmen, journeymen, labourers, women, girls, boys, and all have to say; reasoning with some, laughing with others, and observing all that passes. . . . At the end of a tramp like this you get impressed upon your mind a true picture, not only of the state of the country, but of the state of people's minds throughout the country.' For Cobbett was that new thing among tourists, a man whose interest lay in the people themselves. He was completely incapable of seeing workers in a furnace merely as infernal beings adding a touch of the horrific to a romantic scene, or finding the natives of Wales interesting as a race apart, symbolic of primeval innocence. Such a self-conscious approach was far removed from his robust concern for a people whom he found much like himself, 'born in a farm house, bred up at the plough tail, with a smock-frock on my back, taking a great delight in all the pursuits of farmers, liking their society'. His social conscience and political interests were typical of that group of radicals of which he was so prominent a member, men like Major Cartwright, who had set out to see his country in 1811 saying: 'English gentlemen are perpetually travelling. . . . Some go to see Lakes and mountains. Were it not allowable to travel for seeing the actual conditions of a starving society?'[1]

Cobbett lived simply, not to say austerely, when he travelled. He told his readers with no little complacency after covering nearly 600 miles in the early autumn of 1826 that 'during the whole of this ride, I have very rarely been a-bed after day-light; I have drunk neither wine nor spirits. I have eaten no vegetables, and only a very moderate quantity of meat; and, it may be useful to my readers to know, that the riding of twenty miles was not so fatiguing to me at the end of my tour as the riding of ten miles was at the beginning of it.'[2] Yet there was nothing austere about his enjoyment of what he found, and the enthusiasm, almost buoyancy, of his writing shows the immediate and intense

---

[1] *Life of Cartwright*, I, 45, quoted R. J. White, *Waterloo to Peterloo*, London, 1957, *133*.

[2] *Rural Rides*, London, 1830, *666*.

delight he took in the simple pleasures he found on his road. He caught one such moment as he described how a farmer's wife brought out a loaf and Wiltshire cheese for him and his son at Burghclere one October morning, 'and I took them in hand, gave Richard a good hunch, and took another for myself. I verily believe, that all the pleasure of eating enjoyed by all the feeders in London in a whole year, does not equal that which we enjoyed in gnawing this bread and cheese, as we rode over this cold down, whip and bridle-reins in one hand, and the hunch in the other.'[1] Again the sight of 'thousands upon thousands of clouds, continually coming puffing out from different parts of these hills and towering up to the top of them', would give him a childlike delight. 'I stopped George several times to make him look at them; to see them come puffing out of the chalk downs as well as out of the woodland hills. . . . The first time that I have leisure when I am in the high countries again, I will have a conversation with some old shepherd about this matter.'[2]

Less concerned than Young to notice hoeing and manures, and to remark on the rotation of crops and decent drainage, he could write almost ecstatically as his heart lifted at the sight of the downs, the countryside he preferred above all other. Time and again he came back to his love for them, and particularly that one spot between Heytesbury and Warminster, 'the brightest and most beautiful'; 'for there is, as appertaining to rural objects, *everything* I delight in. Smooth and verdant downs in hills and valleys of endless variety as to height and depth and shape; rich corn-land, unencumbered by fences; meadows in due proportion, and those watered at pleasure; and, lastly, the homesteads and villages, sheltered in winter and shaded in summer by lofty and beautiful trees.'[3] 'This is my taste', he cried as he rode near Winchester, 'and here it has full gratification. I like to look at the winding of a great down, with two or three numerous flocks of sheep on it, belonging to different farms; and to see, lower down, the folds in the fields, ready to receive them for the night.'[4] Even in a description which is little more than a bare list he managed to convey his feeling for a small valley among the downs.

[1] ibid., *293*.
[2] ibid., *658–9*.
[3] ibid., *538–9*.
[4] ibid., *290*.

A most beautiful scene it was! Villages, hamlets, large farms, towers, steeples, fields, meadows, orchards, and very fine timber trees, scattered all over the valley. The shape of the thing is: on each side *downs*, very lofty and steep in some places, and sloping miles back in other places; but each *out-side* of the valley are downs. From the edge of the downs begin capital *arable fields* generally of very great dimensions, and, in some places, running a mile or two back into little *cross-valleys*, formed by hills or downs. After the corn-fields come *meadows*, on each side, down to the *brook* or *river*. The farm-houses, mansions, villages and hamlets, are generally situated in that part of the arable land which comes nearest to the meadows.[1]

The autumnal richness of Surrey delighted him:

Here are some very fine farms, a little strip of meadows, some hop-gardens, and the lakes have given rise to the establishment of powder-mills and paper-mills. The trees of all sorts grow well here; and coppices yield poles for the hop-gardens and wood to make charcoal for the powder-mills. They are sowing wheat here, and the land, owing to the fine summer we have had, is in a very fine state. . . . All the *fall fruit* is excellent, and in great abundance. The grapes are as good as those raised under glass. The apples much richer than in ordinary years. The crops of *hops* has been very fine here.[2]

But he never saw the country entirely in terms of landscape; he was always too much aware of its inhabitants and of their misery or happiness. Thus he could allow a certain beauty to Andover, though he did not in general care for country as open as this, because he found it rich and contented. 'The homesteads in the sheltered bottoms with fine lofty trees about the houses form a beautiful contrast with the large open fields. The little villages, running straggling along the dells (always with lofty trees and rookeries) are very interesting objects, even in the winter. You feel a sort of satisfaction, when you are out upon the bleak hills yourself, at the thought of the shelter, which is experienced in the dwellings in the vallies.'[3]

But much of Cobbett's writing was far from being in such a peaceful vein. Wherever he went he was conscious of the menace of 'the system', his name for everything that, as he saw it, was

[1] ibid., *354*.
[2] ibid., *8–9*.
[3] ibid., *43–4*.

wringing the life-blood out of the old England—game-laws, factories, tolls, the Poor Law, capital punishment . . . Then in a succession of staccato exclamations and wild expletives he would damn, one after another, 'the malignant and tyrannical jolter-heads at Whitehall', 'this vile paper money and funding system', 'the profligate, the trading, the lying, the infamous press of London'. The thought of the day that will see the end of all this filled him with a wild exultation. 'It has lasted a good while, and has done tremendous mischief to the people of England; but, it is *over*; it is *done for*; it will live for a while, but it will go about drooping its wings and half shutting its eyes, like a cock that has got the pip: it will NEVER CROW AGAIN; and for that I most humbly and fervently thank God! It has crowed over us long enough: it has pecked and spurred us and slapped us about quite long enough.'[1] Again and again he gloated over this prospect. 'It is a pleasure, it is real, it is great delight, it is boundless joy to me, to contemplate this infernal system in its hour of *wreck*: sway here: crack there: scroop this way: souse that way: and such a rattling and such a squalling . . . a total blowing-up of the *whole system*, game-laws, new trespass laws, tread-mill, Sunday tolls, six-acts, sun-set and sun-rise laws, apple-felony laws, select-vestry laws, and the whole THING, root and trunk and branch!'[2]

Completely unrealistic, he dreamt of an unsullied England where the fair and the market would still satisfy the needs of the nation: 'Does not every one see, in a minute, how this exchanging of fairs and markets for shops creates *idlers and traffickers*; creates those locusts, called middle-men, who create nothing, who add to the value of nothing, who improve nothing, but who live in idleness, and who live well, too, out of the labour of the producer and the consumer.'[3] When he could actually watch 'the system' encroaching and changing the countryside through which he was passing, as happened at Frome, he lashed out in fury: 'There are here all the usual signs of *accommodation bills*, and all the false paper stuff, called money: new houses, in abundance, half finished; new gingerbread "places of worship", as they are called; great swaggering inns; parcels of swaggering fellows going about, with vulgarity imprinted upon their backs.'[4] The sight of the

[1] ibid., *455*.
[2] ibid., *578*.
[3] ibid., *649*.
[4] ibid., *424*.

valley of Chilworth was gall and wormwood to him since it had
become the scene of the manufacture of gunpowder and banknotes:

> As to gunpowder, indeed, we might get over that. The alders and
> the willows one can see, without so much regret, turned into
> powder by the waters of this valley. But the *Bank-notes*! To think
> that the springs which God has commanded to flow from the sides
> of these happy hills, for the comfort and delight of man; to think
> that these springs should be perverted into means of spreading
> misery over a whole nation; and that, too, under the base and hypo-
> critical pretence of promoting its *credit* and maintaining its *honour*
> and its *faith*![1]

Thus a prosperous scene of grazing oxen at Swindon was spoilt
by bitter reflections upon 'the system':

> They were, some *Devonshire* and some *Herefordshire*. They were
> fatting on the *grass only*; and, I should suppose, that they are worth,
> or shortly will be, thirty pounds each. But the great pleasure with
> which the contemplation of this fine sight was naturally calculated
> to inspire me, was more than counter-balanced by the thought that
> these fine oxen, this primest of human food, was aye, *every mouthful
> of it*, destined to be devoured in the WEN, and that, too, for the far
> greater part, by the Jews, loan-jobbers, tax-eaters, and their base and
> prostituted followers, dependents, purveyors, parasites and pimps....

The stream of vituperation reached its climax at Cheltenham
which, more than any other spot, stood for all that he most hated:

> When I enter a place like this, I always feel disposed to squeeze up
> my nose with my fingers. It is nonsense to be sure; but I conceive
> that every two-legged creature that I see coming near me, is about
> to cover me with the poisonous proceeds of its impurities. To places
> like this come all that is knavish and all that is foolish and all that is
> base; gamesters, pick-pockets, and harlots; young wife-hunters
> in search of rich and ugly and old women, and young husband-
> hunters in search of rich and wrinkled or half-rotten men . . . a
> place to which East India plunderers, West India floggers, English
> tax-gorgers, together with gluttons, drunkards and debauchees
> of all descriptions, *female* as well as male, resort. . . .[2]

This was Cobbett's England, seen at one moment in terms of a
pastoral rhapsody, the next with bitterness and revulsion. A new
farmhouse would make him reflect:

[1] ibid., *109–10*.
[2] ibid., *522–3*.

what a miserable thing the country will be! Those that are now
erected are mere painted shells, with a Mistress within, who is
stuck up in a place she calls a *parlour*, with, if she have any children,
the 'young ladies and gentlemen' about her: some showy chairs
and a sofa (a *sofa* by all means): half a dozen prints in gilt frames
hanging up: a dinner brought in by a girl that is perhaps better
'educated' than she: two or three nick-nacks to eat instead of a
piece of bacon and a pudding. . . .[1]

Although he found the Isle of Thanet with its great barns and
ricks and its heavy crops of wheat 'a garden indeed', he could
not enjoy it after he had seen the wretched houses of the
labourers, and the people themselves:

dirty, poor-looking; ragg'd but particularly *dirty*. The men and
boys with dirty faces, and dirty smock-frocks, and dirty shirts;
and good God! what a difference between the wife of a labouring
man here, and the wife of a labouring man in the forests of Hampshire and Sussex! . . . In this beautiful island every inch of ground
is appropriated by the rich. No hedges, no ditches, no commons,
no grassy lanes: a country divided into great farms; a few trees
surround the great farm-house.[2]

Where Young would have approved of the enclosure, chatted
with the farmer and investigated his use of manure or method of
fencing, Cobbett saw a scene either of human happiness or
misery—and in doing so stood apart from his fellow tourists who,
though they might approve of a human element in the scene
from an aesthetic point of view, would certainly never have dreamt
of describing a landscape with figures, much less of bringing
those figures to the very forefront of the picture.

[1] ibid., *245*.
[2] ibid., *207–8*.

THE PICTURESQUE
AND THE ROMANTIC

The Wye and North Wales

THE countryside which pleased the farmer was regarded by the seeker for the Picturesque with disdain and contempt; the agriculturalist looked at the world for information and possibly edification; the followers of Gilpin saw it aesthetically, as raw material for an artist's palette. So while such sturdy travellers as Young and Cobbett strode the countryside with serious purpose, the disciples of the Rev. William Gilpin were setting out on expeditions of a more aesthetic nature: The search for an ideal landscape.

The cult of the Picturesque is inseparable from its creator, the Rev. William Gilpin, a retiring Hampshire parson, to whom belongs the distinction of having added a third category of beauty to the two established by Burke in 1756 in his *Inquiry into the Origin of Our Ideas of the Sublime and Beautiful*. He recognized that what might be either sublime or beautiful in nature lost this quality when translated into painting. 'Nothing is more delusive, than to suppose, that every view which pleases in nature, will please in painting. In nature, the pleasure arises from the eye's roaming from one passage to another; and making its remarks on each. In painting (as the eye is there confined within certain limits) it arises from seeing some select spot adorned agreeably

123

to the rules of art.'[1] He called the succession of eight books in which he elaborated this theme in different parts of the country *Observations . . . Relative Chiefly to Picturesque Beauty*, showing by his use of the double term that he never clearly distinguished, as Uvedale Price and Payne Knight were to do, between beauty and picturesqueness.

Any scene is picturesque if it will look well in a picture, is well composed and harmoniously coloured. But to find such a scene Gilpin was frequently forced to improve upon nature. His sketches in fact are a glimpse of the ideal. He was certainly willing to allow that wild nature was 'always great in design' but in actual composition she seldom produced a harmonious whole. The task of the artist was therefore to 'adapt such diminutive parts of nature's surfaces to his own eyes as comes within its scope'.[2] The plates which illustrate his books show the essence of picturesque beauty: every unessential detail is omitted, the landscape is composed by the choice and combination of its most suitable features. He allowed liberty but not licence: nothing alien should be introduced. The painter should only make such alterations as the nature of the country allowed and the composition of the picture absolutely demanded.

> Trees he may generally plant, or remove, at pleasure. If a withered stump suit the form of his landscape better than the spreading oak, which he finds in nature, he may make the exchange—or he may make it, if he wish for a spreading oak, where he finds a withered tree. He has no right, we allow, to add a magnificent castle—an impending rock—or a river, to adorn his foreground. These are *new features*. But he may certainly break an ill-formed hillock; and shovel the earth about him, as he pleases, without offence. He may pull up a piece of awkward paling—he may throw down a cottage—he may even turn the course of a road or a river, a few yards on this side or that. These trivial alterations may greatly add to the beauty of his composition; and yet they interfere not with the truth of portrait. Most of these things may *in fact* be altered to-morrow; though they disgust today.[3]

[1] W. Gilpin, *Observations, Relative Chiefly to Picturesque Beauty, Made in the Year 1772, on several Parts of England, particularly the Mountains and Lakes of Cumberland and Westmorland*, London, 1786, I, *146*.

[2] W. Gilpin, *Observations on the River Wye, and several parts of South Wales, 1770*, London, 1782, *18*.

[3] *Observations . . . Cumberland and Westmorland, xxix.*

He is concerned only with the visual aspects of the scene. 'In your *adorned sketch* you must grace them (i.e. "the lines of the country just as you find them") a little, where they run false. You must contrive to hide offensive parts with good; to cover such as are too bald, with bushes; and to remove little objects, which in nature push themselves too much in sight, and serve only to introduce too many parts into your *composition*. In this adjustment the grand merit of your sketch consists. No beauty of light, colouring or execution, can atone for the want of *composition*.'[1] He becomes in fact the arch-architect, arranging whatever he finds as he judges fit. 'I take up a tree here, and plant it there. I pave a knoll, or make an addition to it. I remove a piece of paling —a cottage—a wall—or any removeable object which I dislike.'[2]

Gilpin laid down his canons with such authority and directness that his disciples, when well versed in the rules of the game, had no hesitation in setting out to assess nature's handiwork and, if necessary, to improve upon it. For the aim of the traveller now became to track down the picturesque view, and, when it had been suitably corrected and adorned, to add it to his collection. Thus, with critical faculties sharpened on these new theories, and with an attitude to nature which saw her as little more than a scribbling-pad for their sketches, the Rev. William Gilpin unleashed a fresh stream of ardent tourists upon the English countryside.

The expedition down the river Wye provided the material for the first of Gilpin's *Picturesque Observations*, published in 1782. His account of the rich treasures of picturesque beauty ensured that by the end of the eighteenth century the voyage down the Wye had become one of the most popular tours in the country. Pleasure boats plied between Ross and Chepstow and could be hired for the price of three guineas, together with an additional guinea for provisions for the rowers, two men rowing with a single oar and a third sculling with two. The boats were provided with a covering against the sun, and a convenient table for drawing or writing.[3]

The first part of the journey, immediately after leaving Ross,

[1] *Three Essays on Picturesque Beauty*, London, 1792, 70.
[2] ibid., 68.
[3] Jonathan Gray, 'Tour to the Western Counties and South Wales', 1802, York Public Library MS. T/4.

was, by common consent, serene, sublime and tranquil, the great moment being the first sight of Goodrich Castle, a view which Gilpin allowed to be 'Correctly picturesque; which is seldom the character of a purely natural scene', and which was generally considered to rank as the second grand object of the tour. The river here made one of its boldest sweeps and enabled the tourist to enjoy the sight of these sublime ruins crowning steep and woody banks from a variety of different viewpoints. The landscape below this became increasingly sylvan and picturesque and the cottages scattered here and there on the hillside added 'animation and interest to the scenery: for what real pleasure can arise from the contemplation of wild nature, however inviting her features, if the abodes of men and the comforts of society are excluded?'[1] The views became yet more sublime until at Coldwell, halfway to Monmouth and the stopping point for refreshment, nature appeared at her most majestic amidst the abrupt and amphi-theatric cliffs. 'Here the mouldering perpendicular rocks, which assume the most fantastic forms, are clothed with a profusion of pendent foliage and exhibit such a delicacy and variety of tints, that no efforts of art can equal.' This tone of awe-struck wonder continued for the next few miles. New Weir was one of the finest points:

> The river is wider than usual, in this part; and takes a sweep round a towering promontory of rock; which forms the side-screen on the left; and is the grand feature of the view. It is not a broad, fractured face of rock but rather a woody hill, from which large projections, in two or three places, burst out; rudely hung with twisting branches, and shaggy furniture; which, like mane round a lion's head, gives a more savage air to these wild exhibitions of nature. Near the top a pointed fragment of solitary rock, rising above the rest, has rather a fantastic appearance: but it is not with-out its effect in marking the scene.[2]

After the night spent at Monmouth the tours continued between either vast woody declivities or rich pastures on either side of the river banks, both important features in the picturesque landscape, since, as Gilpin reminded his readers, 'furrowed-lands and waving corn, however charming in pastoral poetry, are ill-accomodated

[1] W. Mavor, 'A Tour through Wales in the Summer of 1805', *British Tourists*, London, 1809, V, *176*.

[2] Gilpin, *Observations . . . 1770, 24.*

to painting. . . . Pasturage not only presents an agreeable surface: but the cattle, which graze it, add great variety, and animation to the scene. The Meadows, below Monmouth, which run shelving from the hills to the water-side, were particularly beautiful, and well-inhabited. Flocks of sheep were every where hanging on their green steeps; and herds of cattle occupying the lower grounds. We often sailed past groups of them laving their sides in the water; or retiring from the heat under sheltered banks.'[1] The climax on this lower stretch of river came with the ruins of Tintern Abbey, most famous of beauty spots on the Wye. But even here Gilpin remained critical, seeing them as always with the eye of an improver and finding them disappointing as a *distant* object.

> Though the parts are beautiful, the whole is ill-shaped. No ruins of the tower are left, which might give form, and contrast to the walls, and buttresses, and other inferior parts. Instead of this, a number of gabel-ends hurt the eye with their regularity; and disgust by the vulgarity of their shape. A mallet judiciously used (but who durst use it?) might be of service in fracturing some of them; particularly those of the cross isles, which are not only disagreeable in themselves, but confound the perspective.[2]

The nearer view was preferable for it showed, still in its wild and native rudeness:

> a very inchanting piece of ruin. Nature has now made it her own. Time has worn off all traces of the rule: it has blunted the sharp edges of the chisel; and broken the regularity of opposing parts. The figured ornaments of the east-window are gone; those of the west-window are left. To these are superadded the ornaments of time. Ivy, in masses uncommonly large, has taken possession of many parts of the wall; and gives a happy contrast to the grey-coloured stone, of which the building is composed. Nor is this undecorated. Mosses of various hues, with lychens, maiden-hair, penny-leaf, and other humble plants, over-spread the surface or hang from every joint, and crevice. Some of them were in flower, others only in leaf; but, all together, they give those full-blown tints, which add the richest finishing to a ruin.

Later tourists were easier to please and left descriptions which spoke in largely conventional terms of the atmosphere of gloom

[1] ibid., *30–1*.
[2] ibid., *32–3*.

and solemnity and the luxuriance of the ivy and mosses. By the time that Jonathan Gray saw it in 1802 it had become the chief show-place of the Wye, preserved for its admiring public in a way that must have cut Gilpin to the heart had he known to what end his praises had led. Amidst carefully maintained ruins, cleared floors and neatly cut grass, numberless 'parties of pleasure' enjoyed the contemplation of the sight and, as one scandalized tourist exclaimed, were 'indecorous enough to take their meals on consecrated ground; hampers, baskets and other vehicles for containing viands, with servants packing and unpacking for the different fêtes, gave the place the appearance of a market'.[1] As the numbers of those who made the tour increased, their aesthetic appreciation became progressively debased and Gilpin's sophisticated assessment and technical appraisal gave place to enthusiastic and unselective enjoyment: the objects seen were merely listed, not assigned parts to play in an artistic composition, while the Wye itself became little more than an excuse to indulge in reflections and moralizings. By 1834 the Rev. Luke Booker could write a lengthy poem, *The Springs of Plynlimmon*, an ecstatic effusion which bore small reference to the reality of the scenery he actually saw:

> Soon the gladly-roving eye
> Kens Goderich Tow'rs with ecstasy:
> For, no where (heav'n and earth between)
> May we behold a lovelier scene.
> Rooted on rock of lordly height,
> That awes, yet charms the wandering sight,
> High, in mid air, the fabric stands,
> As if there plac'd by magic hands;
> And when the storm its head enshrouds,
> It seems descending from the clouds,
> Enchantment's work, where Genie dwell,
> Which nothing earthly may excel.[2]

The tour down the Wye thus offered the tourist a series of picturesque tableaux, which demanded that he follow a closely defined route, and exercise an equally clearly defined aesthetic

---

[1] D. C. Webb, *Observations and Remarks during Four excursions . . . 1810 and 1811*, London, 1812, *318*.

[2] *The Springs of Plynlimmon; a Poem descriptive of scenery and circumstances connected with the Severn, the Wye, and three minor rivers*, Wolverhampton, 1834, *16*.

ROTHERFORD BRIDGE.

BOLTON BRIDGE.
Both by John Byng.

judgement. In the Tour of Wales, however, he found himself presented not only with a bewildering succession of immensely varied scenery, ranging from the pastoral to the starkly dramatic, but also by an entirely different way of life, and one moreover which represented a challenge to the values of his own civilized existence. The fame of Wales developed late; in the middle years of the eighteenth century the impression made upon travellers was still an almost wholly unpleasant one. In 1735 the Rev. J. Milles was complaining bitterly that he was constantly finding himself traversing bleak and barren mountains, and that there were such frequent and rugged ascents and descents in the road as to make it continually disagreeable. In 1756 Bishop Pococke was still talking in terms of mile upon mile of disagreeable mountains, and although he did allow that certain of the elements making up the scene were quite attractive, he made no attempt to interest his readers in them beyond giving a bare list of an 'agreeable variety of rocks, woods, field and meadow, much resembling the lower parts of the Alps towards Chambery'.[1] In 1768 'dreary' was still the only adjective used by Sir Harbottle Grimston in describing his passage through Snowdonia. But by the end of the century Wales had converted many enthusiasts, and appreciation of the country was growing fast. All praised it for its infinite diversity—'the gay attire of fertile vales and woods, the plainer dress of mountains, cataracts and craggy precipices, more beautiful by change, and more pleasing by variety'.[2] The beauties of south and central Wales, however, paled before the prospects offered by the north. Here, Bingley promised, the traveller of taste in search of grand and stupendous scenery would find all that his heart could desire. An anonymous tourist in 1791 could only liken it to Switzerland or North America, 'but still they have not that extravagent wildness, nor have they, if I may be allowed such a liberty of words, the *angry grandeur* of North Wales. Here we meet with a country *sui generis*, singular in its kind, magnificent, striking and superb. I have never seen anything that can be justly compared with it.'[3] Nothing of the

[1] *Travels through England*, (ed.) J. J. Cartwright, Camden Society, 1888 and 1889, II, *179–80*.
[2] Joseph Cradock, *An Account of some of the most Romantic Parts of North Wales*, London, 1777, *1–2*.
[3] *A Tour through the South of England, Wales, and part of Ireland made during the summer of 1791*, London, 1792, *274*.

crude commercialization of the Lakes had yet sullied its natural beauty, and to a considerable extent each tourist was still something of a pioneer, and might reasonably hope to discover some new waterfall or make some ascent hitherto never attempted. Guides there certainly were, and few tourists were so foolhardy as to think that they could dispense with their local knowledge. But only one, Ralph Edwards at Cader Idris, had actually developed the idea of producing a handbill advertising himself and his services. 'CONDUCTOR TO, and over the most tremendous mountain CADER IDRIS, to the stupendous cataracts of CAIN and MAWDDACH, and to the enchanting cascades of DOL-Y-MELYNLLYN, with all the beautiful romantic scenery, GUIDE-GENERAL and MAGNIFICENT EXPOUNDER of all the natural and artificial curiosities of North Wales.'[1] In 1792 Plumptre was accosted by this extraordinary old man, dressed in a blue coat with yellow buttons, a pair of old boots and a cocked hat with a feather of enormous size, who thrust a paper into his hand announcing that Mr. Watt of Soho, Birmingham, recommended future tourists to follow a certain path and so enjoy one of the finest views in North Wales. Led by Edwards, Plumptre followed this advice, and found the spot mentioned marked by a tree bearing the initials of Mr. Watt who had discovered it only three weeks previously.[2] Wales was indeed still the province of the amateur. Mementos and souvenirs had not yet made their appearance, and the nearest approach to the shops springing up in the Lakes was that the widow of a Snowdon guide, who fell a martyr to his too frequent journeys up Snowdon which threw him into a decline, eked out her modest existence by selling his collection of spars and minerals at a few shillings apiece.[3]

This simplicity made tremendous appeal, and the honesty, the absence of worldly ambition of these people living so close to nature, formed the subject of constant comment from admiring tourists. Here the tourists clearly felt they could glimpse something of that Elysian life long since buried elsewhere beneath the weight of corruption and the care of worldly vanities. The very dress of the people seemed in itself to symbolize the gulf between the two

[1] Mavor, *Tour* . . . *1805*, 250–1.
[2] 'A Journal of a Tour through part of North Wales in the year 1792', Camb. Univ. Lib. Add. MS. 5802, f. 130.
[3] Mavor, *Tour* . . . *1805*, 267.

worlds, and they gazed with delight upon the long cloaks, the red silk handkerchiefs and the black beaver hats. Mrs. West, who confessed that she had approached Wales with a beating heart and awakened imagination, was not disappointed in her first sight of its womenfolk. 'The picturesque dress and countenance of the Welsh women we passed on the road delighted me; their clean caps, blue flannel cloaks and black hats, added to their independent way of riding behind each other, bespoke a hardy, useful race who were really the help-mates, not the incumbrances of man.'[1] A road thronged with country folk on their way to market was one of the most typical and colourful scenes. 'In such a barren and apparently uninhabited country it was astonishing to see such numbers pouring down from the mountains. They looked as if they had dropt from the clouds ... Long blue cloaks were now universal, with black beaver hat and striped flannel petticoat. Blue was the general colour, worn by both sexes, even down to the stockings. Children are dressed in a striped flannel gown or frock, with sleeves, sitting close to the waist and pinned before.'[2] Occasionally an enterprising tourist such as Hucks would make his way into one of their cottages and find the family round the hearth. He was considerably startled on one occasion to discover one such small cottage inhabited by thirteen human beings, all in petticoats, though later he learnt that two or three of the children were in fact boys. Delighted with their rosy cheeks and fine skins, with the simple fare of bread and milk provided for him, with the clean clothing and the absence of shoes and stockings, he could only conclude that such a people must be healthy, peaceable and contented. 'I left this race of beauties with a smile upon each face.'[3] It was difficult not to find in the sight of such a life an occasion for moralizing and pious reflection. 'Ambition seems wholly excluded. The dress of the inhabitants is of that kind which never changes for ages. It is made to cover, not for show. . . . I did not see the smallest degree of smartness in the apparel, even of the young females. When a man chuses a wife it must be for the kernel not the shell.'[4] The women, everlasting knitters of

---

[1] 'Tour to Wales and Ireland', 1810, Camb. Univ. Lib. Add. MS. 738, f.10–11.
[2] Mavor, *Tour . . . 1805*, 240–1.
[3] *A Pedestrian Tour through North Wales, in a Series of Letters*, London, 1795, *23–4*.
[4] W. Hutton, *Remarks upon North Wales, being the Result of Sixteen Tours Through that part of the Principality*, Birmingham, 1803, *19–20*.

stockings as the tourists passed them upon the road, showed an industry that was entirely admirable. 'Let the fair daughters of indolence and ease contemplate the characters of the patterns of industry, who are happily unacquainted with the gay follies of life, who enjoy health without medicine, and happiness without affluence. Equally remote from the grandeur and the miseries of life, they participate of the sweet blessings of content, under the homely dwelling of a straw-built cottage.'[1] The difficulty with which they could be prevailed upon to accept money or gifts, and their willingness to give directions in return for no other repayment than a kind word, was regarded as one of their greatest virtues. 'We sometimes gave them a shilling, they received it with an aukward surprise, and were so confounded, that they could only express their thanks in tears of gratitude',[2] reported an anonymous tourist, admiration coupled with amazement. For Mavor and his party, all that they felt about these qualities of simplicity and honesty were summed up in a beautiful little girl of about twelve in her striped flannel gown, who walked barefoot for half a mile to open a gate for them on a wild common, and expected nothing in return. 'The flannel frock was evidently the whole of her dress, and it shewed her shape to great advantage. It reminded us that beauty when unadorned attracts the most.'[3] It was as though she epitomized the innocency and the native dignity of her race.

Such character was deemed to be due in part to surroundings which demanded a hardy way of life and were well calculated to foster a love of liberty and independence, but perhaps even more to an ancestry in which barbarity and virtue were equally coupled. For the tourists never forgot that this was the land of the Ancient Britons, the country where 'liberty made her last stand in these kingdoms against the strides of Roman power, under the gallant Silurian and Ordovician chieftains'.[4] Face to face with such a heritage many stopped to reflect that they were no more than outsiders, mere observers of 'a happiness which none but a native of that country might feel'.

The force of the national way of life made itself felt most

---

[1] Cradock, *Account of North Wales*, 1777, 31–2.
[2] *A Gentleman's Tour through Monmouthshire and Wales in the Months of June and July 1774*, London, 1775, 157–8.   [3] Mavor, *Tour . . . 1805, 241*.
[4] Rev. Richard Warner, *A Walk through Wales in August 1797*, Bath, 1799, 2.

powerfully to the tourists when they first heard the Welsh harpists and were entertained by the singing of traditional sagas. The Welsh language in any case carried with it a certain element of mystery, and those who heard it felt something of its spell. 'It is true there is a sort of Guteral uncoothness in it to *English Ears*', wrote Lady Crewe after attending a service in Welsh, 'but there is also something *grand* & *imposing* in some words wherein many vowels occur to open the mouth freely, & so as to Give Room for *Emphasis* & *Energy* in long sentences.' At the inn in the evening it was the common custom for the local people to gather round the harpist to sing and dance to his playing. 'Nothing is more cheerful nor yet more melancholy than to be greeted as one is at every Inn by venerable blind men who play airs of the country, as wild & yet as harmonious as the beauties they are deprived from seeing.'[1] Moved by the plaintive quality of the music many found themselves dreaming of the past: 'the simplicity of former times struck forcibly upon my mind, and brought back the pleasing recollection of those happy ages, when riches and luxury had not corrupted the heart of man; but when all mankind were brothers. It afforded me a satisfaction I had never before experienced to find myself amongst a people who act with all the simplicity of nature; totally destitute of the assumed appearance and artificial manners of more modern times.'[2]

It was not merely that here was a way of life that seemed close to that of the Garden of Eden; the setting of this paradisical existence was one of unsurpassed natural beauty. 'A Welch tour is surprisingly grand', wrote Hutton quite simply; 'Nature is seen in extreme. The lofty, rough and barren mountains opposed to the beautiful and fertile vallies is a charming contrast.'[3] The richness and variety of the scenery defied any easy generalization, and while one county might be famed for its stupendous, craggy wildness, its neighbour was known for its calm sublimity, richness and beauty. Caernarvonshire was the main goal of every tourist, for here they found themselves face to face with the savage and majestic face of untamed nature, precipitous, rugged, gloomy. The approach to Snowdonia from Bangor beneath the shadow of Penmaenmawr was famous, and looked upon as a test of nerve. Above and below the road the terrified tourist found himself

---

[1] 'A Tour to North Wales, 1795', B.M. Add. MSS. 37,926 f. 139. [2] Hucks, *Pedestrian Tour*, 1795, *32–3*. [3] Hutton, *Remarks upon North Wales*, 1803, *11–12*.

caught between horrid precipices, above his head hung fragments of rock seemingly about to crash down upon him, and it was well known that after a thaw or rains they would give way and roll as convulsive ruins into the sea. Only the presence of a recently built wall reassured him that he too would not find himself flung in the same path. The fact that the native thought nothing of riding along on the very brink of such a desperate site provided little consolation, and Bingley was undoubtedly right in assuming that most traversed it as he did in a state of considerable tremor. Warner admitted that he could not travel it without shuddering, expecting every moment to be crushed to atoms under a torrent of huge stones,[1] and Mrs. West gave a picture of herself crouched at the bottom of her carriage looking in vain for a sight of the sky above the abyss.[2]

As the tourist drew within sight of Snowdon itself the scenery became increasingly grand, the giant peak capped with clouds towering amidst his subject mountains, with grotesque, majestic rocks and dark, sinister lakes below.

I could almost have fancied that nature untamed bore here an uninterrupted sway amidst the gloom & grandeur of these dreary rocks. The scenery was awfully rude. It was one continued series of rocks, infinitely varied in their figure and disposition. The nimble-footed sheep that brouzed on their dark sides, and skipped along their tremendous precipices, looked down upon us with the utmost composure, fearless of any danger from their seemingly precarious situation. I was much pleased with this for I love

'These lonely regions, where, retired
From little scenes of art, great Nature dwells
In awful solitude.'[3]

Most tourists attempted the ascent of Snowdon with feelings of considerable alarm, for it was always made out to be extremely hazardous, demanding a good head and strong nerves, and it was by no means uncommon for ladies to turn faint and giddy in the early stages. With the sudden approach of mists a party would often find themselves surrounded on all sides by desperate precipices and the guides generally delighted at this point to

[1] Warner, *Walk through Wales . . . 1797, 144.*
[2] Camb. Univ. Lib. Add. MSS. 738, f. 20–20b.
[3] Rev. W. Bingley, *A Tour round North Wales; including its Scenery, Antiquities, Customs and . . . Natural History; from excursions . . . during the summers of 1798 and 1801,* London, 1804, I, 260.

recount the terrible accidents that had befallen earlier visitors to that very spot. Standing on the summit, rubbing their faces with brandy (the most popular and widely recommended remedy for the intense cold which was generally held to affect their muscles), the hardy tourists could congratulate themselves that they had now achieved 'the sublime of terror'. Newell was amused to find how many who had made this ascent before him had taken care to record their exploits, carefully packing among the stones at the top scraps of paper with their names and the dates of their excursions. Hutton recounted the epic story of the lady who had climbed it with two companions in 1797, and successfully gained the summit though drenched with rain and clinging to one another to prevent their being blown away. Elated with success she pulled off her hat and cap, and 'huzzaed for joy', only to have them immediately swept from her hands by the gale. Hutton concluded the tale with a moral: 'The amazonian lady, no doubt, was the leader of the party, and designed like some others of her own sex, to govern ours. The lofty Snowdon however reduced the more lofty spirit of the female adventurer. She fell into fits, her life was despaired of, and she was brought in a chaise the next morning to Caernarvon in a state of distress which excited pity.'[1]

The storms and mists which added so much to the perils of the climb frequently meant that the view from the top was obscured, though to the stronger spirits this actually heightened the gloom and grandeur of their situation. Pennant, standing in the midst of swirling fogs, found himself delighted by the mystery which this added to the scene:

It gave the idea of a number of abysses concealed by thick smoke, furiously circulating around us; sometimes they would open only in one place, at others in many at once, exhibiting a most strange and perplexing sight of water, fields, rocks, chasms, in fifty different places. Then they closed at once, and left us involved in darkness; in a small space they would separate again, and fly in wild eddies round the middle of the mountains, and expose, in parts, both tops and bases to our view.[2]

The Rev. Richard Warner felt moved to quote the prophet Joel:

[1] Hutton, *Remarks upon North Wales*, 1803, *157–8*.
[2] T. Pennant, *The Journey to Snowdon*, London, 1781, II, *164*.

'A day of darkness and of gloominess, a day of clouds and of thick darkness, as the morning spread upon the mountains', it produced however an effect that was very sublime. Occasional gusts of wind, which now roared around us, swept away for a moment the pitchy cloud that involved particular spots of the mountain, and discovered, immediately below us, huge rocks, abrupt precipices, and profound hollows, exciting emotions of astonishment and awe in the mind, which the eye, darting down in an immense descent of vacuity and horror, conveyed to it under the dreadful image of inevitable destruction.[1]

An anonymous tourist of 1774 was even prepared to go so far as to admit that several days of continuous mist might prove an enjoyable experience. 'During our abode amid those superb mountains, neither sun nor stars appeared to our sight for several days; and, wrapt up in an impenetrable mist, we were perpetually enveloped with a twilight obscurity. Our situation was like a scene of enchantment, impressing a superstitious extasy on our senses, while we contemplated the sublime operations of nature around us.'[2]

A few made other ascents in the neighbourhood, though Pennant advised that this new and greater toil should only be attempted by those 'who possess a degree of bodily activity as well as strength of head to bear the sight of the dreadful hollows frequent beneath them'.[3] But most of those who had faced Snowdon went on to climb Cader Idris, as Hucks's party did:

We armed our guide with stores, and warlike preparations of all kinds, to wit, ham, fowl, bread and cheese, and brandy, and began the ascent at nine in the morning, and continued to toil for three and a half hours until we reached the top. . . . The summit of the mountain is not of greater extent than the base of a common sized room; and, on one side, falls almost perpendicularly many hundred yards in depth. When I stood upon the edge of this precipice and looked into the frightful abyss of clouds, it put me in mind of the the chaos, or void space of darkness, so finely described in Milton, where the fallen archangel stood at the gates of hell, pondering the scene before him and viewing with horror the profound expanse of silence and eternal night.[4]

[1] Warner, *Walk through Wales* . . . *1797, 130.*
[2] *A Gentleman's Tour*, 1774, *154.*
[3] Pennant, *Journey to Snowdon*, 1781, II, *154–5.*
[4] Hucks, *Pedestrian Tour*, 1795, *113–14.*

Cader certainly came up to the expected standard of savage grandeur, and this was the aspect dwelt on by most tourists, and
reflected in Foley's description of his expedition.

> Sometimes we looked down awful precipices, more awful perhaps
> from the circumstance that our eyes could not penetrate the
> bottom of them, & that all we could see below was now & then a
> fearful crag, or a piece of apparently isolated rock, shewing its
> head thro' the mist, while its juncture with the mountain was
> invisible. No one who has not been in a similar situation can con-
> ceive the effect produced on the mind by looking down on such a
> scene from above, without a spot of earth visible excepting the few
> yards of rocky ground on which we stood.[1]

Having conquered a peak or two, yet one other exercise was
incumbent upon any serious tourist of Wales; one, however,
which demanded less athletic prowess than aesthetic judgement.
Cataracts and waterfalls presented them with horror and grandeur
in another form. 'Language is but ill calculated to convey an
accurate idea of the scene which is here presented to the eye',
wrote Warner at Devil's Bridge. 'The awful height of the fissure
which the bridge bestrides a hundred feet above the observer,
rendered doubly gloomy by its narrowness, and the wood which
overhangs it; the stunning noise of the torrent thundering at his
feet, and struggling through black, opposing rocks, which its
ceaseless impetuosity has worn into shapes strange and grotesque,
fill the mind with a mingled but sublime emotion of astonishment,
terror, and delight.'[2] Newell exclaimed at the sight of the waterfall at Rhydol that 'the height of the precipices, the gloom of
their shadows, the roar of the fall, the confusion of rocky fragments, the age of the trees, all form together a scene that fills the
mind with pleasing breathless wonder'. He next visited Mynach
and was even more impressed. 'Fearful it is to stand upon the
giddy footing of the plank across the chasm, and mark the wild
grandeur of the scenery. The swirling torrent, the fantastic rocks,
scooped into hollows of unknown depth, the barren steep, the
gloomy wood, the spiry mountain tops—while the hollow rush
of the water heard at intervals adds solemnity to the whole.' He
was amongst those who found even greater satisfaction here than

[1] Edward Foley, 'Tour through North and Mid Wales, July–August 1831',
Edward Hall Collection, Wigan Public Library, M965/EHC 173.
[2] Warner, *Walk through Wales . . . 1797, 74.*

upon any mountain top. 'Twice have I staid amidst these terrible beauties, and each time took of them a very unwilling farewell. They have left a more vivid impression on my fancy than any I have seen before or since.'[1] Mavor was similarly moved by these two. 'Every circumstance that enters into the composition of this scene is calculated to inspire fear and horror. Where the eye cannot fathom depths, and noise is heard without being able to trace its cause, fancy is no longer under the control of judgement, and it creates terrors of its own.'[2] Rhaidr Du in the Festiniog Valley was made particularly splendid by water cascading over three great black rocks in different directions. Creeping along the shelving rocks by the side of the stream for half a mile, Bingley soon found himself in what he called an abode of horror. 'Here the banks closed over my head, leaving but a narrow chasm, from which the light was altogether excluded by the dark foliage from each side, and I found myself entering the mouth of a deep and horrid cavern.'[3] Others were less well known, but equally rewarding, and the connoisseur would assess the various elements and then pass judgement upon the quality of the total scene in terms of its setting of dark precipices and overhanging woods, the broken and dramatic disposition of the rocks, the roar of the stream rushing with savage impetuosity from stupendous heights, enjoying as he did so a succession of emotions that ranged from awe and wonder to an almost childlike delight.

[1] Rev. R. H. Newell, *Letters on the Scenery of Wales*, London, 1821, 82-8.
[2] Mavor, *Tour . . . 1805, 225.*
[3] Bingley, *North Wales, 1798 and 1801*, II, 4.

II

THE PLAYGROUND
OF ENGLAND

The Lakes

'To make the Tour of the Lakes, to speak in fashionable terms, is the *ton* of the present hour', declared the *Monthly Magazine* in 1778, and in the 1790's this was the most popular summer excursion in the kingdom, gaining new recruits from those debarred from travel in Europe by the happenings which, in the words of one traveller, had 'rendered part of the continent a scene of horror and devestation'. By 1798 the Lake tourists had become a sufficiently well-known phenomenon to form the subject of a three-act comic opera, *The Lakers*:

> Each season there delighted myriads throng,
> To pass their time these charming scenes among:
> For pleasure, knowledge, many thither hie,
> For fashion some, and some—they know not why,
> And these same visitors, e'en one and all,
> The Natives by the name of LAKERS call.[1]

The two books which are generally taken as heralding the discovery of the Lakes are John Dalton's *Descriptive Poem Addressed to Two Young Ladies at their Return from Viewing the Mines near Whitehaven* in 1755, and Dr. John Brown's *Description of the Lake and Vale of Keswick* in 1767. Neither has great intrinsic

[1] Anon. (Rev. James Plumptre) London, 1797, *prologue.*

literary worth: their significance lies in the fact that they employ for the first time those images and phrases which were to colour all subsequent tourists' accounts. 'Rocks and cliffs of stupendous height, hanging broken over the Lake in horrible grandeur', 'a variety of waterfalls tumbling in vast sheets from rock to rock in rude and terrible magnificence', 'beauty, horror and immensity united'—these are phrases which were to become so much the current coinage that it is difficult to realize the advance that they represent upon the awkward hesitations and fumblings of a Bishop Pococke or Thomas Pennant, who, lacking any adequate vocabulary, put antiquarian or naturalist interest before any appreciation of scenery for its own sake. Even more significant for the opening up of the Lakes were Thomas Gray and Thomas West, for they not merely equipped the tourists with a descriptive vocabulary but blazed a trail for them over the face of the countryside, reducing it to a succession of carefully disposed stations from which the best views might be obtained. Gray made his tour of the Lakes in 1769, writing an account of his experiences there in the form of a journal to his friend Dr. Wharton, though it became famous only after being printed as an appendix to the second edition of West's *Guide to the Lakes* in 1780. He saw the landscape in the form of a pictorial composition, describing it in terms of foreground, middle-distance and side-screens, though he was not yet so completely tied to an aesthetic formula that he was prepared to distort the actual scene to fulfil pictorial demands. He merely simplified and reduced it to its essentials without sacrificing a most genuine enjoyment of what he actually saw. As Mason put it: 'When Mr. Gray described places he aimed only to be exact, clear and intelligible . . . to paint by the eye not the fancy.' The passage of his most frequently quoted, however, is his account of lower Borrowdale, an exaggerated and fantastic piece of writing reflecting the intense nervous agitation which constituted a part, but by no means the whole, of his attitude to the Lakes.

> Soon after we came under Gowdarcrag—the rocks at the top deep-cloven perpendicularly by the rains, hanging loose and nodding forwards, seem just starting from their base in shivers. The whole way down and the road on both sides is strewed with piles of fragments, strangely thrown across each other, and of dreadfull bulk; the place reminds me of those passes in the Alps, where the guides tell you to move with speed, and say nothing,

lest the agitation of the air should loosen the snows above, and bring down a mass that would overwhelm a caravan. I took this counsel here, and hastened on in silence.

This, as West remarked, was mere hyperbole, 'the sports of fancy he was pleased to indulge himself at'. Far more typical were the descriptions written with delicacy and simplicity as on that grey autumn day when he went to see Ullswater and approached it from Dunmallet:

From hence saw the lake opening directly at my feet, majestic in its calmness, clear and smooth as a blue mirror, with winding shores and low points of land covered with green inclosures, white farm-houses looking out among the trees, and cattle feeding. The water is almost every where bordered with cultivated lands, gently sloping upwards from a mile to a quarter of a mile in breadth, till they reach the feet of the mountains, which rise very rude and awful with their broken tops on either hand.

Or again he might indulge in a little gentle conceit.

The air mild as summer, all corn off the ground, and the skylarks singing aloud (by the way, I saw not one at *Keswick*, perhaps because the place abounds in birds of prey). I went up the castle hill; the town chiefly consists of three nearly parallel streets, almost a mile long; except these, all the other houses seem as if they had been dancing a country-dance, and were out; there they stand back to back, corner to corner, some up the hill, some down, without intent or meaning.[1]

West's *Guide* first appeared in 1778, and by 1812 had gone through ten editions, for it remained unquestionably the most popular of all the guides to the Lakes and found its way into the pocket of every assiduous tourist. By now there could be no doubt that the way of looking at the landscape had become formalized, and the picturesque vocabulary hardened into a convention. West knew the district, he could tell the tourist what to look for, where to find it and what he should feel about it. He divided every lake into stations, that is viewpoints, and directed the tourist to make a regular progress of them, and his careful and detailed catalogue soon became quite indispensable for the dedicated sightseer. His descriptions were well calculated to whet the appetite:

[1] Appendix to Thomas West, *A Guide to the Lakes*, 2nd ed., London, 1780, *201, 214.*

From the top of *Castlecrag* in *Borrowdale* there is a most astonishing view of the lake and vale of *Keswick*, spread out to the north
in the most picturesque manner . . . the most extraordinary line of
shore, varied with all the surprising accompanyments of rock and
wood . . . a beautiful mixture of villages, houses, cots and farms,
standing round the skirts of *Skiddaw*, which rises in the grandest
manner from a verdant base and closes this prospect in the noblest
stile of nature's true sublime. From the summit of this rock the
views are so singularly great and pleasing that they ought never
to be omitted. . . . This truly secreted spot is completely surrounded
by the most horrid, romantic mountains that are in this region of
wonders; and whoever omits this *coup d'œil* hath probably seen
nothing equal to it.

'From the *north* side of the island the views are more sublime
and vast', he directed the tourist at his third station at Windermere. 'The lake is here seen both ways. To the south an expanse
of water spreads on both hands, and behind you see a succession
of promontories, with a variety of shore patched with islands, and
the whole encircled by an amphitheatre of distant hills, rising in
noble stile.' At Derwentwater he led the tourist's eyes:

On the floor of a spacious amphitheatre, of the most picturesque
mountains imaginable, an elegant sheet of water is spread out
before you, shining like a mirror, and transparent as chrystal;
variegated with islands adorned with wood, or cloathed with the
forest verdure, that rise in the most pleasing forms above the
watry plane. The effects all around are amazingly great; but no
words can describe the surprising pleasure of this scene, on a fine
day, when the sun plays on the bason of the lake, and the surrounding mountains are illumined by his refulgent rays, and their
rocky summits invertedly reflected by the surface of the water.[1]

'We remarked most of the stations described in West's *Tour to
the Lakes*, a book we had constantly in our hands', wrote Henry
Kett at Coniston in 1798, though he added: 'It would be better if
the descriptions were not so highly wrought, and painted in too
rich colours.' Later, at Ullswater, he was complaining that
Dunmallet, 'so commented by West, is a lumpish mountain,
nearly covered with firs and a broad green road. It is like the
back part of a full-dress wig', he added scornfully. At the station
on the top of Grasmere Hill he felt almost equal disappointment.
'The island he so much commends is an ugly lump of green colour.

[1] ibid., *9–14, 64–5, 85–6.*

The village and the church on the opposite side of the lake are too indistinct to appear to any advantage from this high point.'[1] Yet, although they might at times criticize him quite harshly, the tourists still followed faithfully in West's steps, and even if they showed sufficient independence of mind to 'take some inferior stations and amuse ourselves with our glasses' this formed no more than an appendage to their official pilgrimage.

Thus throughout the 1780's and 1790's the tourists were setting out determined to wring the last drop of aesthetic satisfaction from an expedition to the Lakes. They went fully armed, carrying a Claude-glass, and, if real connoisseurs, probably several other glasses as well, West's *Guide* in their pocket, a sketching-pad to hand. And they came to a countryside well prepared to welcome them, with guides ready to conduct them to West's stations, fleets of boats waiting by the lakeside, and every conceivable tourist attraction from museums to regattas. The Claude-glass formed an indispensable part of the equipment of any serious tourist. A slightly convex mirror, four inches in diameter, on black foil, and bound like a pocket-book, its purpose was to gather any landscape reflected in it into a tiny picture, and by reducing the colours and detail accentuate the tonal values of the scene. 'The person using it ought always to turn his back to the object that he views', advised West. 'It should be suspended by the upper part of the case, holding it a little to the right or left (as the position of the parts to be viewed requires) and the face screened from the sun.' The Rev. Joseph Plumptre added a further refinement by carrying a selection of glasses, and employing them all to produce new effects during his descent from Skiddaw. 'Though the objects were distant yet they were so large as to be seen with effect in the Gray. The Claude Lorraine gave it a most pleasing moonlight. But seen through the dark red or rather orange it was tremendous, and its burning glow called to mind that day "in which the Heavens shall pass away with a great noise, and being on fire shall be dissolved".'[2] That Plumptre could not take himself entirely seriously however is clear from his satires upon such behaviour in his opera *The Lakers*. 'Speedwell, give me my

[1] 'A Tour to the Lakes of Cumberland and Westmorland in August 1798', W. Mavor, *British Tourists*, London, 1809, V, *128*, *134*.
[2] 'A Narrative of a Pedestrian Journey through some parts of Yorkshire, Durham and Northumberland, and home by the Lakes and some parts of Wales in the Summer of 1799', Camb. Univ. Lib. Add. MSS. 5816, f. 17–18.

glasses', demands Miss Beccabunga Veronica in the third scene
set with a view across Derwentwater to Borrowdale.

> Where's my Gray? Oh! Claude and Poussin are nothing. By the
> bye, where's my Claude-Lorraine? I must throw a Gilpin tint
> over these magic scenes of beauty. (*Looks through the glass*) How
> gorgeously glowing! Now for the darker. (*Looks through the glass*)
> How gloomily glaring! Now the blue. (*Pretends to shiver with
> fright*) How frigidly frozen! What illusions of vision! The effect
> is inexpressibly interesting. The amphitheatrical perspective of
> the long landscape; the peeping points of the many-coloured crags
> of the head-long mountains, looking out most interestingly from
> the picturesque luxuriance of the bowery foliage; the delightful
> differences of the heterogeneous masses; the horrific mountains,
> such scenes of ruin and privation . . .

Later in the play she is to look at her prospective husband through
the glasses too. 'I'll throw a Gilpin tint over him. (*Looks through
glass*) Yet, he's gorgeously glowing. I must not view him with the
other lights, for a husband should not be either glaringly gloomy, or
frigidly frozen; nor should I like to be haunted by a blue devil.'[1]

The viewpoints upon which these glasses were to be employed
were not only carefully listed by West, but were often actually
marked upon the hills, either by crosses cut in the turf or by a
summer-house or some other shelter. At West's first station at
Bowness Plumptre found, 'much too finished and artificial', a
building with a caretaker installed on the lower floor. Elsewhere,
however, he felt that the potentialities of the spot had not been
fully exploited, and at Ambleside advocated the throwing of a
rude alpine bridge over the stream and the placing of a rustic
building on the station, while at Skiddaw he discussed with his
guide the possibility of building a small room with a fireplace and
'a long seat on each side to sleep upon, to accomodate those
gentlemen who might wish to remain here any time to see the
sunrise or set—to contemplate from this height the stupendous
world of wonders below amid the golden blaze of noon, or the
crimson resplendence of evening . . . the solemn illumination of
moonlight, and then again to observe the first faint dawning of
morning, its cool and sober mists and colours'.[2]

'He toils day and night during the season, at the desire of

---

[1] *The Lakers*, 1798, *19*, *58*.
[2] Camb. Univ. Lib. Add. MSS. 5815, f. 279–80; 5816, f. 15–16.

PONT Y PAIR OVER THE RIVER CONWAY ABOVE LANTWIST.
By Paul Sandby, from *XII Views in North Wales*, 1776.

strangers, and is judiciously acquainted with Mr. West's stations, having often been with him when he fixed upon them',[1] wrote Joseph Budworth of Hutton, one of the leading Lakes guides. Other tourists mention Robin Partridge: 'a talkative and entertaining old man', said Kett, 'an expert walker in a country where walking is a very different exercise to walking along a level turnpike road'.[2] Filled with apprehension at the hazards of exploring the Lakes on foot most tourists took good care never to venture forth until they had placed themselves in the hands of some competent guide. The local inhabitants naturally took full advantage of the situation, and by 1799 the Hon. Mrs. Murray was warning her readers that they must expect to pay five shillings a day for the attendance of a guide, quite apart from the hire of a horse.[3] Rather than employ such expensive and uncultured natives Plumptre devised an optimistic scheme by which it might be possible to arrange for 'persons of confined circumstances but of liberal manner and information to undertake the office of Guides of the Lakes . . . young Artists would be particularly eligible . . . a series of drawings of the adjacent views (sold at moderate prices) might form an exhibition at their lodgings which might repay their trouble to travellers coming to see and to purchase'.[4] But the 'Guide Business' had come to stay, and Peter Crosthwaite, proprietor of the museum at Keswick, warned Plumptre that any sign-boards, a rather simpler solution, he might put up, would be immediately pulled down by the local men who were by now only too well aware of the financial possibilities of gullible tourists.

While the circuit of West's stations round the hillsides offered the delightful prospect of a succession of panoramic views, an excursion by water presented an alternative attraction, that of hearing the echo resound from rock to rock 'in a sort of aerial perspective', as Gilpin put it. Fleets of boats stood ready at Derwentwater and Ullswater, equipped with brass cannon fitted on swivels, and French horns had been installed at vantage points along the shore. At Lodore it cost 1s. 6d. a time to hear the cannon fired, but with half a pound of gunpowder put in Plumptre

[1] *A Fortnight's Ramble to the Lakes in Westmorland, Lancashire and Cumberland*, London, 1792, *231*.
[2] *Tour . . . 1798, 134*.
[3] *A Companion and Useful Guide to the Beauties of Scotland, to the Lakes of Westmorland, Cumberland and Lancashire*, London, 1799, *18*.
[4] Camb. Univ. Lib. Add. MSS. 5816, f. 25.

reckoned it was well worth while. Gilpin, as always, wrote of his
expedition in terms of a profoundly moving aesthetic experience.
'The grandest effect of this kind is produced by a *successive* discharge of cannon; at the interval of a few seconds between each
discharge. . . . Such a variety of awful sounds, mixing and com-
mixing, and at the same moment heard from all sides, have a
wonderful effect on the mind: as if the very foundations of every
rock on the lake were giving way; and the whole scene, from some
strange convulsion, were falling into general ruin.' But while the
cannon provided 'the music only of thunder', the French horns
gave forth 'a *continuation* of musical echoes; which reverberating
around the lake, are exquisitely melodious in their several grada-
tions; and form a thousand symphonies; playing together from
every part. The ear is not equal to their innumerable combinations.
It listens to a symphony dying away at a distance; when other
melodious sounds arise close at hand.'[1] With a greater zest and
more unsophisticated enjoyment William Hutchinson described
how he was rowed out in barges 'sent there for pleasuring' by the
Duke of Portland, and how, while they enjoyed their noonday
repast, they were regaled with explosions from the six brass
cannon mounted in swivels with which the boat was provided.

> The sound, repeated like a peal of thunder bursting over our heads,
> continued for several seconds, flying from haunt to haunt, till
> once more it gradually declined. At intervals we were relieved
> from this entertainment, which consisted of a kind of wondrous
> tumult and grandeur of confusion, by the music of two French
> horns whose harmony was repeated from every recess which echo
> haunted on the borders of the Lake;—here the breathings of the
> organ were imitated, there the bassoon with clarinets;—in this
> place from the harsher sounding cliffs, the cornet—in that from
> the wood creek, amongst the caverns and the trilling water falls,
> you seemed to hear the soft-toned lute accompanied with the
> languishing strains of enamoured nymphs whilst in the copse and
> groves was still retained the music of the horns.[2]

Adam Walker chose to make his excursion by moonlight, which
naturally encouraged yet greater flights of fantasy. Embarking on

[1] *Observations, Relative Chiefly to Picturesque Beauty, Made in the Year 1772,
on several Parts of England; particularly to the Mountains and Lakes of Cumberland and Westmorland*, London, 1786, II, 60-2.
[2] *An Excursion to the Lakes in Westmorland and Cumberland in August 1773*
London, 1776, 70.

the 'glassy bosom of the lake', ordering the horns to play at intervals, he asked himself, as he rested on his oars: 'Is it a Choir of Angels ascending and descending? Is it a fairy-ground realized? Or an Arabian Nights Entertainment?'[1] 'No consideration should have induced me to repeat the experiment', exclaimed Henry Kett, in a refreshing outburst of obviously genuine feeling, 'the noise was so tremendous, harsh and jarring as to confound all the senses!'

Already by the 1790's all this was beginning to verge on crude commercialization. Peter Crosthwaite at Keswick sold prints and guide-books, made a path to the top of Latrigg, and cut steps in the rocks for the convenience of tourists visiting Scale Force. Few tourists missed seeing his museum which he described in the handbills he circulated to advertise it as the largest house in town. He had glasses fixed in every direction to show him people passing in the street, and he greeted his visitors as they entered with a burst of music. He presented for their inspection an amazing collection of antiquities and curiosities. A Roman altar headed Kett's list, 'an inscription concerning its genuineness I had some doubts—a sword—and spurs—a petrified bamboo—very perfect, found in Cumberland—a species of euphorbium, indigenous in the East Indies and Africa—a petrifaction found in Lancashire—the Gom Gom of terrific sound', and so on.[2] 'More of gimcracks than antiquities', remarked Grant rather censoriously, though he could not deny how delighted he was by 'a number of little reeds, fixed to the foot of a window-sash, through each of which, by applying your eye, you are directed to principal objects at stations on the lake'.[3] As they left to the strains of valedictory music many must have reflected, with Joseph Budworth, that this was a shilling well spent—and indeed it was likely to prove an investment for the rest of their stay since Crosthwaite never allowed any of his visitors to pass his museum again without striking up a tune of acknowledgement.

With such an influx of tourists it was inevitable that inns should begin to put up their prices and that a place such as Keswick, which Hutchinson could describe in 1773 as a mean village without any apparent trade, should be growing into a prosperous

[1] *Remarks made on a Tour from London to the Lakes*, London, 1792, *101–2*.
[2] *Tour . . . 1798, 142.*
[3] 'A London Journal of a Three Weeks Tour in 1797 through Derbyshire to the Lakes', Mavor, *British Tourists*, London, 1809, IV, *281.*

small town. 'Moderation is changed into extortion', wrote Plumptre angrily at Ambleside in 1799 on learning that a wealthy gentleman and his wife from London, sooner than not have everything they wanted, were quite prepared to pay twopence for an egg. 'The diversions of Newmarket are introduced', said Gilpin, his tone for once that of the country parson rather than the prophet of the Picturesque. 'Diversions, one would imagine, more foreign to the nature of this country than any other. A number of horses are carried into the middle of a lake in a flat boat. A plug is drawn from the bottom; the boat sinks, and the horses are left floating on the surface. In different directions they make to land; and the horse which soonest arrives secures the prize.'[1] This admittedly was a particularly crude example, but such regattas and carnivals were fast becoming a regular feature of the Lakes at this time. Well might Plumptre sigh for the days when Vicar's Island on Derwentwater was still corn land with a grove of sycamores, before Mr. Pocklington began to 'improve' it. He, poor man, was condemned out of hand by every tourist who took a pleasure in hurling insults at the head of anyone who could so break the canons of all good taste as to cover his island with such childish monstrosities as a boat-house built to look like a chapel, a Druid circle, a fake church and a fort fitted with cannon. 'Card-buildings of showy hue, tricked out and dizened,' declared Grant, failing, as did all his fellow tourists, to recognize that Pocklington was doing no more than they were doing themselves, merely showing an exuberant enjoyment about it, far removed from the self-conscious and conventional attitudes which governed their own behaviour. When Plumptre satirized Miss Beccabunga Veronica dressing to play her role of a Laker he was in some measure satirizing this self-conscious attitude adopted by so many tourists as part of the whole art of touring the Lakes. A riding-habit would be most inappropriate for the ascent of Skiddaw, she decided, though a Scotch plaid might be possible. 'I have negligently bound up my hair in a silk net, and suffered some tresses to escape to play upon my neck and round my countenance. And then the light drapery of my dress, my straw hat, the veil partially concealing my face, my figure, and my hair, are what might, I think, be copied for a Grecian nymph. . . . It will accord with the scenery round Derwent-water; I shall

[1] *Observations . . . 1772*, II, 68–9.

appear like the Naiad of Lowdore, or the nymph of Borrowdale. . . .'[1]

The tourists' whole approach to the Lakes was dominated by
their determination to see the landscape in pictorial terms or
translated into a canvas of its most appropriate artist. Thus Dr.
Brown had abandoned any attempt to describe Keswick, saying it
would require the united powers of Claude, Salvator and Poussin:
'The first should throw his delicate sunshine over the cultivated
vales, the scattered cots, the groves, the lake and wooded islands.
The second should dash out the horror of the rugged cliffs, the
steeps, the hanging woods; the foaming waterfalls; while the
grand pencil of Poussin should crown the whole with the Majesty
of the impending mountains.' Hutchinson did the same for the
district as a whole: 'The paintings of POUSSIN should describe the
nobleness of HULLS-WATER;—the works of SALVATOR ROSA express
the romantic and rocky scenes of KESWICK;—and the tender and
elegant touches of CLAUDE LORAINE and SMITH pencil forth the
rich variety of WINDERMERE.'[2] But the contemporary topographical artists who actually did attempt such sketches came in
for criticism from the tourists. Although he admitted that the
scenes presented extraordinary difficulty since 'the whole is
sublime and astonishing, but the Parts in general are too ragged
and broken for a Picture,' Adam Walker felt that 'LOUTHERBOURG
has rather given the character of the Country than a Portrait of
its Parts: his blue tints assimilate ill with the black complexion of
these mountains. . . . FARRINGDON has been more faithful, with
less art: his Views make good Prints, but do not give the Character
of the Country. It is difficult to select, where Nature surrounds
you with profusion.'[3] This seems however to have encouraged
rather than deterred the tourists from setting pencil to paper
themselves, and in doing so most of them went to considerable
pains to improve upon nature as Gilpin had taught them they
should. 'If it is not like what it *is*, it is what it *ought* to be',
explained Miss Beccabunga Veronica. 'I have only made it
picturesque. I have only given the hills an Alpine form, and put
some wood where it is wanted, and omitted it where it is not
wanted: and who could put that sham church and that house into

[1] *The Lakers*, 1798, 27.
[2] *Excursion . . . 1773, 182.*
[3] *Observations*, 1791, 78-9.

a picture? It quite *antipathizes*. I don't like such meretricious
ornaments . . . so I have made the church an abbey, the house a
castle, and the battery an hermitage . . .'[1]

Written descriptions presented the tourists with fewer difficulties, for here there was an accepted vocabulary and the right
phrases rose only too readily to their lips. Scenes which were
predominantly great, horrific or sublime lent themselves particularly well to their pens. As she approached the Lakes from
Kendal Mrs. Radcliffe's first impression was 'of simple sublimity,
unmixed with any tint of beauty. The vast, yet narrow, perspective
sweeps in ridges of mountains, huge, barren, and brown, point
beyond point . . .' Ullswater again pleased her for its

> severe grandeur and sublimity; all that may give ideas of vast
> power and astonishing majesty. The effect of Ullswater is that,
> awful as its scenery appears, it awakens the mind to expectation
> still more awful, and, touching all the powers of imagination,
> inspires that 'fine phrensy' description of the poet's eye. . . . The
> abrupt and tremendous height of its rocks, the dark and crowding
> summits of the fells above, the manner in which they enclose it,
> together with the dignity of its breadth, empower it constantly to
> effect the mind with emotions of astonishment and lofty expectation.

Borrowdale gorge was well calculated to instil in the tourist a
sense of gloomy terror. 'Dark rocks yawn at its entrance, terrific
as the wildness of a maniac; and disclose a narrow pass, running up between mountains of granite, that are shook into
almost every possible form of horror. All above resembles the
accumulations of an earthquake; splintered, shivered, piled,
amassed.'[2] 'Borrowdale Fells are an indescribable scene', wrote
Grant before launching himself into a melodramatic account of
them. 'Nature reigns in primeval horror. We only penetrated as
far as Bowdar stone, a prodigious rock, which has either been
there immovable since the deluge, or hurled down by some storm,
or convulsion of the earth. Looking from thence up the dell, we
see nothing but rocks brooding over the path, some of them
naked, and others have parcels of trees among their vents, and
mountains bare and unsearched, crossing each other . . .'[3]

[1] *The Lakers*, 1798, 20–1.
[2] *A Journey made in the Summer of 1794 . . . with Observations During a Tour of the Lakes in Westmorland and Cumberland*, London, 1795, 392–3, 478, 465.
[3] *Three Weeks Tour . . . 1797*, 283–4.

Undoubtedly a sense of imminent danger contributed much to Gilpin's sensations as he passed along Derwentwater under Castellet: 'There is not an idea more tremendous than that of riding along the edge of a precipice, unguarded by any parapet, under impending rocks; which threaten from above; while the surges of a flood, or the whirlpools of a rapid river, terrify below.' Although he was in fact never more than thirty or forty feet above the water he could still congratulate himself on his safe passage. 'As we edge the precipices, we every where saw fragments of rock, large stones scattered about, which being loosened by frosts and rains, had fallen from the cliffs above; and show the traveller what dangers he has escaped.' A favourite word of his when writing of such scenes of terror and grandeur was 'desolation'. Thus from the summit of a steep hill above Rydal he found displayed 'a prospect of desolation in a very dignified form. It was an amphitheatre of craggy mountains, which appeared to sweep round a circumference of thirty miles. . . . The soul involuntarily shuddered at the first aspect of such a scene.' A little farther on however this was to be surpassed by his first view of Helvellyn:

> Of all the rude scenery we had yet visited none equalled this in *desolation*. The whole is one immensity of barrenness. The mountains are universally overspread with cragges, and stones, which are sometimes scattered carelessly over their surfaces; and sometimes appear shivering in cascades of crumbling fragments down their sides. . . . These vast regions, whose parts are thus absorbed in the immensity of a whole, have the strongest effect on the imagination. They distend the mind, and fix it in a state of stupor:
>
> > —These lonely regions, where retired
> > From little scenes of art, great Nature dwells,
> > In awful solitude.[1]

'A repetition of the same images of rock, wood and water,' wrote Mrs. Radcliffe in despair, 'and the same epithets of grand, vast and sublime, which necessarily occur, must appear tautologous on paper, though their archetypes in nature, ever varying in outline, or arrangement, exhibit new visions to the eye, and produce new shades of effect on the mind.' At Derwentwater she found herself faced with a peculiarly difficult problem: 'The beauty of its banks contending with the wildness of its rocks, gives opposite impressions to the mind, and the force of each is,

[1] *Observations . . . 1772*, I, *187-9, 163-4, 170-1.*

perhaps, destroyed by the admission of the other. Sublimity can scarcely exist without simplicity; and even grandeur loses much of its elevating effect when united with a considerable portion of beauty; then descending to become magnificence.'[1]

Pastoral scenes were even more confusing, as Gilpin discovered when he came to write about the vale of Lorton near Buttermere:

> No lakes, no rocks are here, to blend the ideas of dignity, and grandeur with that of beauty. All is simplicity and repose. Nature, in this scene, lays totally aside her majestic frown, and wears only a lovely smile. . . . Scenes of this kind (however pleasing) in which few objects occur, either of *grandeur* or *peculiarity* in a singular manner elude the powers of verbal description. They almost elude the power of colours. The soft and elegant form of beauty is hard to hit.[2]

At Windermere, amongst scenes which she considered tame, Mrs. Radcliffe complained that 'even the rocky fells which rise for six miles from the middle of Windermere shore have nothing either picturesque or fantastic in their shape. Their rudeness softens into insignificance when they are seen o'er the wide channel of the lake; they are neither large enough to be grand, or wooded enough to be beautiful . . .' The only way in fact in which she could bring interest to a quiet glade by. Haweswater was to imagine it as it *might* have been: 'So sequestered and gloomily overshadowed, that one almost expected to see the venerable arch of a ruin, peeping between the branches. It was the very spot, which the founder of a monastery might have chosen for his retirement, where the chantings of a choir might have mingled with the soothing murmur of the stream, and monks have glided beneath the solemn trees in garments scarcely distinguishable from the shades themselves.'[3]

Waterfalls ranked high among the aesthetic pleasures of the Lakes, and any real connoisseur took good care to organize the time of his visit correctly. While some pleased Plumptre best on a fine hot day when he found them refreshing with their shades and soothing noise, he thought Rydal should be seen after a storm, though he clearly regarded this as a sophisticated view, only to be fully appreciated by those far advanced in a taste for the Picturesque. The very words Hutchinson used to describe

[1] *Journey . . . 1794*, 419, 450-1.
[2] *Observations . . . 1772*, II, 7-9.
[3] *Journey . . . 1794*, 473, 404.

the waterfall at Ambleside seemed to have acquired something of
the breathlessness of the waters themselves:

> A craggy rock threw it into two branches, foaming and making a
> horrid noise; but it soon united again, and from then precipitated
> into a deep and dreary gulph . . . from whence it dashed through a
> rough and craggy channel down to the town of Ambleside with a
> mighty sound which shook the air as to give a sensible agitation
> to the nerves, like the effect of a thunder-clap. . . . It was almost
> impossible for the steadiest eye to look upon this waterfall without
> giddiness.[1]

But the greatest experience which the Lakes could offer was
reserved for those tourists who were prepared to climb one of the
peaks, an enterprise fraught with no little danger.

> 'Which way to Watenlath?' said one of our company to a peasant,
> as we left the vale of Borrodale. 'That way,' said he, pointing up
> a lofty mountain, steeper than the tiling of a house. To those who
> are accustomed to mountains, these perpendicular motions may
> be amusing: but to us, whose ideas were less elevated, they seemed
> rather peculiar. . . . To move upwards, keeping a steady eye on the
> objects before us, was no great exercise to the brain: but it rather
> gave it a rotation to look back on what was past—and to see our
> companions below *clinging*, as it appeared, to the mountain's side;
> and the rising breasts and bellies of their horses, straining up a
> path so steep, that it seemed, as if the least false step would have
> carried them rolling many hundred yards to the bottom.[2]

Mrs. Radcliffe's classic account of her ascent of Skiddaw must
rank among the finest pieces of such writing:

> A narrow path now wound along steep green precipices, the beauty
> of which prevented what danger there was of being perceived. . . .
> As we ascended Derwentwater dwindled on the eye to the small-
> ness of a pond, while the grandeur of its amphitheatre was
> increased by new ranges of dark mountains, no longer individually
> great, but so from accumulation; a scenery to give ideas of the
> breaking up of a world. Other precipices soon hid it again, but
> Bassenthwaite continued to spread immediately below us, till we
> turned into the heart of Skiddaw, and were inclosed by its steeps.
> We had now lost all track even of the flocks that were scattered
> over these tremendous wilds. The guide conducted us by many
> curvings among the heathy hills and hollows of the mountain;

[1] *Excursion . . . 1773, 170–2.*
[2] *Observations . . . 1772*, I, 207.

but the ascents were such, that the horses panted in their slowest walk, and it was necessary to let them rest every six or seven miles. . . . Sometimes we looked into tremendous chasms, where the torrent, heard roaring long before it was seen, had worked itself into a deep channel, and fell from ledge to ledge, foaming and shining amidst the dark rock. The streams are sublime from the length and precipitancy of their course, which, hurrying the sight with them into the abyss, act, as it were, in sympathy upon the nerves, and, to save ourselves from following, we recoil from the view with involuntary horror. . . . About a mile from the summit the way was indeed dreadfully sublime, laying, for nearly half a mile along the ledge of a precipice that passed with a swift descent, for probably near a mile, into a glen within the heart of Skiddaw. . . . How much too did simplicity increase the sublime of this scenery, in which nothing but mountain, heath and sky appeared. But our situation was too critical, or too unusual, to permit the just impressions of such sublimity. The hill rose so closely above the precipice as scarcely to allow for a ledge wide enough for a single horse. We followed the guide in silence, and, till we regained the more open wild, had no leisure for exclamation.[1]

After making an almost equally dramatic ascent Hutchinson and his party found the air on the summit:

remarkably sharp and thin compared with that from which we passed in the valley; and respiration seemed to be performed with a kind of asthmatic oppression. . . . Our guide was very earnest with us to quit the mountain, as he prognosticated a storm was collecting, and we should be in danger of being wet, or in hazard of losing our way in the heavy vapour which he assured us would soon cover Skiddaw;—the circumstances was too singular to be left by people curious in their observations on natural events; we desired our guide would take care of himself, and leave us to our pleasure, but the good attendant had a due sense of our impropriety in wishing to be left there, and determined to abide by us.

A moment later they found themselves totally surrounded by mist, looking down upon 'an angry and impetuous sea, hearing its billows, as if boiling from the bottom' and while they were rejoicing in this grand spectacle of nature a violent clap of thunder stunned their senses, the mountains seemed to tremble, and the clouds were instantly illuminated with streams of lightning. 'Our guide laid upon the earth terrified and amazed, in his ejaculations accusing us of presumption and impiety;—danger

[1] *Journey . . . 1794, 454–9.*

made us solemn indeed, we had no where to fly for safety, no place to cover our heads; to descend was to rush into the very inflammable vapour from whence our perils proceeded, to stay was equally hazardous.' When the storm eventually turned away from them they were able to return to despised Keswick, wet and fatigued, and only too thankful to reach a town which now seemed like paradise.[1] Adam Walker and his friends however were bitterly disappointed on climbing Skiddaw that their prayer for a storm of thunder and lightning was not answered, though they did at least have the satisfaction of firing off a gun and hearing its reverberation continuing for twenty seconds, 'thunder in all its horrors', while they drank to their friends in the nether world.

Even on such occasions, when it is quite clear that the tourists were entering into their adventures with a whole-hearted enjoy-ment, they were still seeing the landscape as they had been taught to see it, and writing of it in the terms that they knew were familiar and acceptable. When Wordsworth, hoping to bring others to his own appreciation and understanding of the country-side, insisted that it should be seen for itself, as an organic unity and not as a series of pictorial scenes, he was presenting the tourists with a radically new approach. The Lakes had become stale and stereotyped, reduced to the size of the tourists' minds. Wordsworth's hope was that his *Guide* might encourage 'Habits of more exact and considerate observation than have hitherto been applied to local scenery', and he set the example in his own temperate, almost matter-of-fact, descriptions. The simplicity and directness with which he wrote of a scene which would have sent a tourist of the 1790's into paroxysms of exaggerated delight can be seen in what he said of Loughrigg Tarn near Grasmere. 'It has a margin of green firm meadows, of rocks and rocky woods, a few reeds here, a little company of water-lilies there, with beds of gravel or stone beyond; a tiny stream issuing neither briskly nor sluggishly out of it; but its feeding rills, from the shortness of their course, so small as to be scarcely visible.' Again, of Scafell he wrote: 'I ought to have mentioned that round the top of Scawfell-PIKE not a blade of grass is to be seen. Cushions or tufts of moss, parched and brown, appear between the huge blocks and stones that lie in heaps on all sides to a great distance, like skeletons or bones of the earth not needed at the creation, and there left to

[1] *Excursion . . . 1773, 157.*

be covered with never-dying lichens, which the clouds and dews nourish; and adorn with colours of vivid and exquisite beauty.' He caught the movement of a stormy morning along the shores of Ullswater: 'The wind blew strong, and drove the clouds forward, on the side of the mountain above our heads—two storm-stiffened black yew-trees fixed our notice, seen through or under the edge of, the flying mists,—four or five goats were bounding among the rocks:—the sheep moved about more quietly, or cowered beneath their sheltering places.' Or he could create the very feel of an early autumn morning in a vivid turn of phrase: 'The grass on which we trod, and the trees in every thicket were dripping with melted hoar-frost. We observed the lemon coloured leaves of the birches, as the breeze turned them to the sun, or rather *flash*, like diamonds, and the leafless purple twigs were tipped with globes of shining crystal.'[1]

But before Wordsworth's life was over this freshness was to harden into that seriousness, almost moral earnestness, of the mid-Victorian tourist. The change is reflected in the last edition of his *Guide* which appeared in its final reissue in 1842 with expert geological sections contributed by Sedgwick and botanical lists supplied by John Gough. Here was the fare for the new tourists who left their prosperous middle-class homes and expected their money's worth of good honest scenery, thoroughly documented and without fantasy or extravagance. The hills were no longer an adventure, a discovery. Already Wordsworth was saying of the tourists of his day that 'they deem the district a sort of national property, in which every man has a right and interest who has an eye to perceive and a heart to enjoy'. The Lakes were only setting the pattern which was to be followed elsewhere—stretches of country laid aside, as escape for the town-weary, a reminder of that older world upon which an urban civilization was relentlessly encroaching. Earlier tourists had taken the whole of England for their journeyings, delighting as much in the sight of a field of saffron, a coal-pit blazing on a heath, a Druid circle, a newly installed cotton-mill, a Gothic abbey or a salt-mine. Now the discovery has been made, and that all-embracing curiosity of the earlier tourists has given place to pleasant family expeditions to well-known haunts and carefully preserved beauty-spots.

[1] *A Guide through the District of the Lakes in the North of England, with a Description of the Scenery &c, For the Use of Tourists and Residents,* Kendal, 1835, 74, 155, 162.

BIBLIOGRAPHY

GENERAL

ABBEY, J. R., *Scenery of Great Britain and Ireland in Aquatint and Lithography 1770–1860* (privately printed), London, 1952.

ADDISON, WILLIAM, *English Spas*, London, 1951.

AUBIN, R. A., *Topographical Poetry in XVIIIth Century England*, New York, 1936.

BAYNE-POWELL, ROSAMOND, *Travellers in Eighteenth Century England*, London, 1951.

BURKE, THOMAS, *Travel in England*, London, 1942.
The English Inn, London, 1930.

CLARK, H. F., 'Eighteenth Century Elysiums', *Journal of the Warburg and Courtauld Institutes*, 1943, VI, *165–90*.

FLOWER, ROBIN. 'Laurence Nowell and the Discovery of England in Tudor Times', *Proceedings of the British Academy*, 1935, XXI.

HAY, DENYS (ed.), *The Anglica Historia of Polydore Vergil, A.D. 1485–1537*, Camden Series, 1950, LXXIV.

HUSSEY, CHRISTOPHER, *The Picturesque, Studies in a Point of View*, London, 1927.

KENDRICK, T. D., *British Antiquity*, London, 1950.

KETTON-CREMER, R. W., 'The Tour of Norfolk', *Norfolk Assembly*, London, 1957.

KLINGENDER, FRANCIS G., *Art and the Industrial Revolution*, London, 1947.

LAMBERT, AUDREY M., 'Early Maps and Local Studies', *Geography*, 1956, XLI, *167–77*.

LAMBERT, R. S., *The Fortunate Traveller. A Short History of Touring and Travel for Pleasure*, London, 1950.
(ed.) *The Grand Tour*, London, 1935.

MAXWELL, CONSTANTIA, *The English Traveller in France, 1698–1815*, London, 1932.

MEAD, W. E., *The Grand Tour in the Eighteenth Century*, Boston, Mass., 1914.

MOMIGLIANO, ARNALDO, 'Ancient History and the Historian', *Journal of the Warburg and Courtauld Institutes*, 1950, XIV, Appendix I.

BIBLIOGRAPHY

NICHOLSON, NORMAN, *The Lakers. The Adventures of the First Tourists*, London, 1955.

PARKES, JOAN, *Travel in England in the Seventeenth Century*, Oxford, 1925.

PIGGOTT, STUART, 'Antiquarian Thought in the Sixteenth and Seventeenth Centuries', *English Historical Scholarship in the Sixteenth and Seventeenth Centuries*, (ed.) L. Fox, Oxford, 1956, *93–115*.
'William Camden and the "Britannia" ', *Proceedings of the British Academy*, 1951, XXXVII.
William Stukeley, an Eighteenth Century Antiquary, Oxford, 1950.

PIMLOT, J. A. R., *The Englishman's Holiday*, London, 1947.

SIMMONS, JACK (ed.), *Journeys in England. An Anthology*, London, 1951.

STOYE, JOHN WALTER, *English Travellers Abroad, 1604–1667. Their Influence in English Society and Politics*, London, 1952.

TEMPLEMAN, WILLIAM D., *The Life and Work of William Gilpin (1724–1804), Master of the Picturesque and Vicar of Boldre*, Illinois, 1939.

THOMSON, GLADYS SCOTT, 'Roads in England and Wales in 1603', *English Historical Review*, 1918, XXXIII, *234–43*.

WILSON, FRANCESCA M., *Strange Island. Britain through Foreign Eyes, 1395-1940*, London, 1955.

TRAVEL LITERATURE

I. SECONDARY AUTHORITIES

ANDERSON, JOHN P., *The Book of British Topography. A classified catalogue of the Topographical Works in the Library of the British Museum relating to Great Britain and Ireland*, London, 1881.

COX, EDWARD GODFREY, *A Reference Guide to the Literature of Travel*, Vol. III, *England*. University of Washington Press, 1949.

FUSSELL, G. E., and GOODMAN, CONSTANCE, 'Travel and Topography in 18th-century England. A Bibliography of Sources for Economic History', *Transactions Bibliographical Society*, 1930, 2nd series, X, *84–103*.

FUSSELL, G. E. and ATWATER, V. G. B., 'Travel and Topography in 17th-century England. A Bibliography of Sources for Economic History', *Transactions Bibliographical Society*, 1933, 2nd series, XIII, *292–311*.

MATTHEWS, WILLIAM, *British Diaries. An Annotated Bibliography of British Diaries written between 1442 and 1942*, University of California Press, 1956.

PONSONBY, ARTHUR, *English Diaries from the XVIth to the XIXth century*, London, 1927.

UPCOTT, WILLIAM, *A Bibliographical Account of the Principal Works relating to English Topography*, 3 vols., London, 1818.

II. PRIMARY SOURCES

AIKIN, ARTHUR, *Journal of a Tour through North Wales and part of Shropshire, with Observations on Mineralogy and other Branches of Natural History*, London, 1797.

A Collection of Welch Tours, or, a Display of the Beauties of Wales, Selected principally from Celebrated Histories and Popular Tours, with occasional remarks, London, 1797.

AIKIN, JOHN, *England Delineated; or, a Geographical Description of every county in England and Wales*, London, 1788.

ANONYMOUS, 'Remarkable things which I observed in my Journey thro' Warwickshire, Derbyshire, Nottinghamshire, Cheshire, Flintshire, etc. Anno 1630', B.M. Harl. 1026, m. 13.

'The Relation of a Journey into the West of England, 1637', B.M. Harl. 6494, ff. 128-40.

Drunken Barnby's Four Journies to the North of England, in Latin and English Metre, 1640.

Tour to the Roman Wall, 1697, Hist. MSS. Comm. 13th Report, Part II, 54-7.

'A Tour in Northern England and Scotland', 1704, MS., National Library of Scotland, 2506.

The Comical Pilgrim's Travels thro' England, Wales, Scotland and Ireland, London, 1722.

A Tour through the whole Island of Great Britain, Divided into Circuits or Journies, Giving a Particular and Diverting Account of Whatever is Curious and Worth Observation, By a Gentleman, London, 1724.

[A Cambridge undergraduate] 'A tour from Cambridge to Halifax and Wakefield, returning via Oxford, Bath and Bristol', 1725, Bath Municipal Libraries MS. 38:43.

A Curious and Diverting Journey through the whole island of Great Britain, London, 1734.

'Tour in the North of England and Scotland', 1739, MS. National Library of Scotland, 2144, 2145.

'Itinerary of a Journey from Cambridge to Suffolk, Norfolk, Lincolnshire and Yorkshire', 1741, B.M. Add. MSS. 38,488, ff. 17b-49.

'Some Observations made in a Journey thro' the Eastern and central counties of England, begun June the 7th and finish'd July the 9th 1742', B.M. Add. MSS. 22,926.

'Tour thro' part of England', 1758, Bodleian MS. Top. gen. e. 52.

'Notes of a tour in Nottinghamshire, Derbyshire, etc. in 1766', B.M. Add. MSS. 6767, f. 58.

'Tour to North Wales July 1768', Bodleian MS. Top. Wales e. 1.

An Excursion to the Lakes in Westmorland and Cumberland, August 1773, London, 1774.

BIBLIOGRAPHY

Letters from Snowdon descriptive of a Tour through the Northern Counties of Wales containing the Antiquities, History and State of the Country; with the Manners and Customs of the Inhabitants, London, 1777.

A Journal of First Thoughts, Observations, Characters, and Anecdotes which Occurred in a Journey from London to Scarborough in 1779, London, 1781.

Viator, a Poem: or, a Journey from London to Scarborough, by way of York, London, 1782.

A Tour in England and Scotland in 1785. By an English Gentleman, London, 1788.

'Travel journal of a half-pay naval officer, June–October 1789', Wigan Public Library, Edward Hall Collection.

'Tour through the Highlands and Lowlands, and to Cambridge in the summer of 1789', National Library of Scotland, M.S. 1080.

A Tour from London to the Lakes made in the Summer of 1791, By a Gentleman, London, 1792.

'Journal of Tours in the Midland and Western Counties of England and Wales in 1794, and in Devonshire in 1803', B.M. Add. MSS. 30.172.

'A Tour to the Lakes thro' Derbyshire to Scotland in 1795', Cardiff Public Library MS. 3.276.

'A Journal to the Isle of Wight &c. 1796', Cardiff Public Library MS. 3.276.

'A Tour through North and South Wales, with an Excursion to Dublin, from Holyhead in the year 1798', Cardiff Public Library MS. 3.276.

A Tour of the River Wye and its Vicinity, enriched with two engravings, London, 1798.

Journal of a Tour to Scarborough in the Summer of 1798, Wisbech, 1798.

'Journal of a Tour of the West of England from Salisbury, Wiltshire, 10th April 1801', Cardiff Public Library MS. 4.367.

'Notes on Tours in the Counties of Nottingham and Derby, 1801, 1802', B.M. Add. MSS. 24,466.

Sketch of a Tour from Lancaster round the Principal Lakes in Lancashire, Cumberland and Westmorland, Carlisle, 1803.

Observations, chiefly Lithological, made in a Five Weeks Tour to the Principal Lakes in Westmorland and Cumberland, London, 1804.

A Tour in Quest of Genealogy, through several parts of Wales, Somersetshire and Wiltshire, in a Series of Letters to a Friend in Dublin. By a Barrister, London, 1811.

'A Lady's Summer Driving Tour in North Wales', 1811, Cardiff Public Library MS.

A Tour through England described in a Series of Letters from a Young Gentleman to his Sister with copper plates, 3rd ed. revised, London, 1811.

'A Tour from Suffolk to Wales and the Lake District, and back through Derby, 1812', John Rylands Library, Manchester, English MSS. 421.

'A Tour from Glasgow to the Lake District and the North of England', 1813, National Library of Scotland, MS. 3382.

'Tour to Cambridge, Norwich and Ipswich in the summer of 1815', Bodleian MS. Top. gen. e. 72, 81, and 108.

'A Tour in Glamorganshire and Monmouthshire', 1823, Cardiff Public Library MS.

Journal of Excursions through the most interesting Parts of England, Wales and Scotland, during the summers and autumns of 1819, 1820, 1821, 1822 and 1823, London, 1824.

'A Tour into North Wales via mid Wales', 1825, Cardiff Public Library MS.

Travels in England and Wales, compiled from the most Authentic and Recent Authorities, Dublin, 1825.

Picturesque Tour of the River Thames, illustrated by 24 coloured views', London, 1828.

'A Tour from Tottenham, Middlesex, to Scotland, the Lakes and Derbyshire', 1829–30, St. Andrews University Library MS. DA 627 J7 E29.

'A Tour of Southern England and Wales', 1833, Wigan Public Library, Edward Hall Collection.

AYTON, RICHARD, *A Voyage round Great Britain undertaken in the Summer of the year 1813, and commencing from Land's End Cornwall, with a series of Views illustrative of the Character and Prominent Features of the Coast drawn and engraved by William Daniell A.R.A.*, 2 vols., London, 1814.

BAINES, EDWARD, *A Companion to the Lakes of Cumberland, Westmorland and Lancashire in a Descriptive Account of a Family Tour*, London, 1829.

BAKER, J., *A Picturesque Guide through Wales and the Marches Dedicated by Permission to His Royal Highness the Prince of Wales and countenanced by the Principal Nobility &c. of that Principality*, London, 1794.

BANKS, SIR JOSEPH, 'Journals of Excursions to Eastbury and Bristol, etc.', 1767–8, Camb. Univ. Lib. Add. MSS. 6294.

BARBER, J. T., *A Tour through South Wales and Monmouthshire: illustrated with a map and twenty views*, London, 1803.

BASKERVILLE, THOMAS, 'Journeys in England temp. Charles II', Hist. MSS. Comm. 13th Report, Part II, *263–314*.

BEATKNIFE, RICHARD (ed.), *The Norfolk Tour, or Traveller's Pocket Companion*, London, 1772.

BENNETT, GEORGE J., *The Pedestrian's Guide through North Wales; a Tour performed in 1837. With 20 etchings by A. Clint*, London, 1838.

BINGLEY, REV. W., *A Tour round North Wales, including its Scenery, Antiquities, Customs and some Sketches of its Natural History; Delineated from two Excursions through all the interesting Parts of that Country, during the Summers of 1798 and 1801*, 2 vols, London, 1804.

BLOME, R., *Britannia: or, a Geographical Description of the Kingdoms of England, Scotland and Ireland*, London, 1673.

BLOOMFIELD, ROBERT, 'Ten days tour in the Wye Valley', August 1807, B.M. Add. MSS. 28,267.

BOOKER, REV. LUKE, *The Springs of Plynlimmon: A Poem (with copious notes) descriptive of Scenery and Circumstances connected with the Severn, the Wye and three Minor Rivers which Emanate from that Noble Mountain*, Wolverhampton, 1834.

BOSTOCK, LAURENCE, 'A short diary of Mr Laur. Bostock's Journey towards Cheshire from 7 of October 1581 to the 16 of November following', B.M. Harl. MSS. 2113 H9.

BRAY, REV. WILLIAM, 'Tour through some parts of the Midland Counties into Derbyshire and Yorkshire performed in 1777', W. Mavor, *British Tourists*, London, 1809, II, 207–57.

BRERETON, OWEN SALUSBURY, 'Observations in a Tour through South Wales, Shropshire, etc. 1775', *Archaeologia*, III, 111–17.

BRERETON, SIR WILLIAM, *Travels in Holland, the United Provinces, England, Scotland and Ireland, 1634–1635*, (ed.) Edward Hawkins, Chetham Society, 1894.
'Notes of a Journey through Durham and Northumberland in the year 1635', *Reprints of Rare Tracts and Imprints of Ancient MSS*, (ed.) M. A. Richardson, Newcastle, 1844.

BROME, JAMES, *Travels over England, Scotland and Wales, Giving a True and Exact Description of the Chiefest Cities, Towns and Corporations*, London, 1700.

BROOKE, CHARLOTTE, *A Dialogue between a Lady and her Pupils, describing a Journey thro' England and Wales*, 3rd ed., considerably enlarged by Rev. J. Evans, London, 1812.

BROWN, JOHN, *Description of the Lake and Vale of Keswick*, Newcastle, 1767.

BROWNE, DR. EDWARD, 'Notes taken in a tour through the West of England 1662', B.M. Sloane MSS. 1900, ff. 59–63.

BROWNE, DRS. E. and T., *Journal of Edward and Thomas Browne's Tour into Derbyshire in 1662, Sir Thomas Browne's Works, including his life and correspondence*, (ed.) Simon Wilkin, 1836, Vol. I.

BIBLIOGRAPHY

BROWNE, DR. THOMAS, 'Account of Dr. Thomas Browne's journey into Kent with Dr. Plot, August 1693', B.M. Sloane MSS. 1899, ff. 89–120.

BUDWORTH, JOSEPH, *A Fortnight's Ramble to the Lakes in Westmorland, Lancashire and Cumberland, By a Rambler*, London, 1792.

BURTON, JOHN, 'A Traveller's Reveries, or Journey thro' Surrey and Sussex, prefaced by a Critical Epistle in certain instruction of the Greek Language', B.M. Add. MSS. 11,571.

BURTON, THE HON. —, 'A Tour of England 1759', Royal Irish Academy, Dublin, MS. S.R. 12 F 15.

BUTCHER, E., *An Excursion from Sidmouth to Chester in the Summer of 1803, in a Series of Letters to a Lady*, London, 1805.

BYNG, THE HON. JOHN, *The Torrington Diaries. Tours made between the years 1781 and 1794*, (ed.) C. Bruyn Andrews, 4 vols., London, 1934–8.
The Torrington Diaries, A Selection from the Tours made between the years 1781 and 1794, (ed.) C. Bruyn Andrews, abridged Fanny Andrews, London, 1954.

CAMPBELL, ALEXANDER, *A Journey from Edinburgh through parts of North Britain*, 2 vols., London, 1802.

CLARKE, EDWARD DANIEL, *A Tour through the South of England, Wales and Part of Ireland, made during the Summer of 1791*, London, 1793.

CLARKE, JAMES, *A Survey of the Lakes of Cumberland, Westmorland and Lancashire; together with an Account, Historical, Topographical and Descriptive, of the adjacent country*, London, 1787.

CLERK, JOHN, 'Eight days tour in the West Country', 1779, St. Andrews University Library MS. DA 855.C.6.

CLUTTERBUCK, ROBERT, 'Journal of a Tour from Cardiff, Glamorganshire, through South & North Wales in the summer of 1794', Cardiff Public Library MS. 3.277.
'Journal of a Tour through the North of England & part of Scotland during the summer of 1795', Cardiff Public Library MS. 3.277.
'Journal of a Tour through the Western Counties of England during the summer of 1796', Cardiff Public Library MS. 3.277.
'Journal of a Summer Excursion to the Iron Works at Merthyr Tidvil, Glam., Aberdare, Port Neath Fechan, Neath, Pyle, and Cowbridge from Cardiff A.D. 1799', Cardiff Public Library MS. 3.277.

COBBETT, WILLIAM, *Rural Rides in the Counties of Surrey, Kent, Sussex, Hampshire etc. with Economical and Political Observations relative to matters applicable to, and illustrated by, the state of those counties respectively*, London, 1830.

COBBOLD, MRS., 'Tour in the Lake District, 1795', B.M. Add. MSS. 19,203, ff. 78–90.

163

COLE, REV. WILLIAM, *A Tour with Walpole 1763, Horace Walpole's Correspondence*, (ed.) W. S. Lewis, Yale, 1941, Appendix IV.

COLERAINE, HENRY HARE, 3rd Baron, 'Travel diary 1739', Hist. MSS. Comm. Portland, VI, 70.

COLERIDGE, S. T., *Diary of a Tour to the Lake District October–November 1799, Wordsworth and Coleridge* (ed.) Earl Leslie Griggs, Princeton & Oxford, 1939, *135–65*.

COLLETT, ELIZABETH, 'Three weeks tour from London, 1783', Typescript ed. Henry Collett, Bath Municipal Library.

COLMAN, GEORGE, *A Tour to the North of England in 1775, Memoirs of the Colman Family*, 1841, I, *345–86*.

COMPTON, THOMAS, *The Northern Cambrian Mountains, or, a Tour through North Wales, Describing the Scenery and General Characters of that Romantic Country and embellished with a series of highly-finished Coloured Views, from original drawings*, London, 1817.

CRADOCK, JOSEPH, *Letters from Snowdon: descriptive of a Tour through the Northern Counties of Wales*, London, 1770.
An Account of some of the most Romantic Parts of North Wales, London, 1777.

CREWE, LADY FRANCES ANNE, 'A Tour to North Wales 1795', B.M. Add. MSS. 37,926.

CROMWELL, T. K., *Excursions through England and Wales, Scotland and Ireland*, London, 1818–22.

CRUTTWELL, REV. CLEMENT, *A Tour through the Whole Island of Great Britain, Divided into Journeys interspersed with useful observations and maps*, 6 vols., 1801.

CULLUM, SIR JOHN, 'Journal of a tour to Yorkshire, returning via Manchester, Nottingham, Derby, 1771', Bury St. Edmunds and West Suffolk Record Office, E2/44/1.
'Tour through Several Counties of England and Part of North Wales, 1774', Bury St. Edmunds and West Suffolk Record Office, E2/44/2.1–2.3.
'Tour in the West of England, 1779', Bury St. Edmunds and West Suffolk Record Office, E2/33/2.
'Tour in Wales, returning via Shrewsbury, Lichfield, Leicester etc', N.D., Bury St. Edmunds and West Suffolk Record Office E2/44/5.

CULLUM, SUSANNA, 'Journey from Bury St. Edmunds to Normanton, Yorks, 1799', Bury St. Edmunds and West Suffolk Record Office E2/44/62.
'Journeys Peterborough to Ely, and London, 1800 and 1801', Bury St. Edmunds and West Suffolk Record Office, E2/44/65, 66.

CULLUM, REV. SIR THOMAS GERY, 'Tours in Wales, 1775 and 1811', *Y Cymmrodor* (1927), XXXVIII, *45–59, 60–78*.

'Tour in Devonshire and the West Country 1789', Bury St. Edmunds and West Suffolk Record Office, E2/44/6.

'Tour from Cheltenham to Cardiff via Tenby, 1811', Bury St. Edmunds and West Suffolk Record Office, E2/44/49, 50.

DALE, SAMUEL, 'Journeys from Braintree to Cambridge, 1722–1738', Camb. Univ. Lib. Add. MSS. 3466.

DANIELL, W., *A Voyage round Great Britain, undertaken in the Summer of the year 1813 and commencing from Land's End*', Cornwall, 1814.

DANVERS, CHARLES, 'Tours in the West of England and the Lake District, 3–13 Oct. 1795; 2 July–16 Aug. 1805; 14–23 July 1812', B.M. Add. MSS. 30,929.

DAVIDSON, G. H., *The Thames and Thanet Guide, and Kentish Tourist; containing the History and Description of every place and object between London Bridge and Ramsgate Harbour*, 3rd ed., London, 1838.

DEFOE, DANIEL, *A Tour through England and Wales*, (ed.) G. D. H. Cole, 2 vols., London, 1928.

DENHOLM, JAMES, *A Tour to the Principal Scotch and English Lakes*, Glasgow, 1804.

DENNIS, ALEXANDER, *Journal of a Tour through great part of England and Scotland in the year 1810*, Cornwall, 1816.

DIBDIN, CHARLES, *Observations on a Tour through almost the Whole of England and a Considerable part of Scotland in a series of letters addressed to a large number of Intelligent and Respectable Friends*, 2 vols., London, 1801–2.

DODD, JOHN, 'Journal of a Tour through England, 1735', B.M. Add. MSS. 5957.

DONOVAN, EDWARD, *Descriptive Excursions through South Wales and Monmouthshire, in the year 1804 and the four preceding summers*, 2 vols., London, 1805.

DUGDALE, SIR WILLIAM, 'Things observable in our Itinerarie begun from London, 19 May 1657', B.M. Lans. MS. 722, ff. 29–38.

'Observacouns in my Fen Journey begun 19 May 1657', Bodleian MS. Ashmole 7841.

DUNSFORD, M., *Miscellaneous Observations in the Course of Two Tours through Several Parts of the West of England*, Tiverton, 1800.

EDWARDS, J., *A Companion from London to Brightelmstone*, 1801.

EDWARDS, JOHN, *The Tour of the Dove, a Poem*, London, 1821.

EVANS, REV. JOHN, *A Tour through Part of North Wales in the Year 1798 and at other Times; principally undertaken with a View to Botanical Researches in that Alpine Country*, London, 1800.

Circular Tour from Chester through North Wales, London, 1802.

EVANS, JOHN, *The Juvenile Tourist; or, Excursions through various parts*

of Great Britain, illustrated with maps, in a Series of Letters etc., London, 1804.
An Excursion to Windsor in July 1810, through Battersea, Kew etc. Also a Sail down the River Medway, July 1811, from Maidstone to Rochester, London, 1817.

EVANS, THOMAS, *Cambrian Itinerary, Welsh Tourist*, 1801.

FENTON, RICHARD, *Tours in Wales, 1804–1813*, (ed.) John Fowler, London, 1917.
'A tour through Carmarthenshire 1800'; 'A tour through Montgomeryshire 1808'; 'A tour to Anglesea, Carnarvon etc. 1810'; 'A tour to Denbighshire and Montgomeryshire 1810', Cardiff Public Library MSS.

FERRAR, JOHN, *A Tour from Dublin to London in 1795, through the Isle of Anglesea, Bangor, Conway etc.*, Dublin, 1796.

FIELDING, T. H., *A Picturesque Description of the River Wye from the Source to its Junction with the Severn*, London, 1841.

FIENNES, CELIA, *The Journeys of Celia Fiennes*, (ed.) Christopher Morris, London, 1947.

FOLEY, EDWARD W., 'Tour through North and Mid Wales, by E. W. Foley, Ed Cockey and Thomas Green Simcox, July–August 1831'. Wigan Public Library, Edward Hall Collection, M965/EHC 173.

FORD, WILLIAM, *A Description of the Scenery in the Lake District, intended as a guide to strangers, with maps and plans*, Carlisle, 1839.

FORSYTH, J., 'Fragmentary Notes of Journeys through England between 1751 and 1774', Bodleian MS. Top. gen. e. 55.

FOSBROKE, T. D., *The Wye Tour, or Gilpin on the Wye, with Historical and Archaeological additions, especially illustrations of Pope's Man of Ross, and copious accounts of Ross, Goodrich Castle, Monmouth etc.*, Ross, 1818.

FOWKE, RICHARD, 'Journey into Lincolnshire, 1805', *Transactions Leicestershire Archaeological Society*, 1871–4, III, 364–70.

GALE, ROGER, 'Tour through Several Parts of Britain, 1705', J. Nichols (ed.), *Bibliotheca Topographica Britannica*, London, 1790, III.

GILPIN, REV. WILLIAM, *Observations on the River Wye, and Several Parts of South Wales*, 1770, London, 1782.
Observations on Several Parts of England, particularly the Mountains and Lakes of Cumberland and Westmorland, 1772, 2 vols., London, 1786.
Observations on Several Parts of the Counties of Cambridge, Norfolk, Suffolk, and Essex. Also on Several Parts of North Wales, 1769 and 1773, London, 1809.
Observations on the Coasts of Hampshire, Sussex, and Kent, Relative Chiefly to Picturesque Beauty: made in the summer of the year 1774, London, 1804.

Observations on the Western Parts of England . . . to which are added a Few Remarks on the Picturesque Beauties of the Isle of Wight, London, 1798.

GORDON, ALEXANDER, *Itinerarium Septentrionale: or, A Journey thro' most of the Counties of Scotland, and those in the North of England, containing an Account of all the Monuments of Roman Antiquity; also of the Danish Invasions*, London, 1726.

GRANT, MRS. ANNE, *Letters from the Mountains. Being the real correspondence of a Lady between the years 1773 and 1807*, 3 vols., London, 1807.

GRANT, JOHNSON, 'A London Journal of a Three Weeks Tour in 1797 through Derbyshire to the Lakes', W. Mavor, *British Tourists*, London, 1809, IV, *219–92*.

GRAY, JONATHAN, 'A Tour in Wales 1809'; 'A Tour in Wales and the West 1811'; 'Tours in Shropshire, Wales, Lancashire and the Isle of Wight', York Public Library MSS. J14–24; J41–51; J52a; J52b–h; J57–67; J114–15; J143; T/3; T/4.

GRAY, MARGARET, 'Tour to the Isle of Man, 1822'; 'Tour to the Lake District 1823', York Public Library MSS. T/7; T/8.

GRAY, WILLIAM, 'Tour to York, Bath, Derbyshire etc.', York Public Library MSS. T/5.

GRAY, —., 'Journal, in a Letter to Dr. Wharton, October 18th 1769', Thomas West, *Guide to the Lakes*, 2nd ed., London, 1780, *199–224*.

GRIMSTON, SIR HARBOTTLE, 'A Northern Tour from St. Albans, 1768', Hist. MSS. Verulam, *229–42*.

'A Tour in Wales 1769', Hist. MSS. Verulam, *242–83*.

GROSE, FRANCIS, 'Notes and drawings by Francis Grose in a visit to Christ Church, Hants, 1776; in a journey to Monmouthshire and Glamorganshire, through Oxford, Gloucester etc., 1775; a journey into Sussex, and a journey from London to Thetford, 1777', B.M. Add. MSS. 17,398.

'Account of an Antiquarian tour through the counties of Suffolk, Norfolk, Cambridge and Essex, from 10 Sept. to 19 Dec. 1777, with indian ink drawings', B.M. Add. MSS. 21,550.

[HAMMOND] *A Relation of A Short Survey of 26 Counties Observed in a seven weeks Journey begun on August 11, 1634, By a Captain, a Lieutenant, and an Ancient*, (ed.) L. G. Wickham Legg, London, 1904.

A Relation of a Short Survey of the Western Counties made by a Lieutenant of the Military Company in Norwich in 1635, (ed.) L. G. Wickham Legg, Camden Miscellany, 1936, XVI.

HANWAY, JONAS, *A Journal of Eight Days Journey from Portsmouth to Kingston-upon-Thames, through Southampton, Wiltshire, etc., with Miscellaneous Thoughts, Moral and Religious, in Sixty-Four Letters*, 2 vols., London, 1757.

HARLY, ROBERT, 'Notes of a Journey from Kynsham to London, May–June 1680', Bodleian MS. Eng. Misc. f. 52.

HARRAL, THOMAS, *Picturesque Views of the Severn, with Historical and Topographical Illustrations*, 2 vols., London, 1824.

HART, JAMES, 'Travel diary 1714–5, from Edinburgh to London, through York, Lincoln, Cambridge and Oxford', Edinburgh University Library MS. Dc. 7.80.

HASLAM, MISS SARAH, 'Travel journal Aug.–Oct. 1802', Wigan Public Library, Edward Hall Collection, M969 EHC 177.

HASSELL, J., *A Tour of the Isle of Wight*, 2 vols., London, 1790.
Tour of the Grand Junction Canal, illustrated with a series of engravings with an Historical and Topographical description of those parts of the counties of Middlesex, Hertfordshire, Bucks, Beds, and Northamptonshire, through which the canal passes, London, 1819.

HASTED, E., *Tour through the Island of Thanet and some other parts of East Kent*, 1793.

HATFIELD, MARY, 'Tour to London 1791', John Rylands Library, Manchester, Eng. MSS. 1049.

HEAD, SIR GEORGE, *A Home Tour through the Manufacturing Districts of England in the Summer of 1835*, London, 1836.
A Home Tour through various parts of the United Kingdom, Being a Continuation of the 'Home Tour through the Manufacturing Districts of England', London, 1837.

HEATH, CHARLES, *The Excursion down the Wye, from Ross to Monmouth; including Memories of J. Kyrle, Esq. . . . the Man of Ross*, Monmouth, 1800.

HERRING, BISHOP, 'An Account of Two Journies into Wales, 1737 and 1739', *Annual Register*, XVI, 2000–3.

HOARE, SIR RICHARD COLT, 'Tours in South Wales, 1793, 1803', Cardiff Public Library MS. 3.127.
'Tours in North Wales 1796–1810', Cardiff Public Library MS. 3.127.6.
'Northern Tour, 1800', Cardiff Public Library MS. 3.127.5.
'Tour in South Wales, 1801, 1802', Cardiff Public Library MS. 127.2,1.
'Excursions on the Wiltshire Downs, 1807–14', *Wiltshire Archaeological Society*, 1884–5, XXII, 234–8.

HOLLAND, JOHN, *The Tour of the Don. A Series of Extempore Sketches made during a Pedestrian Ramble along the banks of that river and its tributaries*, 2 vols., London, 1837.

HORNE, T. H., *The Lakes of Lancashire, Westmorland and Cumberland, Delineated in 43 Engravings from Drawings by J. Farington. With Descriptions Historical, Topographical and Picturesque*, London, 1816.

HOUSMAN, JOHN, *A Descriptive Tour and Guide to the Lakes, Caves, Mountains and other Natural Curiosities in Cumberland, Westmorland, Lancashire, and a Part of West Riding of Yorkshire*, Carlisle, 1800.

HUCKS, J., *A Pedestrian Tour through North Wales, in a Series of Letters*, London, 1795.

HUTCHINSON, JOHN, *Tour through the High Peak of Derbyshire*, Macclesfield, 1809.

HUTCHINSON, WILLIAM, *An Excursion to the Lakes in Westmorland and Cumberland, August 1773*, London, 1774.

HUTTON, JOHN, *A Tour to the Caves in the Environs of Ingleborough and Settle, in the West Riding of Yorkshire*, 2nd ed., London, 1781.

HUTTON, WILLIAM, *A Journey from Birmingham to London*, Birmingham, 1785.

'Remarks in a Tour through Wales, 1799', *Gentleman's Magazine*, LXIX, *846–50, 925–8.*

Remarks upon North Wales, being the Result of Sixteen Tours through that part of the Principality, Birmingham, 1803.

A Tour to Scarborough in 1803, 2nd ed., London, 1817.

A Trip to Coatham, a Watering-Place in the North Extremity of Yorkshire, London, 1810.

IRELAND, SAMUEL, *Picturesque Views on the River Medway from the Nore to the Vicinity of its Source in Sussex etc.*, London, 1793.

Picturesque Views on the Upper or Warwickshire Avon, from its Source at Naseby to its Junction with the Severn at Tewkesbury, London, 1795.

Picturesque Views on the River Wye, from its Source at Plinlimmon Hill, to its Junction with the Severn below Chepstow. With Observations on the Public Buildings in its Vicinity, London, 1797.

JOHNSON, SAMUEL, *A Diary of a Journey into North Wales in 1774*, (ed.) R. Duppa, London, 1816.

JOLLIE, *Jollie's Cumberland Guide & Directory: containing a Descriptive Tour etc.*, Carlisle, 1811.

JONES, CAPT. JENKIN, R.N., 'Tour in England and Wales, May–June 1819', *Transactions of the Historical Society of West Wales*, 1911, I, *97–144.*

KEATE, GEORGE, *Sketches from Nature: Taken and Coloured in a Journey to Margate*, 2 vols., London, 1779.

KETT, HENRY, 'A Tour to the Lakes of Cumberland and Westmorland in August 1798', W. Mavor, *British Tourists*, London, 1809, V, *118–57.*

KING, PETER, 'A Journey from London to Dublin, August 1789–January 1790', Manx Museum, Douglas, Isle of Man, MS. 262.

KIRK, THOMAS, 'Journeyings through Northumberland and Durham anno Dom. MDCLXXVII', *Reprints of Rare Tracts and Imprints of Ancient MSS.* (ed.) M. A. Richardson, Newcastle, 1844.

KITCHINIR, WILLIAM, M.D., *The Traveller's Oracle, or, Maxims for Location, containing Precepts for Promoting the Pleasures and Hints for Preserving the Health of Travellers,* 2 vols., London, 1827.

LAMBARDE, WILLIAM, *Perambulation of Kent,* London, 1576.

LAUDER, SIR JOHN, *Notes of Journeys in London, Oxford and Scotland 1667–1670, Journals of Sir John Lauder,* (ed.) Donald Crawford, Edinburgh, 1900, *167–205.*

LEEDS, FRANCIS GODOLPHIN OSBORNE, Fifth Duke of, 'Tour to the West 1791, accompanied by the Duchess and others', B.M. Add. MSS. 28,570, ff. 38–54.

LEIGH, EDWARD, *England Described; or, the Several Counties and Shires thereof briefly Handled. Some things also Promised, to Set Forth the Glory of this Nation,* London, 1659.

LELAND, JOHN, *The Itinerary of John Leland in or about the years 1535–1543,* (ed.) Lucy Toulmin-Smith, 5 vols., London, 1907–10.

LE NEVE, PETER, 'An Essay towards the Direction of Sir John Percivale Bart. in his Travells thro' the Countys of Essex, Suffolk, Norfolk and Cambs, June 1701', B.M. Add. MSS. 27,989, ff. 49–122.

LIPSCOMB, GEORGE, *A Journey into Cornwall from Hampshire through the Counties of Southampton, Wilts, Dorset, Somerset and Devon,* Warwick, 1799.
A Journey into South Wales, through the Counties of Oxford, Warwick, Worcester, Hereford, Salop, Stafford, Buckingham and Hertford, in 1799, London, 1802.

LOVEDAY, JOHN, *Diary of a Tour in 1732 through Parts of England, Wales, Ireland ond Scotland, ed. by his grandson,* Roxburghe Club, London, 1889.

LYTTLETON, LORD GEORGE, 'An Account of a Journey into Wales in Two Letters to Mr Bower', *Annual Register,* 1774, XVII, *160–4.*

MACKAY, CHARLES, *The Thames and its Tributaries; or, Rambles among the Rivers,* 2 vols., London, 1840.

MACKEY, —., 'Mr Mackey's original M.S. of his Journey through Worcestershire and other Counties, given to Mr Warburton by Captain Berkeley', B.M. Lans. MS. 825, 179–84.

MACKY, JOHN, *A Journey through England. In Familiar Letters from a Gentleman here to a Friend Abroad,* 2 vols., London, 1722–3.

MACRITCHIE, REV. WILLIAM, *Diary of a Tour through Great Britain in 1795,* London, 1797.

MALCOLM, J. P., *Excursions in Kent, Gloucestershire, Herefordshire Monmouthshire and Somersetshire made in the Years 1802, 1803 and 1805; Illustrated by Descriptive Sketches of the most Interesting*

Places and Buildings in those Counties, and Delineations of Character in Different Ranks of Life, London, 1807.

MALKIN, B. H., *The Scenery, Antiquities, and Biography of South Wales, from Materials Collected during Two Excursions in the year 1804. With Views*, London, 1804.

MANNERS, JOHN HENRY, Duke of Rutland, *A Journal of Three Years' Travels through different Parts of Great Britain in 1795, 1796, and 1797*, 3 vols., London, 1805.
A Journal of a Tour to the Northern Part of Great Britain, London, 1813.

MARRIOTT, J., 'A Journey to London with S. A. Mərriott in Search of Health, accompanied by Louisa and Margaret in Search of Pleasure, and followed by Tom Hobson in Search of his Wife', 1834, Wigan Public Library, Edward Hall Collection, M997/EHC 197.

MASON, J., 'A Tour into the North of England, 1779', Bury St. Edmunds and West Suffolk Record Office, E2/42/5.
'A Western Tour, 1780', Bury St. Edmunds and West Suffolk Record Office, E2/42/5.

MATON, DR. WILLIAM GEORGE, *Observations relative chiefly to the Natural History, Picturesque Scenery and Antiquities of the Western Counties of England, Made in the years 1794 and 1796*, 2 vols., Salisbury, 1797.
A Sketch of a Tour from London to the Lakes made in the Summer of the year 1799.
'Summer tours made in 1799, 1822, 1824, 1826 and 1829', B.M. Add. MS. 32,442–3.

MAVOR, WILLIAM, 'A Tour through Wales in the Summer of 1805', Mavor, *The British Tourists*, London, 1809, V, *149–255*.
The British Tourists; or, Traveller's Pocket Companion through England, Wales, Scotland and Ireland, 6 vols., London, 1798–1810.

MAWMAN, JOSEPH, *An Excursion to the Highlands of Scotland, and the English Lakes, with Recollections, Descriptions and References to Historical Facts*, London, 1805.

MEYRICK, LLEWELLYN, 'Journal of a Tour through part of England and North Wales in the summer of 1821', B.M. Add. MSS. 28,802.

MILLES, REV. JEREMIAH, 'Summer tours to Wales and the Southern Counties, 1735–43', B.M. Add. MSS. 15,776.

MORGAN, MRS., *A Tour to Milford Haven in the year 1791*, London, 1795.

MORRIS, MOULE, 'A three months tour in 1789 from Cambridge to Edinburgh, the Lakes and Dublin', Chetham's Library, Manchester, MS. Mun. A2 34.

MOUNT, —, 'A Tour in Kent, 1759', (ed.) F. Hull, *Archaeologia Cantiana*, 1955, LXIX, *171–8*.

BIBLIOGRAPHY

MUNDY, PETER, *A Petty Progress through England and Wales, and his Tour round the Coast, 1639,* Hackluyt Society, 1925.

MURRAY, THE HON. MRS., *A Companion and Useful Guide to the Beauties of Scotland, to the Lakes of Westmorland, Cumberland, and Lancashire; and to the Curiosities of the District of Craven in the West Riding of Yorkshire,* London, 1799.

NEWELL, REV. R. H., *Letters on Scenery of Wales; including a Series of Subjects for the Pencil, with their Stations determined on a General Principle; and Instructions to Pedestrian Tourists,* London, 1821.

NEWTE, THOMAS, *Prospects and Observations on a Tour in England and Scotland,* London, 1791.

NICHOLS, ANN SUSANNAH, *Journal of a Very Young Lady's tour from Canonbury to Aldborough through Chelmsford . . . and back through Harwich, Sept. 13th–21st 1804,* London, 1804.

OLIVER, PETER, 'Journal of a Voyage to England in 1776, and of a Tour through Part of England', B.M. Eg. MSS. 2672–3.

ORD, CRAVEN, 'Journal of Tours by Craven Ord in the Counties of Norfolk and Suffolk, commenced in 1781 and continued till 1797', B.M. Add. MSS. 14,823.

OXFORD, Second Earl of, 'Journeys in England, 1723–38', Hist. MSS. Comm., Portland, VI, *74–81.*

OXFORD, HENRIETTA CAVENDISH, Countess of, 'Journey through Yorkshire, Durham &c into Scotland in 1745', Hist. MSS. Comm., Portland, VI, *182–91.*

PADMAN, —, 'A few observations made upon Journies taken in the years 1776, 1779, 1781, 1783, 1786, 1790, 1796, 1799 & 1811', Bodleian MS. Top. gen. e. 54.

PARNELL, SIR JOHN, 'Tours through England and Wales, 1769–83', London School of Economics, MS. Coll. Misc. 38.

PATCHING, R., *Four Topographical Letters written in July 1755 upon a Journey through Bedfordshire, Northamptonshire, Leicestershire, Nottinghamshire, Derby and Warwick,* Newcastle, 1757.

'PEDESTRES', *A Pedestrian Tour of Thirteen Hundred and Forty Seven Miles through Wales and England,* 2 vols., London, 1836.

PENNANT, THOMAS, *A Tour in Wales, 1770,* London, 1778.
A Tour from Downing to Alston-Moor, 1773, London, 1801.
A Tour from Alston-Moor to Harrogate and Brimham Crags, 1773, London, 1804.
The Journey to Snowdon, London, 1781.
A Journey from Chester to London, London, 1782.
A Journey from London to the Isle of Wight: Vol. I, *From London to Dover;* Vol. II, *From Dover to Land's End,* London, 1801.

PEPYS, SAMUEL, 'Tour to the West June 4th–17th 1668', *Diary,* (ed.) H. B. Wheatley, London, 1899, VIII, *35–48.*

BIBLIOGRAPHY

PHILLIPS, WILLIAM, 'Account of a Journey made by William Phillips of Broadway, co. Worcester, from Broadway to Manchester and Liverpool, and back; 13–31 May 1792', B.M. Add. MSS. 30,173.

PLAYFAIR, WILLIAM HENRY, 'Notes of a Journey from Edinburgh to Saltcoats, 1811', Camb. Univ. Lib. Add. MSS. 6305.

PLUMPTRE, REV. JAMES, 'A Journal of a Tour through part of North Wales in the year 1792', Camb. Univ. Lib. Add. MSS. 5802.

'A Journal of a Tour into Derbyshire in the year 1793', Camb. Univ. Lib. Add. MSS. 5804.

'A Narrative of a Pedestrian Journey through some parts of Yorkshire, Durham and Northumberland to the Highlands of Scotland, and home by the Lakes and some parts of Wales in the summer of 1799', 3 vols., Camb. Univ. Lib. Add. MSS. 5814–16.

'A Journal of a Tour to the Source of the River Cam made in July 1800 by Walter Blackett Trevilyan Esq. A.B. of St. John's College, and the Revd. James Plumptre A.M. Fellow of Clare Hall, Cambridge', Camb. Univ. Lib. Add. MSS. 5819.

POCOCKE, BISHOP RICHARD, *The Travels through England of Dr. Richard Pococke, successively Bishop of Meath and of Ossory during 1750, 1751, and later years*, (ed.) James Joel Cartwright, 2 vols., Camden Society, 1888 and 1889.

Northern Journey of Bishop Richard Pococke, 1760, North Country Diaries, II, Surtees Society, 1915, CXXIV, *199–253*.

PRATT, SAMUEL JACKSON, Gleanings in England, 3 vols., London, 1804.

PRICE, JOHN, 'Journies in Oxfordshire, Gloucestershire, South Wales, and the Eastern counties, 1760, 1761, 1763', Bodleian MSS. Top. gen. f. 33–4.

PUGH, EDWARD, *Cambria Depicta; a Tour through North Wales, illustrated with Picturesque Views. By a Native Artist*, London, 1816.

QUINCY, THOMAS, *A Short Tour in the Midland Counties of England, performed in the Summer of 1772, with an account of a Similar Excursion undertaken September 1774*, London, 1774.

RADCLIFFE, MRS. ANNE, *A Journey made in the Summer of 1794 through Holland and the Western Frontier of Germany, with a Return down the Rhine, to which are added Observations During a Tour of the Lakes in Westmorland and Cumberland*, London, 1795.

RICHARDS, WILLIAM, *Wallography, or, The Briton Described, being a pleasant Relation of a Journey into Wales, By William Richards, a mighty Lover of Welsh Travels*, London, 1682.

RISTE, GEORGE, 'Journal of a Tour thro' England, 1735', B.M. Add. MSS. 5957, f. 1.

ROBERTSON, ARCHIBALD, *A Topographical Survey of the Great Road from London to Bath and Bristol*, London, 1792.

ROBINSON, JOHN, *A Guide to the Lakes in Cumberland, Westmorland and Lancashire*, London, 1819.

ROGERS, R. [pseudonym of Brome], *An Historical Account of Mr Rogers' Three Years Travels over England and Wales, giving a True and Exact Description of all the chiefest Cities, Towns and Corporations, etc.*, London, 1694.

ROSCOE, THOMAS, *Wanderings and Excursions in North Wales, with 51 engravings by Radclyffe, from drawings by Cattermole, Cox, etc*, London, 1836.
Wanderings and Excursions in South Wales, including the Scenery of the River Wye, 48 engravings by Radclyffe, from drawings by Cox, Harding, etc., London, 1837.

RUTLAND, JOHN HENRY MANNERS, Fifth Duke of, *Journal of a Tour through North and South Wales, the Isle of Man, &c, &c*, London, 1805.
Journal of a Tour round the Southern Coasts of England, London, 1805.
Journal of a Tour to the Northern Parts of Great Britain, London, 1813.
Journal of Three Years' Travels through different parts of Great Britain, in 1795, 6 and 7, 3 vols., London, 1805.

SALMON, N., *A New Survey of England*, 2 vols., London, 1728–9.

SANDERSON, T., *The Companion to the Lakes in Lancashire, Westmorland, and Cumberland*, Carlisle, 1807.

SANDS, W., 'Diary of a journey to Stratford, Oxford, Woodstock, etc. 1832', Birmingham Reference Library, 259856.

SAVAGE, JOHN, 'Tours in Northern England and the West Country, 1767–1794', Typescript, Central Library, Ipswich.

SELWYN, MRS. ELIZABETH, *Journal of Excursions through the most Interesting Parts of England, Wales and Scotland, during the Summers and Autumns of 1819, 1820, 21, 22, & 23*, London, 1824.
Continuation of Journal of Excursions, Kensington, 1830.

SHAW, STEBBING, *A Tour to the West of England in 1788*, London, 1789.

SHEPHARD, CHARLES, 'A Tour through Wales and the Central Parts of England', *Gentleman's Magazine*, 1798, LXVIII, *303–4, 390–2, 486–90, 560–3*; 1799, LXIX, *452–6, 755–8, 851–4, 932–5, 1036–40, 1098–1102*.

SHEPHEARD, FRANCIS, 'Journal of a Tour through England in 1735', B.M. Add. MSS. 5957.

SKINNER, REV. JOHN, 'Copy of a Journal kept by the Rev. John Skinner, of a Tour to Wells, Bridgwater, Taunton, Exeter, Sidmouth, Oakhampton, and in Cornwall from 20 Sept. to 25 Nov. 1797', B.M. Add. MSS. 28,793.
'Tour to the Lakes, 1801', B.M. Add. MSS. 33,639.

'Excursion from Camerton by Sandhurst to London, thence to Peterborough and Lincoln in the Summer of 1825', B.M. Add. MSS. 33,683.

SKRINE, H., *Two Successive Tours throughout the whole of Wales; with several of the Adjacent English Counties, so as to form a Comprehensive View of the Picturesque Beauty, the Peculiar Manners, and the Fine Remains of Antiquity in that interesting part of the British Island*, London, 1798.

Three Successive Tours in the North of England and great part of Scotland; interspersed with Descriptions of the Scenes they Presented, and Occasional Observations on the State of Society and the Manners and Customs of the People, London, 1795.

SMITH, B. P., *A Journal of an Excursion round the South-eastern Coast of England*, London, 1834.

SOMERSET, Duke of, *The Tour of the Duke of Somerset and the Rev. J. H. Michell, through Parts of England, Wales and Scotland, in the Year 1795*, London, 1795.

SOTHEBY, W., *A Tour through Parts of Wales, Sonnets, and Odes, and other Poems. With Engravings from Drawings taken on the spot, by J. Smith*, London, 1794.

SPENCE, ISABELLA E., *Summer Excursions through Parts of Oxfordshire, Gloucestershire, Warwickshire, Staffordshire, Herefordshire, Derbyshire and South Wales*, 2nd ed., London, 1809.

SPENCER, N., *The Complete English Traveller; or, a New Survey and Description of England and Wales*, London, 1771.

STEWART, MRS. T., 'Travel diary July 1813 and July 1814, Durham to Bath and Bath to Weymouth', Wigan Public Library, Edward Hall Collection.

STUKELEY, WILLIAM, *Itinerarium Curiosum, or, an Account of the Antiquitys and Remarkable Curiositys in Nature or Art, Observ'd in Travels thro' Great Britain. Illustrated with Copper Prints, Centuria I*, London, 1724.

'Iter Oxiense May 1730', B.M. Add. MSS. 688.

Iter Boreale, Itinerarium Curiosum, Centuria II, London, 1776.

SULLIVAN, R. J., *Observations made during a Tour through Parts of England, Scotland, and Wales, in a Series of Letters*, London, 1780.

SYKES, SIR CHRISTOPHER, 'Tour in Wales 1791', National Library of Wales, Add. MSS. 2258c.

TAYLOR, JOHN, *Part of this Summers Travels. Or News from Hell, Hull and Hallifax, from York, Linne, Leicester, Chester, Coventry, Lichfield, Nottingham and the Divells Ars, Works of John Taylor the Water Poet*, 1639, Spenser Society, Manchester, 1868.

John Taylors last Voyage, and Adventure Performed from the twentieth of July last 1641 to the tenth of September following. In which time he past, with a Scullers Boate, from the Cittie of London, to the Cities and Townes of Oxford, Gloucester, Shrewsbury, Bristoll, Bathe, Monmouth and Hereford, Works, 2nd Collection, Spenser Society, Manchester, 1869.

Tailors Travels, from London to the Isle of Wight, with his Returne, and Occasion of his Journey, 1648, Works, 4th Collection, Spenser Society, Manchester, 1876.

Wanderings to See the Wonders of the West. How he Travelled neere 600. Miles, from London to the Mount in Cornwall, and beyond the Mount, to the Lands end, and home againe, 1649, London, 1670.

A Short Relation of a Long Journey made Round or Ovall by Encompassing the Principalitie of Wales, 1652, (ed.) J. O. Halliwell, London, 1859.

TAYLOR, JOSEPH, *A Journey to Edenborough in Scotland in the Yeare 1705,* (ed.) William Cowan, Edinburgh, 1903.

THOMPSON, G., *A Sentimental Tour Collected from a Variety of Occurrences from Newbiggin . . . to London,* Penrith, 1798.

THOMSON, WILLIAM, *A Tour in England and Scotland in 1785, by an English Gentleman,* London, 1788.

THORESBY, RALPH, *The Wayfarings of Ralph Thoresby in the North of England,* 1682, *Reprints of Rare Tracts and Imprints of Ancient Manuscripts,* II, Newcastle, 1899.

THRALE, MRS. HESTER, 'Tour in Wales, July–September 1774', A. M. Broadey, *Dr Johnson and Mrs Thrale,* London, 1910, *155–219.*

'Travel book 1789. Journey to the North of England', John Rylands Library, Manchester, Eng. MSS. 623.

TORBUCK, JOHN, *A Collection of Welsh Travels and Memoirs of Wales,* London, 1737.

TRAVERS, BENJAMIN, *A Descriptive Tour to the Lakes of Cumberland and Westmorland in the Autumn of 1814,* London, 1816.

TUNNICLIFF, WILLIAM, *A Topographical Survey of Hants, Wilts, Dorset, Somerset, Devon and Cornwall,* Salisbury, 1791.

TURNER, THOMAS, *Narrative of a Journey, associated with a Fly, from Gloucester to Aberystwith, and, from Aberystwith through North Wales in 1837,* London, 1840.

VERDON, J., 'Tour through England and Wales 1699', Cardiff Public Library MSS.

VERTUE, GEORGE, 'Travel diaries 1731–47', B.M. Add. MSS. 23089.

WALFORD, T., *The Scientific Tourist through England, Wales and Scotland,* 2 vols., London, 1818.

WALKER, ADAM, *Observations, Natural, Oeconomical and Literary made in a Tour from London to the Lakes in the Summer of 1791,* London, 1792.

WALPOOLE, G. A., *The new British Traveller; or, a complete display of*

Great Britain and Ireland: being a new . . . tour through England, Wales, Scotland, Ireland, the Isles of Man, Wight, etc., London, 1784.

WALPOLE, HORACE, *Journals of Visits to Country Seats*, (ed.) Paget Toynbee, Walpole Society, 1928, XVI, *9–80*.

WANDBY, A. J., *Sketches on the Wye*, London, 1839.

WARNER, A., 'A few notes, scraps, remembrances and c of a Journey of pleasure taken by A.W. & J.S.T. 1832', Bodleian MS. Top. gen. f. 35.

WARNER, REV. RICHARD, *A Walk through Wales in August 1797*, Bath, 1799.
A Second Walk through Wales, in August and September 1798, Bath, 1799.
A Walk through some of the Western Counties of England, Bath, 1800.
Excursions from Bath, 1800, London, 1801.
A Tour through the Northern Counties of England and the Borders of Scotland, London, 1802.
A Tour through Cornwall in the Autumn of 1808, London, 1809.

WEBB, DANIEL CARLESS, *Observations and Remarks during Four Excursions made to various parts of Great Britain in the years 1810 and 1811, performed by Land, by Sea, by Various Modes of Conveyance, and partly in the Pedestrian Style*, London, 1812.

WEBB, WILLIAM, 'Tour from Cambridge to the Highlands and back to Liverpool, June–September 1838', Camb. Univ. Lib. Add. MSS. 5871.

WEBBER, MARY, 'Tour to Wales, 1835', Bodleian MS. Top. gen. e. 59.

WEST, MRS., 'Extracts from Mrs West's Manuscript Tour to Wales and Ireland, c. 1810', Camb. Univ. Lib. Add. MSS. 738.

WEST, THOMAS, *A Guide to the Lakes in Cumberland, Westmorland and Lancashire*, 2nd ed., London, 1780.

WESTALL, W., and OWEN, S., *Picturesque Tour of the River Thames illustrated by twenty four coloured views from original drawings taken on the spot*, London, 1828.

WHALEY, JOHN, 'Journal of a Tour through England in 1735, with notes by W. Cole', B.M. Add. MSS. 5842, 5957.

WHEATON, N. S., *A Journal of a Residence during several months in London: including Excursions through various parts of England in the years 1823 and 1824*, Hartford, 1830.

WHITE, JAMES, 'Tour into South Wales in 1805', *Transactions Honorable Society of Cymmrodorion*, 1937, *331–7*.

WIGSTEAD, HENRY, *Remarks on a Tour to North and South Wales in the year 1797*, London, 1800.

WIGSTEAD, HENRY, and ROWLANDSON, THOMAS, *An Excursion to Brighthelmstone made in the year 1789*, London, 1790.

WILKINSON, THOMAS, *Tours to the British Mountains*, London, 1824.

WILLETT, MARK, *An Excursion from the Source of the Wye*, Chepstow, 1820.

WILLIAMS, ESTHER PHILLIPS, 'Tour into Glamorganshire and South Wales, 1836', Cardiff Public Library MSS.

WILLIAMS, J. F. L., 'SILURIAN REMINISCENCES, with Legendary Tales of the Cambrian Border . . . by the late Marmaduke Mandeville in 1823. An account of a tour by J. F. L. Williams, under the above pseudonym, from London into Monmouthshire and Herefordshire, with historical notes of places and families, 1833–4', B.M. Add. MSS. 33,500.

WILLIAMS, WILLIAM, *Observations on the Snowdon Mountains*, London, 1802.

WINDHAM, W., 'Journal of a Tour through Surrey, Wiltshire, Dorset, Devon, Somerset, Wales, Worcestershire etc., 7 June–21 August 1779', B.M. Add. MSS. 37,926.

WINSTANLEY, WILLIAM, *Poor Robin's Perambulation from Saffron-Walden to London, performed this month of July, 1678*, London, 1678.

WOODWARD, G. M., *Eccentric Excursions; or Literary & Pictorial Sketches of Countenance, Character, & Country in different parts of England and South Wales. Embellished with prints* [by G. Cruickshank], London, 1807.

WORDSWORTH, WILLIAM, *Topographical Description of the Country of the Lakes, anonymous introduction to Rev. Joseph Wilkinson, Select Views in Cumberland, Westmorland and Lancashire*, London, 1810. [Third edition published separately September 1822.]
A Guide through the District of the Lakes in the North of England, Kendal, 1835.

WRIGHT, LUCY, 'A Tour through Wales to the South Coast, 1806', Wigan Public Library, Edward Hall Collection, M 842 EHC 73.

WYNDHAM, HENRY PENRUDDOCKE, *A Gentleman's Tour through Monmouthshire and Wales. In the months of June and July 1774*, London, 1774.

YOUNG, ARTHUR, *A Six Weeks Tour through the Southern Counties of England and Wales. Describing, particularly I. The present state of agriculture and manufacture, II. The different methods of cultivating the soil . . . In several letters to a friend*, London, 1768.
A Six Months Tour through the North of England. Containing, an Account of the Present State of Agriculture, Manufactures, and Population, in Several Counties of this Kingdom, 4 vols., London, 1770.
The Farmer's Tour through the East of England, being the Register of a Journey through various Counties of this Kingdom to Enquire into the State of Agriculture etc., 4 vols., 1771.

INDEX

INDEX